Assault on the Small Screen

Assault on the Small Screen

Representations of Sexual Violence on Prime-Time Television Dramas

Molly Ann Magestro

ROWMAN & LITTLEFIELD
Lanham • Boulder • New York • London

Published by Rowman & Littlefield
A wholly owned subsidiary of The Rowman & Littlefield Publishing Group, Inc.
4501 Forbes Boulevard, Suite 200, Lanham, Maryland 20706
www.rowman.com

Unit A, Whitacre Mews, 26-34 Stannary Street, London SE11 4AB

British Library Cataloguing in Publication Information Available

Library of Congress Cataloging-in-Publication Data

Magestro, Molly Ann, 1982–
Assault on the small screen : representations of sexual violence on prime-time television dramas / Molly Ann Magestro.
pages cm
Includes bibliographical references and index.
ISBN 978-1-4422-5397-1 (hardback : alk. paper) — ISBN 978-1-4422-5398-8 (ebook) 1. Television broadcasting—Social aspects—United States. 2. Television serials—United States. 3. Violence on television. 4. Sex on television. I. Title.
PN1992.6.M299 2015
302.23'450973—dc23
2015011655

∞ ™ The paper used in this publication meets the minimum requirements of American National Standard for Information Sciences Permanence of Paper for Printed Library Materials, ANSI/NISO Z39.48-1992.

Printed in the United States of America

For Henry James Krueger,
who has already made the world better,
and for the ones in six and ones in thirty-three
and everyone fighting with them to do the same

Contents

Acknowledgments

I could not be more thankful to the following people:

Everyone who ever read something I wrote and told me how it could be better and everyone who ever let me do the same for them.

Anyone who listened to me talk about or who critiqued any part of this book, especially Peg Mudroch, Anne Widmayer, Bill Malcuit, David Ostrenga, Eric Harding (librarian extraordinaire), Sarah Rodenberg, Jenny Cruse, Emilie Lindeman, Aviva Cristy, Jessica Van Slooten, Chris Yogerst, Jennifer Chamberlain, David Beard, Kim Behnke, David Yost, Jackie Lee, Barb McKeough, Kara Bivens Vorwald and John Vorwald, Alyssa Lawson, Stacy Barner, and all my students, colleagues, and friends at the University of Wisconsin–Washington County and the UW Colleges English Department.

Jen Adler, Rachel Barger, Michael Dean Clark, and Jennifer Heinert, because without their encouragement, insights, friendship, and an occasional phrase or two this project would be much less.

My family—Jim and Ann Magestro; Tony Magestro; Emily, Dan, and Henry Krueger; Bonnie McKeough; my uncles, aunts, cousins in all variations—who give me the courage to aim because they're always with me, even if I miss.

Introduction

My history with police procedural dramas goes back to the nights I used to spend watching television with my mom when I was young. Weekly, we would tune in to watch *Walker, Texas Ranger*, *Nash Bridges*, *Law and Order*, and *NYPD Blue*, to name a few. I don't remember us ever talking much, maybe exchanging a few words during commercial breaks, but watching those shows together always made me feel closer to her. It wasn't just the shared narrative experiences, either, though knowing the same stories is one thing that ties people together. Rather, as a child, I felt closer to my mom after watching all those television cops because she was a cop.

In 1978, my mom, who is retired now, was the first female police officer to be hired by the Brown County Sheriff's Department. She had to fight for the opportunity, a story I pieced together over the years as I grew older. Watching those shows with her night after night when I was young, I began to wonder about her life outside our home, beyond our quiet television time as we watched Chuck Norris roundhouse-kick another suspect in the face or Don Johnson lament the ax someone had swung into the hood of his yellow 1971 Cuda.

I watched these shows as a child, feeling like I was developing an understanding of my mom's job and what she might be like when we weren't together. And it wasn't just her. My father is also a retired police officer, having served the Ashwaubenon Public Safety Department from 1980 until 2002. These shows seemed like windows into my parents' time at work even though I knew the television cops weren't real. But surely some of it reflected a version of their reality: there had to be car chases, gunshots, interrogations in mirrored rooms, one neatly solved crime after another.

So one night I asked her. *NYPD Blue* was on a commercial break, and I spoke. "Hey, Mom, is this show what your job is like?"

She laughed. "No! And that's what I like about it."

* * *

I kept up with *Law and Order* even after I moved out of my parents' house. My mom never made the transition to *Law and Order: SVU*, but I did in college. Frequently over the years, when I would visit my parents' house, my mom and I would find ourselves back in front of the television, watching whichever cop shows she was into at the time. She was the one who turned me on to *NCIS*, *Criminal Minds*, and *The Closer*. I would sit down to watch an episode here and there, just enough to develop an interest in the lives of the recurring characters, but not enough of an interest to keep up with the shows after I returned home. At least, that was the case until the summer of 2012.

In addition to the feeling of connection to my mom, what drew me in to most of the series under consideration in this book were the personal relationships between some of the regular characters. I was particular interested in the romantic undertones that run through Derek Morgan and Penelope Garcia's relationship on *Criminal Minds*. While Morgan fills the role of handsome charmer and Garcia is quirky and funky, they have a close, suggestive relationship that pushes right up against the boundaries of romance. Their connection is unexpected for the same reasons it is interesting: She is lovely but not thin, he loves her but isn't in love with her, they depend on each other in difficult times, and neither one of them is concerned about the fact that their relationship is far from professional even when the circumstances of a case are dire. The desire to know more about their relationship than the glimpses I had previously seen, in the sporadic episodes of the show I had watched with my mom or whenever I happened to catch a marathon on television, led me to binge-watch all previous seasons of the show that summer. A similar relationship, this one between *NCIS'* Tim McGee and Abby Sciuto—interesting because he seems so straitlaced and she seems so not—drew me into that show. When I finished watching all of the available seasons of *Criminal Minds*, I selected *NCIS* to watch next.

* * *

The 2012 election cycle was long and contentious (as most are). One of the issues that received quite a bit of media attention in the months leading up to November was women's health and access to Planned Parenthood and specific health care services. In an interview, Missouri Representative Todd Akin infamously referred to a woman's body's ability, in cases of "legitimate rape," "to shut that whole thing down" and stop unwanted pregnancy.[1] His claim was just one of a seeming barrage of similar comments that suggested that *real* victims of *actual* rapes wouldn't become pregnant as a result. In her essay "How We All Lose" from the book *Bad Feminist*, author Roxane Gay reminds readers to "consider the many different kinds of rape we have learned about over the past few years as conservative politicians blunder through trying to explain their stances on sexual violence and abortion."[2] Her discussion of the blundering includes Akin, of course, as well as a state representative from my home state of Wisconsin, Roger Rivard, whose comments to the press in response to the sexual assault of a fourteen-year-old girl included the warning his father passed down to him: "Some girls, they rape so easy."[3] While Gay doesn't mention him, another, more famous Wisconsin politician, vice-presidential candidate Paul Ryan, referred to rape as a "method of conception."[4] Additionally, several candidates discussed pregnancies resulting from rape as gifts from God, or the circumstances that constituted "forcible rape," or their desire to deny abortion access to all women, including rape and incest victims. While Ryan retained his seat in the U.S. House of Representatives, he lost his bid for the vice-presidency, and most of the other candidates—including Rivard and Akin—lost their races as well.

I paid close attention to the election cycle due to the political climate in my state, and throughout the weeks and months during which these rape comments made headlines, I was pleasure-watching *Criminal Minds* and *NCIS* in my free time. Then I attended a screening of Kirby Dick's documentary *The Invisible War* at the Milwaukee Film Festival. A film about the issue of military sexual trauma (MST), *The Invisible War*[5] presents personal narratives of several former military personnel who are survivors of MST, statistics from the military and Department of Justice, interviews with military representatives (including members of the real-life Naval Criminal Investigative Service), and a look into the current, ongoing battle in Washington, D.C., as the survivors fight to bring more attention to the problem. The film, which was nominated for an Academy Award in 2013, was an extremely discomforting viewing experience but made me think about how much worse it would be for those who had lived those experiences.

It was the combination of these three things—the shows, the politics, and *The Invisible War*—that led me back to an episode of *NCIS* that had bothered me the first time I watched it. In Season Two, Episode Four, "Lt. Jane Doe," one scene in particular arrested my attention even before I was looking specifically at how the show represented rape and rape victims. It was really something rather small, just a matter of word choice, but I am an English teacher, after all. Tony DiNozzo, one of the show's main characters, when explaining what happened to a rape/homicide victim, stated that "she got herself raped and killed."[6] And that one three-letter verb, that word "got," which is usually the opposite of provocative, became the crux of my exploration of the representation of rape and rape victims on prime-time police and legal dramas, the subject of this book.

* * *

Since its creation, television has made the world smaller. Broadcasting world events, bringing them into the homes of far-flung citizens, creates a space in which people who have never met and may never meet become a group: a simultaneous audience. Anyone with access to a television set can bear witness to happenings in the world that are far removed from their everyday lives and experiences. David Sarnoff, founder and former president of the Radio Corporation of America (RCA), hoped that television would be the "greatest opportunity ever given us for creating close ties of understanding among the peoples of the world" at the same time as he cautioned citizens about the place of television in "the intimate background of one's home."[7] People watching television were letting the world, with all its capacity for good and for evil, into their homes and the stories shared through the medium into their heads.

Today's television programming might have been difficult for Sarnoff, who died in 1971, to imagine. With hundreds of channels and thousands of shows to choose from, television audiences today have a much different viewing experience than audiences in the 1940s and 1950s, and not just because of the proliferation of options. While television was largely government-regulated until the 1980s,[8] the state has passed control over to the large-scale media conglomerates. According to Toby Miller, professor of media and cultural studies at the University of California, Riverside, and author of the book *Television Studies*, "90 percent of the major cable networks [are] owned by five conglomerates, which also own many of the companies that make the shows they buy."[9] This privatization and concentration of television production and regulation has influenced the variety of shows available to audiences and the goals of television as a medium for the mass production of information.

Because whatever else changes, that is still what television does: shares information with mass audiences. In a report by the Nielsen Company, 114.7 million households in the United States, or 96.8%, are television households.[10] The messages portrayed through this ubiquitous medium are worthy of in-depth study and attention if for no other reason that millions of people welcome those messages into their living rooms, their family rooms, and even their bedrooms every day. These are messages viewers share with their friends and coworkers, parents and children. And they are messages that have the potential to both reflect and influence the ways we understand the world we live in, including parts of that world that would otherwise be outside of our ability to experience.

* * *

There aren't many individuals interested in arguing about the United States' near-total television saturation. However, rape culture is a phenomenon that is just as widespread, far more insidious, and a very contentious topic. While the term has gained enough traction that it may not strictly require a definition, it is worth interrogating given the importance of everything it entails for the underlying premises of this project. As a pervasive set of socially accepted ideas that increase tolerance for and normalization of rape and sexual violence, "rape culture" also incorporates gender and sexuality-based stereotypes, fixed and rigid gender roles for women in particular, and the long list of rape myths that proliferate in society and popular culture. The idea that rape victims have done something to set themselves up for the violence committed against them stems from concerns and excuses regarding what victims are "asking for" when they wear something particular or go particular places or drink or behave in particular ways. As malevolent as rape culture is, however, plenty of the ways it manifests itself appear innocuous: dismissing violent behavior in male children as "boys will be boys," the conventional "wisdom" taught to little girls that boys who pull their hair or tease them do so because they like them. Less innocuous is the fact that pay inequality is still a significant issue in most sectors of the workforce and that women are still vastly underrepresented in politics and many professional fields. These facts convey some of the truths of what society holds on to in terms of what is appropriate behavior for women and where the appropriate spaces for women to occupy exist.

Then there are the facets of rape culture closer to the surface of the actual issue at hand: rape narratives on scripted television shows and in movies, as well as represented in the mainstream media, that victim-blame or refuse to accept the reliability of a victim's word. Real-world examples such as the media coverage on the day the verdict came down in the Steubenville, Ohio, rape case, when an anchor and news correspondent on CNN mourned the potential that was wasted by sending the high school–age perpetrators of a particularly disgusting and well-documented rape to jail.[11] That is rape culture, as is the series of events that led to that point—when the rapists videotaped their crimes and adults seemed to be involved in attempting to cover the whole thing up. Rape culture is when women who are college age or who are serving in the military are routinely being taught how to avoid being raped instead of living in a society that works to address the cause of the problem: rapists themselves. When new examples of collegiate athletes allegedly perpetrating or assisting in covering up instances of rape frequently make breaking news[12] and when the people put in positions of power to investigate sexual harassment and rape turn out to be some of the worst offenders.[13] When a joke about dropping the soap doesn't raise a single red flag, as if simply moving inside the walls of a prison erases the fact that rape is a violent crime. And if a woman uses her media platform to try and raise awareness about these facts, fellow Internet users meet her determination with rape threats.[14] The culmination of all these examples, and the set of circumstances that brought them into being, is rape culture.

Rape is severely underreported, and in most circles, it is well established that rape victims who do decide to report the crimes committed against them to the authorities must be ready to face an onslaught of new victimizations. First they must repeatedly recount the story of an immensely intimate crime. This requires a willingness to trust that their stories will be accepted by the authorities, who are most likely strangers and who, conventional wisdom tells women, will most likely be suspicious and disbelieving. Then there are invasive physical examinations that essentially replicate the initial crime for the purpose of gathering evidence. After these steps, which are often humiliating for already traumatized victims, the decision about whether to move forward with pressing charges rests on the district attorney, who can decide not to pursue a trial regardless of the wishes of the victim. Because rape cases are not always supported by physical evidence of force, they are frequently discussed through the overly simplistic framework of "he said/she said," which puts the burden on the victim, not only to prove the accused's guilt but also, frequently, her own innocence.[15]

Parts of society believe that rape is something that happens when solitary, drunk women wearing short skirts encounter strangers in dark alleys. People say things like "It could have been worse" or "You should take it as a compliment" to victims of sexual harassment. People ask what a rape victim was wearing and what she had been drinking. But rape is not a crime about sexual desire or passion. It is a crime about power and control and violence. Perhaps rape is less scary if we can think about it as something that happens when one person leads the other on or doesn't say "no" stridently enough. If that is the case, we feel like we can avoid situations like that and protect ourselves. If rape is really about taking power and control, about committing violence against another person, we don't know how to stop it from happening to us, to people we know.

But it does happen to people we know. According to statistics from the Federal Bureau of Investigation, in 2013, "there were an estimated 79,770 rapes (legacy definition) reported to law enforcement."[16] The "legacy definition" referred to in that statistic reflects the fact that up until 2013, the FBI's definition of rape included the term "forcible." It wasn't until 2013 that the definition changed to remove that word and address its redundancy. We also know that the statistic only includes rapes that have been reported; the Department of Justice numbers suggest that 67% of rapes and sexual assaults go unreported.[17] And we know more about rape than what these numbers tell us. The facts about rape include that most, but not all, victims are women. Nearly all rapists are men. Men who rape other men are not necessarily gay.

Most rape victims have personal relationships with their rapists. Many victims blame themselves for what was done to them, and all of those victims learned that behavior from rape culture. They worry they should have said "no" more clearly. They shouldn't have worn that or drunk so much or put themselves in that situation. They shouldn't have flirted or teased or suggested. But here is the reality: A woman standing naked in a dark alley so drunk she cannot see straight is not asking to be raped. A sex worker is not asking to be raped. A prison inmate is not asking to be raped. And no one deserves it.

A close friend of mine recently confided in me that she had been raped. That fact does not make either of us unique, neither me as the confidante nor her as the survivor. In college, we both heard the rumors, we knew which house parties and bars to avoid because girls said they had been drugged, raped there. We knew not to accept open drinks from strangers. We knew to go out and come home with friends, never by ourselves in the dark. But everything we knew about rape after countless warnings about protecting ourselves from various avenues—both real-world and fictional—didn't protect us. Didn't protect her. The only thing that protected me was luck, and I'll never know why I was lucky where she wasn't.

* * *

The specifics of what happened to my friend wouldn't be very surprising to most women. The stories told about rape by the majority of shows airing during prime time most likely wouldn't be either. And maybe that is part of the reason why it is important to look closely at what the rape narratives shown on television are actually portraying.

I don't know what it says about American society that so many shows that include these narratives thrive, that *Law and Order: SVU*, for instance, is so popular. I don't have the means at my disposal to even begin a project that sorts through such an extremely complex issue. What I do have is the ability and inclination to look critically at the rape narratives presented to us in an attempt to come to some understanding or draw some conclusions about the messages entering our lives through these small screens that proliferate in most American households, that bring these traumatic events (or, more frequently, the suggestion of the actual trauma with more direct emphasis on the aftermath) into our homes. These representations of rape narratives aren't just happening on television; they play out in our living rooms, kitchens, and even bedrooms. Someone needs to pay attention to what those stories say and show, the ways in which they are empowering or problematic, and to consider what we can learn about, and possibly from, them.

Two examples of such work are Lisa M. Cuklanz's *Rape on Prime Time: Television, Masculinity, and Sexual Violence* and Sarah Projansky's *Watch-*

ing Rape: Film and Television in Postfeminist Culture. These projects—
though different from each other and my own in at least two important
ways—served as examples of how to approach representations of rape
through a critical lens. They also laid the groundwork on which this project is
built. Cuklanz's book focuses on prime-time television from 1976 to 1990 as
"the key period of change in prime time's representations of rape"[18] toward
rape narratives that were much more likely to present rape through a lens of
feminism and the anti-rape work of feminists. Cuklanz explains that "our
popular culture has consistently depicted rape and sexual assault, often
graphically, prompting many to inquire about the relationship between popular representation and general attitudes toward rape. The importance of the
complex and contested relationship between media representations of rape
and social attitudes about it cannot be underestimated."[19] Laying out the
connections between social attitudes and rape narratives represented on the
shows she is considering, Cuklanz's conclusions address what she calls a
"basic change" to the end that "most programs began [. . .] to depict date or
acquaintance rapes where the victim knew her attacker, no extreme violence
or weapons were used, and there was no need for a detective to 'solve' the
crime by discovering the rapist's identity."[20] The narrative elements Cuklanz
calls attention to as plot points in rape narratives are quite familiar to us now,
perhaps even to the point where audiences of most shows would expect
episodes containing rape narratives to include such characteristics.

     In the introduction to Sarah Projansky's *Watching Rape*, the author draws
on Cuklanz's observations about the culturally held, traditional assumptions
regarding rape prior to the shift Cuklanz's book addresses: "that women who
report rape often lie; that rape only takes place between people who do not
know each other; that women who dress or behave in particular ways are
'responsible for their own attacks'; that all rapists are 'abnormal, depraved,
or marginal men'; that women who are raped are placed on trial and forced to
prove their 'moral purity' through discussions of their previous sexual activities; and that African American men are more likely to rape than white
men."[21] Projansky's book accounts for the counterformulations Cuklanz discusses and then takes the consideration of rape narratives in both television
and film a step further, picking up essentially where Cuklanz left off: with
representations of rape post-1980s through the end of the 20th century.
Watching Rape draws on a "poststructuralist theoretical assumption that public discourses have material effects and that representations are as important
to understanding what rape and feminism 'are' as are laws, theory, activism,
and experience,"[22] and the goal of Projansky's project is to use examples to
draw overarching conclusions that can be broadly applied to the ways in
which postfeminist thinking have disrupted the forward momentum anti-rape
activists had gathered.

My project does something different. First, the earliest show I consider began airing in 1999, so the time frame is clearly later, spanning from that year through 2014. Additionally, the work that has been done to this point—addressing the feminist progress (Cuklanz) and the postfeminist backlash (Projansky)—allows me, I believe, to narrow my focus from conclusions that can be applied on a cultural level to critiques of the particular arguments being created about rape through its representations on individual shows.

There are important lessons to be learned from the close reading of any text. While the main ideas and topics of discussion do not always require close reading, the benefits of the practice include a better understanding of how a text works. Looking not just at the messages about rape presented on select prime-time television shows but also at how those messages are created can lead to a better understanding of the messages that go out to millions of television viewers each week. The shows chosen here have something in common: they all deal with violent crimes—either investigating them, litigating them, or both. They are important not as representations of reality, since most television audiences are sophisticated enough to recognize the world on television as one re-created to resemble our own but not actually to represent it. Instead, these stories are important because messages meant to reach such massive audiences are important for their own sake, regardless of how little or how much the world they exist in represents our own.

This project covers shows chosen for a variety of reasons. Several were chosen due to their popularity: *CSI*, for instance, is one of the most-viewed shows around the world. *NCIS* is also extremely popular, reaching the largest audience of any scripted television show in the United States. *Law and Order: Special Victims Unit* was a natural choice, if for no other reason than the unique way the whole show focuses mostly on sexually based offenses. All of the other shows considered deal with rape narratives on a far less consistent basis. Several of the shows I have chosen use a team-based approach to investigation, and I have also selected shows with female protagonists such as *The Closer* and *Rizzoli & Isles*. These eight shows—those already mentioned here along with *Criminal Minds*, *Dexter*, and *The Good Wife*—are by no means to be considered an exhaustive or even wholly representative list for the consideration of this topic. There are plenty of other shows to consider as well as plenty else to explore within these shows beyond the narrow scope I have set up for this project. Lines had to be drawn somewhere, though, and these are the lines I chose.

The book is divided into chapters by show, and its structure unfolds in several different ways. The first three chapters are about CBS heavyweights *NCIS*, *Criminal Minds*, and *CSI*. They are long-running (the shortest among them is in the middle of airing Season Nine as I write this), have wide audiences, and use a similar team-based format that makes comparisons between them reasonable. Additionally, the earliest chapters deal exclusively with the investigation of rape—*NCIS* and *Criminal Minds* never show the inside of a courtroom, but almost always show the inside of an interrogation room. *CSI*, on the other hand, occasionally shows characters prepping for or even testifying in court. These three shows also represent different points on a spectrum of how rape narratives are addressed through character growth and development.

From there, two chapters leave network television. Chapter Four looks to basic cable, specifically TNT for *The Closer* and *Rizzoli & Isles*, and Chapter Five to Showtime, a premium channel, for *Dexter*. These shows represent shifts not just in where they are aired but also in terms of what television can be.[23] Content-wise, these three shows have several things in common. Even though they have the same team-based style of investigation, there are clearly distinguished main characters established in the titles. Additionally, they approach the prosecution of crime a bit more directly. While *The Closer* mostly just refers to court instead of actually going there, the title of the show itself refers to the fact that the show's main character always gets a confession from suspects, and thus the audience knows the verdict of forthcoming court proceedings without the courtroom drama. Neither *Rizzoli & Isles* nor *Dexter* makes courtroom proceedings a large part of the show, but viewers do catch glimpses of characters from those shows preparing to provide or actually providing testimony in court periodically.

These first five chapters take us beyond the halfway point of the book. *Law and Order: SVU* isn't just special in terms of the kinds of victims it deals with. It is also special in terms of this project insofar as it is the only one of these shows that purports to focus specifically on sexually based offenses in the opening monologue that rolls before every episode. The sheer volume of episodes containing rape narratives sets this series apart from the others—171 of the show's 343 episodes over fifteen seasons fit my criteria for consideration.[24] But its focus and the numbers are only part of the reason why *Law and Order: SVU* will get two chapters in this study. The other reason is the show's format. In the traditional *Law and Order* style, approximately the second half of each episode (sometimes more, sometimes less) focuses on the actual prosecution of the crimes the first half investigates. Chapter Six focuses on the investigations—and on one investigator in particular. Chapter Seven focuses on how the show re-creates and represents rape trials and the prosecution of rapists.

After the transition *Law and Order: SVU* allows us to make from investigation to full-on prosecution, Chapter Eight stays in the courtroom, switching to a straight legal drama and back to CBS for *The Good Wife*. The titular character on this show is a defense attorney with specific and very personal ties to the state's attorney's office, and she works toward different ends than most of the characters on the rest of the shows. *NCIS* and *Criminal Minds* deal with federal agencies while *CSI*, *The Closer*, *Rizzoli & Isles*, *Dexter*, and

Law and Order: SVU all follow characters tied to specific local police departments. Nearly all those characters work on the side of the prosecution—though *CSI* and *Dexter* both showcase analysts whose job is specifically to interpret objective evidence. When it comes to most of the cases, the main character on *The Good Wife* fights against the prosecution; when it comes to rape, however, there are often extenuating circumstances, which we will look at more closely in Chapter Eight, to complicate which side this particular group of defense attorneys represents.

There is one last method that I loosely followed when putting these chapters together in this particular order. In addition to all the reasons I have already mentioned, *NCIS* seemed like a solid place to start because it contains the smallest percentage of episodes with rape narratives and, of all the shows considered here, does the poorest job of representing and dealing with victims. As the book progresses, it is arguable that the shows become increasingly more considerate of victims' experiences when specifically addressing the single area of concern central to this project. *Criminal Minds* and *CSI* are comparable, with perhaps a slight edge going to *Criminal Minds*; *The Closer* and *Rizzoli & Isles* are about equal; and *Dexter* is a bit of an anomaly wherever it fits into the book's structure. Given the sheer number of opportunities, it is probably expected that *Law and Order: SVU* takes care to represent all aspects of rape narratives in ways that are respectful and considerate of victims and their rights. But it is my contention that *SVU* doesn't do quite as well as *The Good Wife* when it comes to taking a strong stance for victims, which is another reason I felt *The Good Wife* would work well as the final chapter.

Combined, the sixty-nine seasons of these eight shows offered 342 hour-long episodes of prime-time television that included some kind of rape narrative. Coming to this number was not as straightforward a prospect as I would have hoped when initially considering the 1,409 total episodes. I made several decisions to help narrow the field of episodes to be considered for this project. The first such decision was to limit my consideration to episodes dealing with adult victims of rape and sexual assault. When thinking about rape episodes of most shows that present such offerings, there are several themes viewers are accustomed to seeing: rape as a war crime, rape on a college campus, a false accusation of rape. Another thing quite a few shows include is the sexual assault or rape of a child. I drew a pretty hard line to keep out victims under the age of eighteen because of the multitude of additional issues and concerns raised in examples of child molestation and statutory rape. The second decision I made was to exclude most episodes that addressed sex trafficking and forced prostitution. Rape is clearly a significant component of both crimes, but as with victims who are minors, there are other issues and concerns involved that my discussion is not equipped to address. The additional complexities presented by the other aspects of these types of crime make already unstable ground even more treacherous.

In each chapter, I included as many episodes of the show(s) being considered as space constraints and the chapter's central argument allowed. For *NCIS*, the small number of rape-related episodes meant I could consider them all and draw conclusions about the full scope of rape narratives on the show. The same cannot be said for *Law and Order: SVU* or *CSI*. The number of episodes of these shows that included rape narratives represented approximately one-fourth of all the episodes initially considered; I have done my best here to develop arguments that take them all into consideration whether or not they are mentioned specifically.

* * *

The idea for *Assault on the Small Screen* arose from a series of coincidences. I made connections between *The Invisible War* and *NCIS* at the same time that a string of politicians made headlines with their absurd comments about rape. Through all that, there was one question I couldn't let go: What does it mean when there are representations of rape narratives on prime-time television that include comments like NCIS agent Tony DiNozzo's that the victim of a rape/homicide "got herself raped and killed"?

Asking the question is easy. Answering it, on the other hand, is not. It led to other questions—how do characters on other shows talk about and talk to rape victims? How do the various representations of rape and rape victims across shows work toward justice for victims of sex crimes? What can media consumers learn from these representations, particularly the ones that might be based on true stories? What does our apparent interest in these narratives say about us as individuals or as a society? I don't have answers to all those questions here. In fact, this project is just the first step in the direction of potential answers. Before we can answer the big questions, though, we first have to know what it is we are dealing with. By applying close-reading techniques to the content of the shows considered here, I hope to present a clearer picture of what it is we are confronted with when these shows become and inform part of our lives.

The list of most-popular rape-related headlines as I write this includes the series of decades-old accusations against Bill Cosby that are gaining traction in the mainstream media[25] and the in-depth look by *Rolling Stone* at the University of Virginia's history of mishandling rape[26] and the resulting controversy.[27] It is a list that has changed dozens of times in the three years I have been working on this project, and by the time you are reading these words, it will certainly have changed again. The ways the media discuss rape might be changing, as might society's attitudes toward the victims of rape and sexual assault. And even as attitudes seem to be shifting, it is important to pay close attention to how rape narratives work, even—or perhaps especially—on prime-time television, in order to ensure that we are aware of the messages being broadcast into our homes and our heads.

NOTES

1. Charles Jaco, "Jaco Report: Full Interview with Todd Akin," *Fox 2 Now—St. Louis*, last modified August 20, 2012, accessed January 2, 2015, http://fox2now.com/2012/08/19/the-jaco-report-august-19-2012.

2. Roxane Gay, "How We All Lose," in *Bad Feminist: Essays* (New York: Harper Perennial, 2014), 99.

3. Patrick Marley, "Rep. Roger Rivard Criticized for 'Some Girls Rape Easy' Remark," *Milwaukee Journal Sentinel*, October 10, 2012, http://www.jsonline.com/news/statepolitics/state-legislator-criticized-for-comments-on-rape-hj76f4k-172587961.html.

4. Dave Smith, "Paul Ryan Calls Rape a 'Method of Conception,' Echoes Controversial Todd Akin Comments," *International Business Times*, August 28, 2012, http://www.ibtimes.com/paul-ryan-calls-rape-%E2%80%9Cmethod-conception%E2%80%9D-echos-controversial-todd-akin-comments-video-759465.

5. Kirby Dick, director, *The Invisible War* (Los Angeles: Docurama Films, 2012), DVD.

6. Steven Long Mitchell et al., "Lt. Jane Doe," *NCIS*, season 2, episode 4, directed by Dan Lerner, aired on October 19, 2004 (Hollywood: Paramount Home Entertainment, 2006), DVD.

7. David Sarnoff, "Our Next Frontier . . . Transoceanic TV," in *Mass Communication and American Social Thought: Key Texts, 1919–1968*, ed. John Durham Peters and Peter Simonson (Lanham, MD: Rowman & Littlefield, 2004), 309–310.

8. Toby Miller, *Television Studies: The Basics* (London: Routledge, 2010), 55.

9. Ibid., 66.

10. Nielsen Company, "Nielsen Estimates Number of U.S. Television Homes to Be 114.7 Million," last modified May 3, 2011, accessed January 2, 2015, http://www.nielsen.com/us/en/insights/news/2011/nielsen-estimates-number-of-u-s-television-homes-to-be-114-7-million.html.

11. "Guilty Verdict in Steubenville Rape Trial; Matt Lauer Faults NBC; Iraq War Anniversary," *CNN Reliable Sources* transcript, aired on March 17, 2013, http://transcripts.cnn.com/TRANSCRIPTS/1303/17/rs.01.html.

12. See Matt Baker and Tia Mitchell, "Statement: Police Warned Accuser about Pursuing Jameis Winston Matter," *Tampa Bay Times*, November, 20, 2013, http://www.tampabay.com/sports/college/statement-police-warned-accuser-about-pursuing-jameis-winston-matter/2153364; also see Greg Botelho, "Vanderbilt's Chris Boyd Pleads Guilty in Cover-Up of Alleged Gang Rape," CNN, September 14, 2013, http://www.cnn.com/2013/09/13/justice/vanderbilt-football-player-rape-case/.

13. See Luis Martinez, "Air Force's Sexual Assault Prevention Officer Charged with Sexual Battery," *ABC News*, May 6, 2013, http://abcnews.go.com/Politics/air-forces-sexual-assault-prevention-officer-charged-sexual/story?id=19120383.

14. See Nick Wingfield, "Feminist Critics of Video Games Facing Threats in 'GamerGate' Campaign," *New York Times*, October 15, 2014, http://www.nytimes.com/2014/10/16/technology/gamergate-women-video-game-threats-anita-sarkeesian.html/_r=0.

15. The use of feminine pronouns here is not to suggest that women are the only potential victims of rape. Rather, I use those specifically gendered pronouns here to reflect the fairly well-established societal assumption that rape is primarily a women's problem.

16. United States Department of Justice, *Crime in the United States, 2013: Rape*, Fall 2014, http://www.fbi.gov/about-us/ucr/crime-in-the-u.s.-2013/violent-crime/rape/rapemain_final.pdf.

17. United States Department of Justice, *Rape and Sexual Assault Victimization among College-Age Females, 1995–2013*, December 2014, http://www.bjs.gov/index.cfm?ty=pbdetail&iid=5176.

18. Lisa M. Cuklanz, *Rape on Prime Time: Television, Masculinity, and Sexual Violence* (Philadelphia: University of Pennsylvania Press, 2000), 4.

19. Ibid., 12.

20. Ibid., 28.

21. Sarah Projansky, *Watching Rape: Film and Television in Postfeminist Culture* (New York: New York University Press, 2001), 8.

22. Ibid., 16, 17.

23. As will be discussed in Chapter Four, *The Closer* was a pioneer of sorts for the type of basic-cable programming that is now fairly ubiquitous. *Dexter*, on the other hand, was the first premium cable series to have an entire season aired on a broadcast network. Though heavily edited for content, CBS aired the first two seasons of *Dexter* in response to 2008's television writers' strike. Lynette Rice, "*Dexter* to Air on CBS Starting Feb. 17," *Entertainment Weekly*, January 7, 2008, http://insidetv.ew.com/2008/01/07/dexter-to-out-o/.

24. The other half include most, if not all, instances of statutory rape and child molestation as well as sex trafficking cases and the other assorted crimes that fall under the SVU's purview.

25. See Barbara Bowman, "Bill Cosby Raped Me. Why Did It Take 30 Years for People to Believe My Story?" *Washington Post*, last modified November 13, 2014, accessed January 2, 2015, http://www.washingtonpost.com/posteverything/wp/2014/11/13/bill-cosby-raped-me-why-did-it-take-30-years-for-people-to-believe-my-story/?tid=pm_pop.

26. See Sabrina Rubin Erdely, "A Rape on Campus: A Brutal Assault and Struggle for Justice at UVA," *Rolling Stone*, last modified November 19, 2014, accessed January 2, 2015, http://www.rollingstone.com/culture/features/a-rape-on-campus-20141119.

27. See Ashley Fantz, "Advocates: Rolling Stone Controversy a Distraction from Rape Problem," CNN, December 11, 2014, http://www.cnn.com/2014/12/08/us/uva-rape-jackie-rolling-stone/.

REFERENCES

Baker, Matt, and Tia Mitchell. "Statement: Police Warned Accuser about Pursuing Jameis Winston Matter." *Tampa Bay Times*, November, 20, 2013. http://www.tampabay.com/sports/college/statement-police-warned-accuser-about-pursuing-jameis-winston-matter/2153364.

Botelho, Greg. "Vanderbilt's Chris Boyd Pleads Guilty in Cover-Up of Alleged Gang Rape." CNN, September 14, 2013. http://www.cnn.com/2013/09/13/justice/vanderbilt-football-player-rape-case/.

Bowman, Barbara. "Bill Cosby Raped Me. Why Did It Take 30 Years for People to Believe My Story?" *Washington Post*, November 13, 2014. http://www.washingtonpost.com/posteverything/wp/2014/11/13/bill-cosby-raped-me-why-did-it-take-30-years-for-people-to-believe-my-story/?tid=pm_pop.

Cuklanz, Lisa M. *Rape on Prime Time: Television, Masculinity, and Sexual Violence*. Philadelphia: University of Pennsylvania Press, 2000.

Dick, Kirby, director. *The Invisible War*. DVD. Los Angeles: Docurama Films, 2012.

Erdely, Sabrina Rubin. "A Rape on Campus: A Brutal Assault and Struggle for Justice at UVA." *Rolling Stone*, November 19, 2014. http://www.rollingstone.com/culture/features/a-rape-on-campus-20141119.

Fantz, Ashley. "Advocates: Rolling Stone Controversy a Distraction from Rape Problem." CNN, December 11, 2014. http://www.cnn.com/2014/12/08/us/uva-rape-jackie-rolling-stone/.

Gay, Roxane. "How We All Lose." In *Bad Feminist: Essays*, 96–108. New York: Harper Perennial, 2014.

"Guilty Verdict in Steubenville Rape Trial; Matt Lauer Faults NBC; Iraq War Anniversary." *CNN Reliable Sources* transcript. Aired on March 17, 2013. http://transcripts.cnn.com/TRANSCRIPTS/1303/17/rs.01.html.

Jaco, Charles. "Jaco Report: Full Interview with Todd Akin." *Fox 2 Now—St. Louis*, August 20, 2012. http://fox2now.com/2012/08/19/the-jaco-report-august-19-2012.

Marley, Patrick. "Rep. Roger Rivard Criticized for 'Some Girls Rape Easy' Remark." *Milwaukee Journal Sentinel*, October 10, 2012. http://www.jsonline.com/news/statepolitics/state-legislator-criticized-for-comments-on-rape-hj76f4k-172587961.html.

Martinez, Luis. "Air Force's Sexual Assault Prevention Officer Charged with Sexual Battery." *ABC News*, May 6, 2013. http://abcnews.go.com/Politics/air-forces-sexual-assault-prevention-officer-charged-sexual/story?id=19120383.

Miller, Toby. *Television Studies: The Basics*. London: Routledge, 2010.

Mitchell, Steven Long, Craig W. Van Sickle, Donald P. Bellisario, and Grant Gill. "Lt. Jane Doe." *NCIS*. Season 2. DVD. Directed by Dan Lerner. Aired on October 19, 2004. Hollywood: Paramount Home Entertainment, 2006.

Nielsen Company. "Nielsen Estimates Number of U.S. Television Homes to Be 114.7 Million." May 3, 2011. http://www.nielsen.com/us/en/insights/news/2011/nielsen-estimates-number-of-u-s-television-homes-to-be-114-7-million.html.

Projansky, Sarah. *Watching Rape: Film and Television in Postfeminist Culture*. New York: New York University Press, 2001.

Rice, Lynette. "*Dexter* to Air on CBS Starting Feb. 17." *Entertainment Weekly*, January 7, 2008. http://insidetv.ew.com/2008/01/07/dexter-to-out-o/.

Sarnoff, David. "Our Next Frontier . . . Transoceanic TV." In *Mass Communication and American Social Thought: Key Texts, 1919–1968*, edited by John Durham Peters and Peter Simonson, 309–310. Lanham, MD: Rowman & Littlefield, 2004.

Smith, Dave. "Paul Ryan Calls Rape a 'Method of Conception,' Echoes Controversial Todd Akin Comments." *International Business Times*, August 28, 2012. http://www.ibtimes.com/paul-ryan-calls-rape-%E2%80%9Cmethod-conception%E2%80%9D-echos-controversial-todd-akin-comments-video-759465.

United States Department of Justice. *Crime in the United States, 2013: Rape*. Fall 2014. http://www.fbi.gov/about-us/ucr/crime-in-the-u.s.-2013/violent-crime/rape/rapemain_final.pdf.

———. *Rape and Sexual Assault Victimization among College-Age Females, 1995–2013*. December 2014. http://www.bjs.gov/index.cfm?ty=pbdetail&iid=5176.

Wingfield, Nick. "Feminist Critics of Video Games Facing Threats in 'GamerGate' Campaign." *New York Times*, October 15, 2014. http://www.nytimes.com/2014/10/16/technology/gamergate-women-video-game-threats-anita-sarkeesian.html/_r=0.

Chapter One

"She Got Herself Raped and Killed"[1]

Victim-Blaming and Silencing on NCIS

CBS' 2012–2013 promotional materials referred to *NCIS* as television's most-watched show. *NCIS* became the number-one scripted drama during the 2009–2010 season and remained such through 2013[2] when the second half of the show's tenth season aired. The show, which started in 2003, is about the Naval Criminal Investigative Service's Major Case Response Team led by main character Leroy Jethro Gibbs. Gibbs' team includes Special Agents Tony DiNozzo, Caitlin "Kate" Todd (Seasons One and Two), Tim McGee (Season Two on), and Ziva David (Seasons Three through Ten); medical examiner Donald "Ducky" Mallard; Ducky's assistant Jimmy Palmer; and forensic scientist Abby Sciuto. The Major Case Response Team investigates violent crimes that fall under the jurisdiction of the naval chain of command.

The agency's acronym—NCIS—often goes unrecognized by the fictional civilians who inhabit the show's universe, and this lack of recognition suggests that television's most-watched show is about the underdog of federal investigative agencies. NCIS lacks some of the status and authority of the FBI, CIA, Secret Service, or Homeland Security, all of which play roles in certain narratives throughout the show's first ten seasons. On a show that reaches an average of 21.48 million viewers each week,[3] NCIS is portrayed as the younger, smaller, less intimidating sibling agency, but *NCIS* the show is clearly a heavyweight. The January 15, 2013, episode alone attracted an audience of more than 25 million people.[4]

A spin-off of *JAG* (1995–2005), *NCIS*' similar focus on military justice sets it apart from other procedurals. While the law enforcement officers on this show are not exactly police officers by name, the show still employs the police-procedural format by offering viewers a glimpse of the crime being committed and then focusing on the process of investigation and eventually apprehending the offender. Many episodes of *NCIS* include complications stemming from military procedure or hierarchy, but the overall tone celebrates the military and those who serve in it. Donald P. Bellisario, creator of both *JAG* and *NCIS*, explained that one of his goals for *JAG* was to "show that the values of middle America are the same values we have in the military."[5] This goal was then transferred to *NCIS*, and based on the show's ratings, a fair percentage of the American television audience seems to agree.

While there is certainly some of the male-centric attitude one might expect from a military cop show, *NCIS* does a fair job of representing female characters in a lot of ways. Viewers see high-ranking female military officers, female politicians, strong, well-developed female characters who can more than hold their own regardless of their company. Special Agents Kate Todd and Ziva David both have impressive backgrounds before they even join Gibbs' team: Kate guarded the president of the United States of America while working for the Secret Service, and Ziva was a high-ranking agent in the Israeli Mossad. While these two women both join Gibbs' team, viewers see examples of other, comparable teams led by women over the years. For three seasons, Gibbs' boss is a woman—Director Jenny Shepard was once Gibbs' partner in the field and rose to become the first female director of NCIS. Additionally, fan favorite Abby Sciuto excels at her work, processing evidence as the team's go-to forensic scientist. Though frequently infantilized by her male colleagues,[6] Abby is a prime example of what women can be in the *NCIS* universe: she is intelligent, independent, multifaceted, and flawed. Many of the women on *NCIS* can be, and often are, presented as strong and capable.

However, if one of the things *NCIS* sets out to do is reflect middle America's values, then middle America may need to adjust its thinking about rape. The one group of women that is consistently treated poorly within the *NCIS* universe is women who have been raped. In the first ten seasons of *NCIS*, 10 of the 234 total episodes include one or more rape narratives as part of their central investigation or relevant backstory. While each story is unique, what they all do have in common is a recurring silencing of the voices of women who have been raped.[7] When these women are given the chance to speak, the ways they are allowed or compelled to do so diminish their agency and further take away their individual control over their experiences and stories.

Central to *NCIS*' treatment of women who have been raped is Leroy Jethro Gibbs. As a demanding, stern boss whose team views his skill as near superhuman, Gibbs is more than just the show's central character. All members of his team view him in at least some small way as a father figure and seek to emulate his behavior. Thus, his actions, attitude, and approach almost always exert direct influence over his team's behavior. Gibbs' treatment of the limited number of women who have been raped informs the response and treatment these women receive from his whole team and perhaps from the show itself. While there may have been a shift in the treatment of rape as an issue in the real-world military in recent years, *NCIS* has yet to catch up, and the result is ten rape narratives that all contribute to a pattern of silencing and victim-blaming that persists through the first ten seasons of the show.

It is fitting, then, that the first time *NCIS* viewers are led to believe a rape is about to occur, they are misled. In Season One, Episode Eighteen, "Un-SEALed,"[8] a prisoner escapes from Fort Leavenworth. He has been incarcerated after being convicted of murdering his wife. The fact that he was wrongly convicted does not change the way the episode's opening scene plays out.

"UnSEALed" begins with a man and a woman asleep in bed. When a noise wakes them, the man goes to investigate. Viewers know, because of the formula they expect from a procedural drama, that something bad is about to happen. Anticipating that a crime is about to be committed, viewers are not surprised when the man who returns to the bedroom is not the same man who left. At this point, Vicki Spain is still in bed, and there is a stranger in her bedroom. He has a baseball bat. Viewers assume one of two things will happen to Vicki Spain before they even learn her name. The stranger in her bedroom will either kill her or rape her. Viewers expect this kind of opening scene from a procedural drama; the investigators need a crime to investigate, after all.

The intruder orders Vicki to turn over onto her stomach, tells her that if she does what he says, she won't get hurt, and viewers' expectations are met: the trajectory of the plot is confirmed. When the man begins to unbutton and then remove his shirt, viewers know what is about to happen. The fact that the scene flashes back and forth between Vicki on the bed in her nightgown and glimpses of the man's white boxer shorts and bare skin furthers their belief that they know what comes next. But nothing happens. After a short time, Vicki rises up enough to glance over her shoulder, and the man is gone, leaving behind a jumpsuit stamped with the words "Fort Leavenworth." He actually meant what he said; he didn't break in to hurt Vicki—he broke in for new clothing to aid his escape from military prison.

Most viewers, particularly those with previous experience and understanding of the way procedurals work, assume that a woman wearing just a nightgown alone with a strange man in a bedroom is in danger of being sexually assaulted. It is a reasonable conclusion when the scene draws so much attention to the bed—showing first the sleeping couple, then the rumpled sheets, the empty space next to Vicki Spain when the stranger enters the room. All the clues are there to lead the audience to read that danger into the scene. While developing dramatic tension by subverting viewers' expectations of rape would be a smart move, this scene is telling in terms of *NCIS'* overall treatment of rape. The episode comes late in the first season and marks the first time the show includes even the suggestion of rape. In and of itself, the scene is a relief; Vicki Spain was not sexually assaulted and pre- sumably would discover later that the man who broke into her home hadn't actually committed the crime for which he was incarcerated. And while the experience was most likely traumatic for the character, she made it through physically unscathed. As a part of the show's overall portrayal of rape, how- ever, this scene is troubling in its dismissiveness.

What the subverted expectations of rape suggest is that even when view- ers see it coming, when there doesn't seem to be any other logical assump- tion to make about what comes next, the viewer is wrong. Rape is not a real issue in this scene, even though the show has set viewers up to believe that it will be. Viewers are led to believe the nature of this incident is going to be one thing and are surprised and relieved when it is not. Vicki Spain might be shaken up—her home was broken into while she slept, after all—but she was not raped and, while she didn't know it at the time, she most likely wasn't in any real danger during the ordeal. Taken by itself, the outcome of this scene is positive. But in terms of the precedent it sets, in terms of preparing viewers to dismiss their assumptions about what visual cues will or will not lead to rape and about what they know about when a rape will happen, this scene is damaging as it suggests that even when we see it coming, we are wrong.

The next scene in this episode shows NCIS agents DiNozzo and Kate[9] discussing not the case, as they have yet to be assigned it, but the expecta- tions of an audience during a horror movie. While the two agents consider the possibilities for misleading viewers, what this metacommentary really does is dismiss the potential act of rape from the previous scene in Vicki Spain's home—it breaks the fourth wall and suggests that not only are the writers aware of the subverted expectations, but they are counting on their ability to lead viewers to the wrong conclusion. While the scene does add dramatic tension to the episode, it also suggests that expectations of rape are misguided even when viewers have been led there by the events of the episode itself. As mentioned previously, this scene in and of itself might not be a cause for concern, and this analysis might seem overwrought. But when considered as the establishing scene for the pattern *NCIS* creates when repre- senting rape and the women who suffer because of it, the opening scene of "UnSEALed" is troubling in its dismissiveness, evidenced even further by the fact that Vicki Spain's name only ever appears in the credits; she is never named in the episode.

After a single instance of not-rape in Season One, *NCIS* had five episodes containing rape narratives in Season Two. The first was Season Two, Epi- sode Two, "The Good Wives Club."[10] This episode begins when a construc- tion crew discovers an underground bunker that contains a woman's body. There are no obvious signs of sexual trauma on Carolyn Figgis' body as she is too badly decomposed for the medical examiner to determine the full extent of what happened to her, but she was found chained to a bed, dressed in a wedding gown, and had been held captive for months prior to her death. This episode builds on the groundwork laid by "UnSEALed" in that it finds ways to erase the cues viewers see as signs of rape: Carolyn and others who suffered in the same way were held in replicas of a 1950s bedroom and used to fulfill the role of dutiful "wife" for their captor. It seems improbable that sexual assault wasn't a part of the ordeal these women suffered. Yet the idea is never mentioned as part of the team's investigation. While it makes sense that the team's attention would be focused on the fact that these women had been abducted and murdered, especially once it is determined that another victim might still be out there and alive, the lack of even a mention of sexual assault as a possibility in these circumstances is suspect.

"The Good Wives Club" is the first rape-related episode to deal with a likely example of military sexual trauma (MST), a phenomenon that will receive much more attention throughout this and other chapters and that refers to sexual assault suffered by active military personnel, typically at the hands of other active military personnel. Carolyn Figgis and Barbara Swain—the victim Gibbs' team is able to rescue by the end of the episode—were abducted and held captive by a military chaplain. This is the only example in the first ten seasons of *NCIS* that most likely deals with an actual case of MST, in which both victim and perpetrator are military personnel. The most disconcerting part of this is the fact that it is never labeled as such nor is the possibility even discussed. Further, by the time Barbara Swain is rescued by Agent DiNozzo, she is suffering from Stockholm syndrome and attacks him with a lamp as he is attempting to free her. Her likely sexual assault is never called such; she has physically assaulted DiNozzo, whom viewers see as her rescuer; and even though she is clearly a victim in so many ways, her potential rape is couched within a totally unequal and nonconsensual "relationship." The episode has set up a series of distractions that call most of the viewers' attention away from the fact that whatever else is true about her, she is most likely a rape survivor.

In Season Two, Episode Four, "Lt. Jane Doe,"[11] the show deals forthrightly with a rape narrative for the first time. A woman's body is found on the ground near the Norfolk Naval Base; she is dressed in a navy lieutenant's uniform. She has no identification, but in addition to rape and murder, the crimes committed against her include branding the back of her neck with a trident. These details remind Ducky of a series of similar crimes with the same signature from years earlier. The perpetrator of those earlier crimes was caught and imprisoned; the team discovers he has recently been released.

While canvassing the area near where the body was found, DiNozzo enters a bar. He is interviewing potential witnesses who might be able to identify the victim. When he shows a male bartender a picture of the dead woman, the bartender asks what she has done. DiNozzo's response is that "she got herself raped and killed." What might seem like a minor matter of word choice is in fact a loaded example of the subtle victim-blaming that takes place throughout *NCIS*. DiNozzo's "got" suggests that the woman who is eventually identified as Janice Santos was in some way responsible for what happened to her. This phrasing implies that something Janice did led to her rape and then her death, that had she acted differently, she might have avoided being raped and killed and that she in some way deserved what happened to her since she put herself in a bad situation. DiNozzo's goal with that remark seemed to be to shock the bartender into cooperating. What he couldn't have intended was sparking this in-depth look at how *NCIS* talks about and represents rape.

Janice Santos is not an officer in the military even though her body was found dressed as one. She did not serve in the military in any capacity. The person responsible for her death did, though. While it seems like the team has a promising suspect early on, as the episode unfolds, they discover that the man who committed the earlier crimes Ducky remembers could not have raped and killed Janice on account of his own death weeks prior to hers and shortly after his release from prison. While there were plenty of crimes the dead man was guilty of, he was framed for Janice Santos' death, and the individual responsible for her "rape" and murder, the person who dressed her in a lieutenant's uniform and dumped her body, was a military serviceperson. Naval Petty Officer Cynthia Cluxton works for NCIS and was the first to arrive on the scene when the body was discovered. She was also Janice Santos' girlfriend. Cluxton removed evidence from NCIS to use in covering up her own crime. This revelation is troubling for several reasons. While it does shed light on the possibility that women can in fact perpetrate rape, this petty officer is the only example of an active military service member whose crime is investigated and called rape. According to data from the *2012 Workplace and Gender Relations Survey of Active Duty Members* conducted by the Defense Manpower Data Center for the Department of Defense, only 1% of all offenders within the military were reported as female only.[12] While there is not and probably should not be an expectation that the world created on a television show directly reflect real-world statistics, it is unsettling that instead of focusing on, or even providing a single clear and specific example of, the 94% of offenders who are male only,[13] *NCIS* highlighted the 1% in this episode. While there is a real-world basis for including female offenders, the specifics of this episode, when considered as a part of the overall treatment of rape on the show, contribute to a skewed representation. Additionally, this episode sets a bad precedent: viewers are introduced here to the first of several examples of women who lie or are accused of lying about rape. In this instance, the woman who lies about rape is not the victim but rather the "rapist."

The quotations marks are in no way meant to diminish the severity of the crime Cluxton committed against Santos. Instead, because the "rape" was staged, those quotations marks call attention to the need for further consideration of what to call the violation of Janice's body. From the beginning of the episode, Gibbs' team, with Cluxton's assistance, has been investigating a rape/homicide. When it is discovered that Cluxton herself murdered Janice and then injected her body with the stolen semen of a rapist, it is still clear that a violation has occurred. Would it still be defined as rape, though? Perhaps not legally, as Janice was dead when the forcible entry of her body occurred, but that seems more a technicality than anything else.

Further complicating the issue is the fact that Cluxton, who was clearly aware of Janice's sexual preferences, disregards her ex-lover's lesbianism by inserting a man's sexual fluid into her body. As one of the rare examples of a homosexual couple on a show about the military, it seems like the show is sending an unfortunate message about lesbians when the only one viewers see over an extended period murdered her lover and staged her rape as well.

In addition to these complicating factors, by the end of "Lt. Jane Doe," one thing that is clear about the violation of Janice Santos' body is that it is not an example of MST. This episode is another example of erasure insofar as viewers disassociate Janice Santos from the military once it is revealed that she was merely dressed as a navy lieutenant and had never actually served as one.

Season Two, Episode Nine, "Forced Entry,"[14] centers around an attempted rape of Laura Rowens, a military wife. While her husband is deployed overseas, Laura is surprised in her home by an intruder. She attempts to fight him off, but he shoves her onto the couch and begins to remove his clothing. During their struggle, he refers to her "enjoying the rough stuff" and declares, "This is going to be good." Laura produces a gun from behind the couch cushions and aims it at the intruder, holding it on him for several seconds—long enough for him to suggest she take it easy—before shooting him twice. The scene fades to the opening credits with a shot of the intruder sprawled on the floor, gasping and bleeding.

This episode is the first in which Gibbs has any prolonged contact with a victim of sexual assault. This case is an attempted rape, and the majority of the episode calls that fact itself—and Laura Rowens and her account of events—into question. When the intruder/would-be rapist talks to DiNozzo and Kate in the hospital, he claims the whole scenario was supposed to be a game, that Laura Rowens had invited him to her house and that they had a prior romantic relationship online. Some of the physical evidence seems to support his claims: There are no signs of forced entry at the house, and later, the team will find messages supposedly exchanged between the two on Laura Rowens' computer.

But even before his team discovers that evidence, Gibbs is suspicious of Laura Rowens. While it is, of course, his job to investigate when an attempted rape occurs on a military base, even as he is waiting to speak to

Laura for the first time, he is reading instant messages that pop up on her computer screen. When she arrives, he accepts her offer of coffee and they talk about what happened. Gibbs reassures Laura that she is not in any trouble for shooting the intruder—she did what she had to do to keep herself safe. Laura confides in Gibbs that she did not want to kill the man; she just wanted him to go away.

When their conversation is over, Gibbs makes an offer that seems considerate: He tells Laura Rowens that she can call or email him day or night. There are two issues, though, that make a critical viewer doubt Gibbs' motives. First, the mention of email calls to mind the interest he took in her instant messages. Second, and perhaps more importantly, Gibbs' technophobia and the fact that he does not check his email have been well established by this point in the series. By adding email to his offer, Gibbs seems to be sending a message to the viewer: There is more going on with the technology scattered throughout that scene—and the rest of the episode—than what meets the eye. Gibbs already suspects something isn't right with the story he is being told.

As the episode develops, the would-be rapist's claims align with Gibbs' suspicion. Laura Rowens' next conversation with Gibbs takes place in interrogation—not the nicely appointed conference room that the team frequently uses to talk with other victims and witnesses. Before the conversation begins, viewers see Laura Rowens through the two-way mirror and watch her over the shoulders of Kate, McGee, and DiNozzo. The team has discovered Laura's profile on a dating website, and rape fantasies are listed among her interests there. Viewers watch the team watch Laura Rowens as she wrings her hands. They have the following discussion:

Kate: What kind of woman is into rape fantasies?

McGee: Well, actually, it's not all that uncommon, Kate.

Kate: Well, actually, it's sick and disturbing, McGee. [15]

Viewers are often expected to align themselves with Kate, who frequently serves as a conscience for her coworkers. And in this case, her assessment of "sick and disturbing" seems apt but not her application of those adjectives to Laura Rowens. In this episode, *NCIS* has created a military wife whose husband is on active duty overseas. The fact that she has a profile on an online dating site is damaging; it is difficult to sympathize with a woman cheating on her soldier husband. Additionally, when viewers hear about the character's supposed interest in rape fantasies and Kate's response, two things are likely to occur. First, the revelation adds substance to doubt that already exists about Laura Rowens' account. Second, it serves as a very literal manifestation of the "she was asking for it" rape myth that suggests there are things women do to put themselves in a position where they deserve to be raped. Laura Rowens no longer seems like the victim of an attempted crime; she isn't trustworthy and admits to Internet flirtations behind her husband's back. It becomes more difficult to view her as a victim because she is in interrogation, viewers are looking at her through a two-way mirror, and the evidence is suggesting that she is some sort of black widow, luring a man to her home and then shooting him for trying to play the game or take what she supposedly offered him.

At the end of "Forced Entry," however, the team discovers Laura Rowens was telling the truth the whole time. The would-be rapist falsified the correspondence with Laura Rowens, and he was not only a serial rapist but also a murderer. There is no mention of the dating profile, which Laura did admit was her own, so it isn't entirely clear whether the interest in rape fantasies was actually Laura's or if it was part of the illusion created by the would-be rapist. With the man and his partner in custody, the team is gathered in the office, discussing the case. Kate says, "I can't believe we almost let those two get away."[16] There is no concern for Laura Rowens or the fact that they wrongly believed she lied or that they might possibly owe her an apology for making an already traumatic experience more so. Instead, she has vanished from the episode entirely, and viewers never see any attempt to make amends for the way the team judged her and painted her as a liar. The last time viewers saw her was in that interrogation room being treated like a criminal. Of course, this mirrors real life all too often when the victim's credibility and sexual history, which are called into question after a rape (or attempted rape), have been reported to the authorities.

There is another example of an attempted rape in Season Two, Episode Thirteen, "The Meat Puzzle."[17] In this case, the rape narrative is part of the backstory for the current investigation. Navy Lieutenant Sylvia Waksal was nearly raped, then beaten to death when her civilian attacker was unable to perform the sex act. This closed case comes to the attention of Gibbs' team when bodies of individuals involved in the prosecution of Waksal's killer are discovered cut to pieces and stuffed into steel drums. Dr. Mallard was the medical examiner whose testimony led to the conviction; he is in danger for most of the episode, and saving him is the central focus throughout. Viewers do not learn much more about what happened to Sylvia Waksal; the crimes committed against her aren't developed and are hardly even discussed. They do, however, contribute to two trends that exist across all instances of rape throughout *NCIS*. First, the episode contributes to the attempts to erase, or in this case minimize, sexually violent crime. Using the distance provided by time and putting Ducky's familiar face in peril creates a remove between viewers and what happened to Lt. Waksal. Second, this episode serves as another example of the show's message that men in the military are not rapists: even when a female rape victim is a military serviceperson, her attacker is not.

In Season Two, Episode Twenty-Two, "SWAK,"[18] *NCIS* attempts to shine a light on several important issues related to real-life rape statistics: In addition to addressing the possibilities of persisting psychological trauma for victims, the episode addresses low prosecution rates of offenders. According to information gathered from the Department of Justice and the National Center for Policy Analysis, for every hundred rapes that occur, only forty-six will be reported, nine rapists will be prosecuted, five will be convinced of felonies, and only three will go to prison.[19] While the episode does not directly discuss these issues, it tries to provide an example that addresses them. Two years earlier, Hanna Lowell's daughter Sarah reported being raped after she was found tied to a bed in a room at the Admiral Bay Hotel two days after the attack. The investigating agents had dozens of naval suspects who were also staying at the hotel, but DNA evidence cleared them all. "SWAK" uses this incident as backstory for the events of the present day: DiNozzo opens an envelope containing an activated biological agent that Hanna, who owns a pharmaceutical company, mailed to NCIS because she is convinced NCIS is lying about the DNA results to protect its own. The envelope she used to mail the *Y. pestis* (pneumonic plague) contained a message with the case number for the investigation of Sarah's rape. It is the investigation into the biological attack that is the central focus of this episode.

NCIS agent Cassie Yates, who only appears in this single episode, worked the original rape case. When she arrives to assist Gibbs' team with the current investigation, she explains that even though she was a probationary agent two years ago, she was the one who interviewed the victim, Sarah, since she was female and fairly young and would therefore be easier for Sarah to talk to. As Cassie tells Gibbs the story of what happened to Sarah, viewers see a montage of images from the hospital two years ago: Sarah Lowell crying, her mother screaming, flashes of the hospital room and the drama of those moments. Cassie explains that Sarah suffered from traumatic amnesia and had trouble remembering anything that happened to her. She was unable to identify her rapist.

This scene is one of the few examples throughout the first ten seasons of *NCIS* in which a rape victim is treated carefully. Neither Cassie nor her partner doubted the victim's story, they did the best they could to think of what would make her most comfortable during her interviews, and they worked the case until they ran out of leads and there was nothing more they could do. It says something pretty damning about Gibbs' team, and possibly the show itself, that the first example of this kind of treatment of a rape victim happened at a remove of two years, under the guidance of agents not associated with Gibbs' team, and in the background of an episode focused on an attempt to indiscriminately kill NCIS agents.

Once they have all the information they need to confront Sarah's mother, the woman who nearly killed DiNozzo, Hanna admits to the biological attack and to her motivation, accusing NCIS of covering for her daughter's rapist and declaring that Sarah "never recovered from the horror of that weekend." But the worst of what this episode does in terms of the overall representation of rape is what comes next: In another interview with Cassie Yates in another hospital, Sarah Lowell begins to cry and admits that she was never raped. Her boyfriend, who had tied her to the bed as a joke during sex, never returned to their hotel room after he was hit and killed by a car. When Cassie asks Sarah why she lied about the rape, Sarah's response trivializes everything rape victims endure during and after they are attacked: "I was tied naked to a bed. What else could I tell my mother?"[20]

Instead of admitting that she made sexually adventurous choices that may have been mildly embarrassing outside of the bedroom, Sarah Lowell invented a rape scenario that nearly led to the death of one of the main characters of *NCIS*. In what was arguably the most sympathetic portrayal and treatment of a rape victim in ten seasons, the overall message of the episode seems to be "Look at what happens when we are nice." Sarah Lowell's lie and the threat to DiNozzo's life almost act as a justification for the callous way in which the majority of this show's rape narratives treat victims. Not only has this episode provided a textbook example of the rape myth about women who are later embarrassed about their sexual activities "crying rape," but it also acts to justify the suspicion leveled by the members of Gibbs' team at rape victims from this point in the series on.

"SWAK" does quite a bit of work to distance viewers from the trauma suffered by actual rape victims. As previously mentioned, the "attack" took place in the past, in the background of a current case that has put a significant character at risk. Even before discovering that Sarah lied about her attack, viewers' concern was at best split between discovering the identity of her rapist and worrying about DiNozzo's declining health in quarantine. More likely, though, viewers are much more concerned about DiNozzo, whom they have known for nearly two full seasons by this point, than they are about Sarah Lowell, who has only just been introduced and whose life is not in any immediate danger. And once her lie is revealed, she is easily dismissed as a selfish person whose lack of regard for possible consequences nearly killed DiNozzo.

The most reasonable and seemingly accurate data available about the number of real-world false rape accusations comes from the Department of Justice: "In 1995, 87% of recorded forcible rapes were completed crimes and the remainder were classified as attempts. Law enforcement agencies indicated that about 8% of forcible rapes reported to them were determined to be unfounded and were excluded from the count of crimes."[21] While there are other statistics to suggest the percentage might be as low as 2% or as high as 40% (even some as high as 90%), the studies from which those numbers were drawn seem dubious to a critical eye—be it due to flawed methodology or sample sizes that were too small. The 8% discussed by the Department of Justice in 1997, however, was based on data from sixteen thousand law enforcement agencies on local, county, and statewide levels.[22] Of the ten episodes considered for this chapter, there are eleven named victims (this number does not include Vicki Spain from "UnSEALed," who was named only in the credits). Three of the eleven were killed in rape/homicides and were clearly in no position to lie about their assaults. Of the remaining eight, four, or 50% of victims who survive their attacks,[23] are either accused of or actually lying about what happened to them. Sarah Lowell may be the most straightforward example of a rape "victim" lying, but she is only one specific instance in a disturbing trend on *NCIS*: portraying and/or treating women who report rapes as liars.

While Season Two contained five episodes (of twenty-three total episodes—nearly 22% of the season) that included a rape narrative, Seasons Three, Four, and Five contained none. It isn't until Season Six, Episode Twelve, "Caged,"[24] when another rape narrative becomes part of an investigation. This episode takes place primarily inside a women's prison. While rape is clearly defined as a crime in the *NCIS* universe, when forced sexual contact takes place within the walls of a prison, it seemingly becomes less so. This mirrors attitudes about prison rape in many police dramas and even the real world; prison rape is used as a threat or a joke in many instances. But rape among incarcerated persons is a very real and significant problem within the prison system. Cindy and David Struckman-Johnson, in their report "Sexual Coercion Rates in Seven Midwestern Prisons for Men," explain that "one in five male inmates has experienced a pressured or forced sex incident" while "women inmates, who tend to be assaulted by male staff members, experience rates of abuse ranging from 8 to 27 percent."[25] This episode is a missed opportunity where *NCIS* could have addressed sexual assault as an issue within incarcerated populations, an issue that is rarely given the kinds of attention it deserves.

When the body of a navy officer is found in a park, McGee is sent to a women's prison to interview an inmate, Celia Roberts. She is incarcerated for a series of murders with a signature similar to the new victim. McGee is after Celia's confession. While McGee questions her, a riot breaks out in the visitors' center. Several guards are hurt; one is killed. The inmates, including Celia Roberts and Sharon Bellows, take control of the visitors' center. Gibbs' team comes in to help the warden and his staff address the hostage situation as McGee is among the hostages.

There are three different ways rape enters into the plot of this episode. The first is a nearly casual mention of it early in the investigation into which inmate was responsible for the deadly stabbing of a guard: One of the inmates mentions that the male guard had been in the bathroom with one of the female inmates. The implication is that this kind of activity happens all the time, and there is no discussion of the fact that any sexual contact between a prison guard and an inmate, due to the unequal nature of their relationship and the power one party has over the other, would likely be considered rape under color of authority. The lack of response to that information on the part of the NCIS agents is just the first example of how Gibbs' team mishandles instances of rape in this episode.

Later in "Caged," when questioning one of the prison guards, DiNozzo makes a poorly veiled threat. If a prison guard were to end up on the other side of the bars, DiNozzo says, he would be like the prom queen on prom night. There are multiple ways in which DiNozzo's statement is problematic. First of all, while it may not be his intention, DiNozzo is suggesting that a high school–age female is expected to have sex on prom night. Not just sex, though, because this is actually a rape threat. Indirectly, DiNozzo is comparing prom queens to rape victims, which seems to imply that prom queens who are raped on prom night should expect such treatment. Second, in order to obtain this guard's cooperation, DiNozzo threatens him with a traumatic and violent crime. The way DiNozzo treats prison rape as an expected occurrence and uses it to get the information he needs from the guard adds credence to the idea that prisoners should be sexually violated as some necessary part of their incarceration or as a part of paying their debt to society. The fact that this rape threat is used as a bargaining tool—by a federal agent, no less—is troubling.

These two mentions of rape in "Caged" make it clear that law enforcement on *NCIS* is aware of but unwilling to do anything about the issue of prison rape. Viewers instead see law enforcement officers who perpetuate the crime—the guards who sexually assault female inmates and DiNozzo himself taking advantage of widespread ideas about sexual assault by making threats. The third and most prominent role rape plays in this episode, though, involves the dead prison guard and the daughter of one of the inmates. Zoe Bellows is a high school student whose mother, Sharon, is incarcerated for killing her boyfriend after years of physical and emotional abuse. During their investigation, Gibbs' team finds provocative pictures of Zoe Bellows on the dead guard Trimble's cell phone. Viewers see the pictures of Zoe, who is clearly distraught, sitting on Trimble's lap on the edge of a bed and in other suggestive positions she is obviously uncomfortable with. When questioned in the conference room at NCIS, Zoe explains that the first time the guard raped her, she was so disgusted she threw up. But Zoe doesn't call what happened to her "rape"; her exact words were "the first time it happened."[26]

The agents on Gibbs' team seem to take their cues from her; none of them call what happened between Zoe and the guard—who threatened to kill Sharon if Zoe told anyone—rape. While questioning Sharon to determine what she knew about the situation, McGee actually refers to the "relationship" between Zoe and Trimble.[27] It is Sharon who has to articulate that her daughter clearly does not want to be there. But she doesn't call it rape either. It becomes obvious, though, that it was Sharon who killed Trimble, in retaliation for his repeated rape of her daughter.

As the hostage situation is ending, while waiting outside for Trimble's killer to turn herself over to the prison warden, DiNozzo and Ziva David[28] discuss the unpleasantness of this particular case.

DiNozzo: Sometimes this job sucks.

Ziva: Sharon Bellows was in for killing an abusive boyfriend.

DiNozzo: And while she's inside, her daughter's being abused.[29]

While "abused" is certainly much closer to "raped" than the "relationship" McGee referred to earlier, it still doesn't name the specific crime committed against Zoe Bellows. The fact that the sexual contact Trimble forced on Zoe Bellows might even be statutory rape, given her age, regardless of whether she consented only amplifies the problem. This is carried even further when, only moments later, Celia Roberts, the convicted murderer McGee went in to interview and the woman who confessed to Trimble's murder as well, is the only person to name what happened to Zoe Bellows: "Trimble was raping Sharon Bellows' daughter," she announces to the prison warden.[30] One of the things viewers know about investigative dramas like *NCIS*, though, is that we aren't supposed to relate to the criminals; putting that word, "rape," only in Celia's mouth gives her power but diminishes the weight of the truth of Zoe Bellows' ordeal.

In Season Six, Episode Fifteen, "Deliverance,"[31] viewers get a glimpse into Gibbs' past and discover a young pregnant woman who saved Gibbs' life in Colombia twenty years earlier. The son she had, who was the product of rape, is enmeshed in the investigation of a present-day murder. Rose Tamayo is a rape victim who survived being attacked and with whom Gibbs had a brief romantic relationship. Though this rape narrative is relegated to the background of this episode, there are several aspects of it worth consideration in light of the overall patterns *NCIS* establishes when dealing with such stories. First of all, Rose Tamayo died several years prior to the present action in the episode. As such, viewers hear about what happened to her several times removed from her own testimony. Even in the flashback scenes to Gibbs' memories of what happened in Colombia, Rose has no voice—she literally never speaks, much less speaks out about her assault. That she was raped is also important because of the questions this backstory raises about how male investigators seek justice for rape victims. Gibbs, a military sniper at the time, was sent to Colombia to assassinate the man who raped Rose for other crimes he committed, not because of the rape. Even so, Gibbs' romantic entanglement with Rose gives viewers room to question the role of the male detective character and representations of justice for rape victims. In *Rape on Prime Time: Television, Masculinity, and Sexual Violence*, Lisa M. Cuklanz explores the roles played by male detectives in prime-time television from 1976 to 1990. She discusses the idea that "masculinity solves, atones for, and soothes victims after rape [. . .]. Detectives frequently play a nurturing role in relation to rape survivors."[32] She continues to address the issue at hand in the episodes of shows she studied, but her findings can be applied to this episode of *NCIS*: "These episodes portray a world in which connections among women are rare and in which the proper response to rape involves male caretaking of helpless victims as well as male concern with 'justice' for what has been done to them."[33] Gibbs easily steps into the role of male caretaker; however, it is worth noting that the justice he sought was not actually for her. He did not kill her rapist as a result of the specific crime that had been committed against her—which seems to fit Cuklanz's use of "justice" in quotation marks. Rose Tamayo was the helpless victim—made more so by the fact that she was pregnant, since pregnancy is often equated with fragility, but less so by the fact that she is the only reason Gibbs survived that trip. While it would seem that Gibbs' previous relationship with a rape victim would influence his interaction with and understanding of other victims, it seems instead that the series focuses on broader applications of the ways viewers are distanced from Rose Tamayo rather than on Gibbs' connection to her.

To this point, the *NCIS* episodes containing rape narratives have been considered in the order in which they aired. With two more episodes for consideration, the more recent of the two is another example of rape narrative as backstory. In Season Ten, Episode Seventeen, "Prime Suspect,"[34] Gibbs' barber Frank confides that he suspects his son, Cameron, may be the serial killer sought by the police. The established timeline of the murders corresponds with Cameron's time at a nearby college and the three-year break between victims aligns with the time Cameron was away when he enlisted in the navy. Gibbs' team determines that Cameron is not the killer, but the course of their investigation does reveal accusations of sexual assault in Cameron's past.

Frank: Do you remember when he left college, middle of his sophomore year?

Gibbs: Yeah, he got hurt. Lost his scholarship. The best left-handed quarterback to come out of the D.C. high schools.

Frank: I was too ashamed to tell you the truth. Cameron was accused of date rape. Now eventually the charges were dropped, but he was thrown out.

Gibbs: Long time ago, Frank.[35]

Viewers might respond to Gibbs that it was approximately three years ago, which isn't all that long. Beyond that, though, Gibbs' dismissiveness of the charges is telling; whatever happened in Cameron's past at school, there was sufficient cause for concern that he was expelled as a result. In the real world, an awareness exists that campuses frequently mishandle sexual assault complaints, to the point that it may serve as a deterrent to reporting when an assault takes place, as explained by the findings of a study funded by the Department of Justice in 2002: "Contributing to the low reporting rates among college students may be the traditional lack of responsiveness of colleges and universities in handling complaints of sexual assault."[36] Given the prevalence of headlines in the real-world media as well as representations in television and movies, the majority of college students are aware that "even in cases where the alleged student perpetrator is found responsible for the assault, punishment is often light (such as community service) and, at worst, includes expulsion from the institution."[37] With that understanding of how campus sexual assault is typically handled, an informed viewer should be skeptical that Cameron would have been expelled from school for a sexual assault complaint with no standing. That Gibbs is so dismissive is upsetting but aligns with his overall attitude toward sexual assault.

When Ziva uncovers the allegations, she reports to Gibbs: "Cameron Dean's life started falling apart after high school. In his second year of college, a sorority girl accused him of date rape. The charges were eventually dropped. He left college and enlisted in the Navy."[38] By providing such limited additional detail, "Prime Suspect" withholds not only justice from Cameron's accuser, but her very identity. Describing the victim only as a "sorority girl," Ziva's account of the incident changes the narrative of Cameron's departure from school: she says he left, whereas his father said he was kicked out. Her report lacks a clear acknowledgment of the victim's identity at the same time that her wording shifts the causality between the events themselves, erasing or at least further obscuring the crime that likely took place—since dropped charges against a campus athlete don't actually exonerate the accused.

And it is the accused that Gibbs and his team want viewers to sympathize with. As the only example of a campus rape narrative, this episode flips the most likely script in real campus rape situations: the campus football star getting away with rape with very few, if any, consequences. While this single instance might not prove anything, the absence of any additional campus rape narratives that portray the reality of this crime in this setting does present a skewed understanding of this very real issue.

The final episode of *NCIS* that deals with a rape narrative is Season Seven, Episode Twenty-Three, "Patriot Down."[39] NCIS agent Lara Macy has been murdered, and Gibbs' team is searching her open cases for clues when they discover Macy had been investigating the rape of navy sailor Kaylen Burrows at the time of her death. They pick up the investigation in order to determine whether or not the case had anything to do with Macy's murder, not because—or at least not solely because—Kaylen Burrows deserves justice.

Kaylen's situation is almost unique in the rape-related episodes. She is the only military serviceperson who survives rape and has the violent crime that happened to her labeled as such by the investigating agents. Carolyn Figgis and Barbara Swain, victims in Season Two, Episode Two, "The Good Wives Club," were military, but Carolyn died and Barbara was never labeled a rape survivor. Lt. Sylvia Waksal, whose attempted rape and murder served as backstory in Season Two, Episode Thirteen, "The Meat Puzzle," wasn't actually raped; the perpetrator in that episode beat her to death in response to his inability to rape her. All of the rest of the rape victims—most of whom were not actually raped but instead threatened with rape—were civilians, even though one of them (Laura Rowens from Season Two, Episode Nine, "Forced Entry") was married to a serviceman and attacked on a military base.

In 2013, Academy Award nominee for Best Documentary *The Invisible War* worked to shed light on the reality of military sexual trauma faced by both women and men serving in the armed forces. Using statistics from the Department of Defense, *The Invisible War* establishes a clear problem of sexual assault within the military and shines a spotlight on the issue. According to the *2012 Workplace and Gender Relations Survey of Active Duty Members*, 6.1% of women and 1.2% of men "indicated they experienced unwanted sexual contact in 2012."[40] Only 17% of individuals reported the incident.[41] So while Kaylen Burrows is the only example of a military serviceperson—female or male—who is explicitly labeled as a sexual assault survivor on *NCIS*, she would be far from alone in the real-world military, where MST is a significant problem.

Kaylen is also the only military serviceperson given the opportunity to contribute to the investigation into what happened to her. For all the ways Kaylen's role in a rape narrative is unique, one way it is not is in regard to the way her statement and credibility as a witness are questioned. She is portrayed as a resistant witness, refusing to cooperate with Agent Macy and later with Gibbs' team. Because the rape investigation is a part of his investigation into Agent Macy's death, Gibbs will not allow Burrows to drop her complaint. When DiNozzo and Ziva visit Kaylen's ship to question her, viewers notice, as do the investigators, that two of Kaylen's shipmates seem particularly interested in their conversation. They hover nearby while the agents talk with Kaylen and even attempt to interrupt the conversation to suggest that she needs to report for duty. The way they attempt to insert themselves into the investigation is enough to raise suspicion and leads viewers to wonder if perhaps they are so concerned because they have something to hide. Whether an individual viewer is aware of the prevalence of military sexual trauma in the real armed forces, the show creates a scenario that asks viewers to consider these two men as suspects. Kaylen refuses to talk to NCIS at this point, which adds credence to the possibility that she is worried about who might overhear her saying what.

Later, in the interrogation room where she is brought for questioning, Kaylen names a college student as her attacker. This is not the first time a rape victim has been questioned in interrogation, but it is interesting in this case because the team does not doubt Kaylen's word that she was attacked. Instead, Gibbs uses the interrogation room as a strategic tool, a way to remind both Kaylen and the viewer that what is really at stake in this episode is justice for Agent Macy, not for Kaylen Burrows.

Gibbs' exact words are "I'm not forcing you to do anything here. I get the kind of pressure you're under. Don't let someone get away with this. It's not just about you."[42] By framing his interrogation that way—doesn't Kaylen owe it to Agent Macy, who was only trying to help her when she was killed?—Gibbs convinces Kaylen to name her attackers. Even while suggesting that he understands the pressure she is under, which seems improbable, he adds to that pressure in disturbing ways that mimic the kind of victim-blaming too often associated with rape investigations. His approach constitutes force, and he is pressuring her to do something she clearly is not comfortable with. Gibbs claims that "Macy died trying to arrest whoever did this to you."[43] The end of the episode reveals, however, that Macy was killed as part of a planned attack on Gibbs himself; her death had nothing to do with Kaylen Burrows. While not the most straightforward example of victim-blaming, Gibbs' word choice and implications are in line with that particular and inappropriate response to rape—indirectly suggesting that if Burrows hadn't gotten herself raped, then Macy wouldn't have had to investigate and she wouldn't have ended up dead.

After the interrogation, NCIS agents visit the home of the college student Kaylen named as her attacker, where they are confronted by his angry father. When the agents begin their questioning, the father accuses Kaylen of lying about his son's involvement in her assault. The family already has a lawyer present at the house, and he is the one to explicitly address several important points that viewers are most likely considering. It is the lawyer who explains that Tyler, the accused rapist, didn't actually commit the crime but rather witnessed it. The story is that Tyler, a witness, was beaten up because the two navy men knew he could identify them as Kaylen's rapists. The lawyer's exact words to explain why she would accuse Tyler instead of naming her real attackers: "She's afraid, intimidated. They're on that ship together twenty-four seven."[44] This reasoning makes sense to a viewer, and apparently to the NCIS agents as well, as they discuss it later back at the navy yard.

DiNozzo: What if the lawyer is right?

Ziva: Then I understand why Burrows kept her mouth shut.

McGee: I don't. Why would you let someone get away with rape?

Ziva: Perception. Burrows is in the military. If a woman cries rape, no man on that ship would ever totally trust her again.[45]

Between the sixth and seventh seasons of *NCIS*, Agent Ziva David was held captive by a group of terrorists in the Middle Eastern desert and subjected to torture. Even faithful viewers of the show are not sure the extent of what she suffered while being held. When she was rescued by DiNozzo, McGee, and Gibbs in the Season Seven premiere, there was abundant evidence of physical violence, but the show never addressed whether the trauma she experienced included sexual violence. It certainly seems possible if not even probable that her captors would have used rape as a weapon. Whether her own past experience included sexual violence, though, Ziva's response, and the understanding of rape in the military it represents, is troubling. Instead of worrying about Kaylen and her state of mind while recovering from the trauma she experienced or how she would be able to trust her fellow sailors if two of them committed this crime against her, Ziva's comments focus on how the other, male sailors would respond to Kaylen—and this is when the agents do not doubt that she was actually attacked. But Ziva's choice of words—"if a woman cries rape"—suggests that Kaylen could be lying and that even if she isn't, the difficulties she will face in the future won't involve trusting others but instead being trusted by them. Ziva creates a very clear framework for potential victim-blaming. By choosing to focus on how others will or will not trust Kaylen instead of how she will move beyond her traumatic experience and by not expressing any concern over whether such reactions are appropriate or fair, DiNozzo, McGee, and especially Ziva suggest that perhaps a woman who reports rape has done something worthy of lost trust. Additionally, the lack of understanding McGee shows in this exchange about the realities of what a rape victim in the military (or otherwise) would face is disconcerting. As a trained federal agent for whom part of his job would be responding to such cases, he should be more aware of the fact that reporting a sexual assault is a difficult experience for victims for a multitude of reasons.

So either Kaylen Burrows lied or she would have zero credibility left with her fellow sailors if her attackers were also military. If that is truly the case, it seems impossible to disagree with Ziva's earlier claim—that she understands why Kaylen would want to keep quiet about the truth. If those were the only possible outcomes for Kaylen if she spoke up, of course she would choose silence.

When Tyler Hammond and his angry father are brought to interrogation for further questioning after Kaylen reveals Tyler's father also raped her, Gibbs gets a confession along with more victim-blaming. "That Navy girl," he says, "she was drunk, but she wanted it."[46] Here viewers are exposed to concrete examples of two rape myths—first, that whether or not Kaylen had been drinking influences whether or not she was raped, and second, that she must have wanted the sexual contact or been asking for it in some way. Gibbs takes offense at this claim, pushing the man back against the two-way mirror so forcefully, it cracks and breaks behind his head. Given the way Gibbs himself blamed Kaylen for the outcome of the situation she found herself in, even if that was for the "right" reasons, his violent reaction to the father's suggestion seems out of place and insincere.

This is the episode that comes closest to a narrative representing military sexual trauma. Not only is it not actually an example once the specifics become clear—navy sailor Kaylen Burrows was raped by two civilians while in France on liberty—but the agents investigating the case address the possibility in such a way that it would be exceedingly difficult for viewers to recognize the real stakes for a victim of such a crime either in the *NCIS* universe or in the real world. Instead of offering a meaningful opportunity to address and perhaps redress rape myths, the secrecy and uncooperativeness of the victim, in addition to comments made by both the perpetrators and investigators of the crime, support the idea that Kaylen Burrows is ultimately responsible or should be held accountable for what has been done to her.

NCIS is clearly doing something right if its longevity and popularity are any indication. Narrative arcs on the show typically include heinous crimes, yet the procedural formula allows viewers to feel secure in the knowledge that criminals will be apprehended and the end of each episode will redress whatever wrongs have been committed. Viewers see enough of the personal lives of the agents on Gibbs' team to invest in their well-being to the point that they care not only for the characters but also for the actors who play them. In fact, in 2013, Cote de Pablo and Pauley Perrette, the actresses who play Ziva David and Abby Sciuto, respectively, were named among the ten most appealing celebrities[47] —which speaks to the cultural significance of the show. In addition to being well liked, these actresses play well-developed, strong female characters. *NCIS* portrays women in nearly every light—as federal agents and directors of federal agencies, as terrorists and traitors, as sailors and marines, as wives, mothers, lesbians, and as victims and killers. The show presents a vast array of women whose stories are complicated and land at every point on the spectrum from innocent to guilty.

That being said, one area in which the show requires improvement is its treatment of rape and rape victims. While rape is clearly defined as a crime, the story lines and characters of *NCIS* are usually careless with and suspicious or dismissive of women who are raped. Nearly all of the women who report being raped throughout the show are either lying or accused of it, and it is the women who aren't suspected of lying who actually are (Sarah Lowell in "SWAK"). This bolsters the need for NCIS agents to treat rape victims with suspicion. What viewers see are repeated examples of women lying about rape, and they are thus trained to question the stories women on the show tell in episodes involving rape narratives, whether those women are civilian or military and whether they were attacked or, as in one case, the attacker (Cynthia Cluxton in "Lt. Jane Doe").

All this suspicion stems from Leroy Jethro Gibbs, the show's central character. His lack of sensitivity or sympathy for women who are raped is made evident through interrogations in hostile environments and the pressure he puts on them to discuss the things they are not comfortable with to further his own ends rather than for their own benefit. The fact that his team speaks so carelessly about rape victims—Kate when she asks what kind of woman would be turned on by rape fantasies in "Forced Entry," DiNozzo when he states that Janice Santos "got herself raped and killed" in "Lt. Jane Doe," McGee and Ziva in their oblivious conversation about trust in "Patriot Down"—mirrors Gibbs' carelessness at best and hostility at worst.

On *NCIS*, a show about military crime, most narratives that include rape present the crime as a civilian issue; only two of the rapists discussed here were military—the chaplain in "The Good Wives Club" and Cynthia Cluxton in "Lt. Jane Doe"—and both of those examples were complicated by the specific circumstances of the crimes actually committed and named. There were also no examples or even mentions of the possibility of male victims of sexual assault, with the single exception of the threat of prison rape leveled at a guard by Agent DiNozzo in "Caged."

By convoluting rape narratives to the point where there are several examples of what appears to be rape that turn out to be something else, and by relegating other examples to the distant past or backstory, the show does an excellent job of subverting viewers' expectations regarding sexual assault at the same time that it works to effectively erase or diminish it. By not calling instances of rape by that name and by ignoring the trauma faced by victims, *NCIS* manages to call limited attention to the effects of this particular crime even in the stories that supposedly deal with it.

On *NCIS*, investigating rape is a means to an end, but that end is rarely justice for rape victims. While every episode that includes a rape narrative does identify and punish the rapist, the show uses portrayals of rape and rape victims to add drama and tension to story arcs that are almost always about something other than the rape itself: murder (sometimes, but not always, of the woman who was raped), kidnapping, and even biological weapons attacks. Rarely are women who are raped in the *NCIS* universe given the opportunity to meaningfully assist investigations into the crimes committed against them, and when they are, the women are often portrayed as liars or discredited as witnesses.

As the seasons of *NCIS* go on, the characters do not show any additional understanding of the women who are raped; they make the same dismissive, careless assumptions about them and their stories in Season Ten as in Season One. Though this chapter proceeds in chronological order for the most part, shuffling the narratives wouldn't create any issues in continuity regarding rape narratives. Gibbs and his team act the same toward victims and their stories from the series premiere on. This is true even after the possibility is introduced that one of the characters—Ziva—was sexually assaulted herself during events that took place between two seasons. The repeated poor treatment of rape victims over the first ten seasons of *NCIS* is important to consider because human beings learn about experiences different from their own through the representations they seek out. When the average number of viewers for a weekly episode of *NCIS* is more than twenty million, the messages the show presents about rape and the negative effects those messages might have are worth our time and attention. The characters who make up Gibbs' team may grow and develop in other areas but not in this one. Maybe as the real United States military is beginning to take more direct action to address sexual assault within its ranks, it is time for *NCIS* and the military in its universe to follow suit.

NOTES

1. Steven Long Mitchell et al., "Lt. Jane Doe," *NCIS*, season 2, episode 4, directed by Dan Lerner, aired October 19, 2004 (Hollywood: Paramount Home Entertainment, 2006), DVD.

2. Amanda Kondolojy, "*NCIS* Renewed by CBS for 11th Season," *TV by the Numbers*, February 1, 2013, http://tvbythenumbers.zap2it.com/2013/02/01/ncis-renewed-by-cbs/167648.

3. Ibid.

4. Ibid.

5. John Meroney, "The Leatherneck behind *JAG*," *American Enterprise* 9, no. 5 (Sept/Oct 1998): 796.

6. In addition to the fact that she is routinely patted on the head and kissed on the cheek as part of a typical workday, Abby names her equipment and keeps in her lab a stuffed hippopotamus that farts and is named Bert.

7. While rape is certainly not a crime that only affects women, there is a complete erasure of even the possibility of men being raped through *NCIS*' first ten seasons. This is problematic in its own right for a variety of reasons, including the fact that more than half of the people

raped while serving in the military are men. James Dao, "In Debate over Military Sexual Assault, Men Are Overlooked Victims," *New York Times*, June 23, 2013, http://www.nytimes.com/2013/06/24/us/in-debate-over-military-sexual-assault-men-are-overlooked-victims.html.

8. Thomas L. Moran, "UnSEALed," *NCIS*, season 1, episode 18, directed by Peter Ellis, aired on April 6, 2004 (Hollywood: Paramount Home Entertainment, 2006), DVD.

9. It is my intention to refer to characters as they are most frequently referred to on the show. Typically on *NCIS*, the male characters are addressed by last name, and it is usually first names for the female characters. One definite exception is Ducky, the medical examiner, whose nickname is a reference to his surname, Mallard.

10. Gil Grant, "The Good Wives Club," *NCIS*, season 2, episode 2, directed by Dennis Smith, aired on October 5, 2004 (Hollywood: Paramount Home Entertainment, 2006), DVD.

11. Mitchell et al., "Lt. Jane Doe."

12. United States Department of Defense, *2012 Workplace and Gender Relations Survey of Active Duty Members*, survey note prepared by Defense Manpower Data Center, March 15, 2013, http://www.sapr.mil/public/docs/research/2012_Workplace_and_Gender_Relations_Survey_of_Active_Duty_Members-Survey_Note_and_Briefing.pdf.

13. The remaining 5% of offenders are male and female working together. Ibid.

14. John C. Kelley and Jesse Stern, "Forced Entry," *NCIS*, season 2, episode 9, directed by Dennis Smith, aired on December 7, 2004 (Hollywood: Paramount Home Entertainment, 2006), DVD.

15. Ibid.

16. Ibid.

17. Frank Military, "The Meat Puzzle," *NCIS*, season 2, episode 13, directed by Thomas J. Wright, aired on February 8, 2005 (Hollywood: Paramount Home Entertainment, 2006), DVD.

18. Donald P. Bellisario, "SWAK," *NCIS*, season 2, episode 22, directed by Dennis Smith, aired on May 10, 2005 (Hollywood: Paramount Home Entertainment, 2006), DVD.

19. RAINN (Rape, Abuse and Incest National Network), "Reporting Rates," accessed May 14, 2013, http://www.rainn.org/get-information/statistics/reporting-rates.

20. Bellisario, "SWAK."

21. Emily Bazelon and Rachael Larimore, "How Often Do Women Falsely Cry Rape?" *Slate*, posted October 1, 2009, accessed May 14, 2013, http://www.slate.com/articles/news_and_politics/jurisprudence/2009/10/how_often_do_women_falsely_cry_rape.html.

22. Ibid.

23. Of the total number of named victims, those four represent 36%.

24. Alfonso Moreno, "Caged," *NCIS*, season 6, episode 12, directed by Leslie Libman, aired on January 6, 2009 (Hollywood: Paramount Home Entertainment, 2009), DVD.

25. Lara Stemple, "HBO's *Oz* and the Fight against Prisoner Rape: Chronicles from the Front Line," in *Third Wave Feminism and Television: Jane Puts It in a Box*, ed. Merri Lisa Johnson (New York: I.B. Tauris, 2007), 170.

26. Moreno, "Caged."

27. Ibid.

28. Though Ziva joined the main cast of *NCIS* in Season Three, "Caged" is the first rape narrative in which she plays a role.

29. Moreno, "Caged."

30. Ibid.

31. Dan E. Fesman and Reed Steiner, "Deliverance," *NCIS*, season 6, episode 15, directed by Dennis Smith, aired on February 10, 2009 (Hollywood: Paramount Home Entertainment, 2009), DVD.

32. Lisa M. Cuklanz, *Rape on Prime Time: Television, Masculinity, and Sexual Violence* (Philadelphia: University of Pennsylvania Press, 2000), 77.

33. Ibid., 77, 78.

34. George Schenck and Frank Cardea, "Prime Suspect," *NCIS*, season 10, episode 17, directed by James Whitmore Jr., aired on March 5, 2013 (Hollywood: Paramount Home Entertainment, 2013), DVD.

35. Ibid.

36. Heather M. Karjane, Bonnie S. Fischer, and Francis T. Cullen, "Campus Sexual Assault: How America's Institutions of Higher Education Respond," final report to the National Institute of Justice, RAINN, 2002, https://www.rainn.org/pdf-files-and-other-documents/Public-Policy/Legislative-Agenda/mso44.pdf.

37. Ibid.

38. Schenck and Cardea, "Prime Suspect."

39. Gary Glasberg, "Patriot Down," *NCIS*, season 7, episode 23, directed by Dennis Smith, aired on May 18, 2010 (Hollywood: Paramount Home Entertainment, 2010), DVD.

40. United States Department of Defense, *2012 Workplace and Gender Relations Survey of Active Duty Members*, 2.

41. Ibid, 3.

42. Glasberg, "Patriot Down."

43. Ibid.

44. Ibid.

45. Ibid.

46. Ibid.

47. Reuters, "Actress Betty White Named America's Most Appealing Celebrity," April 10, 2013, http://www.reuters.com/article/2013/04/10/entertainment-us-celebrities-idUS-BRE9390WM20130410.

REFERENCES

Bazelon, Emily, and Rachael Larimore. "How Often Do Women Falsely Cry Rape?" *Slate*, October 1, 2009. http://www.slate.com/articles/news_and_politics/jurisprudence/2009/10/how_often_do_women_falsely_cry_rape.html.

Bellisario, Donald P. "SWAK." *NCIS*. Season 2. Directed by Dennis Smith. Aired on May 10, 2005. Hollywood: Paramount Home Entertainment, 2006.

Cuklanz, Lisa M. *Rape on Prime Time: Television, Masculinity, and Sexual Violence*. Philadelphia: University of Pennsylvania Press, 2000.

Dao, James. "In Debate over Military Sexual Assault, Men Are Overlooked Victims." *New York Times*, June 23, 2013. http://www.nytimes.com/2013/06/24/us/in-debate-over-military-sexual-assault-men-are-overlooked-victims.html.

Fesman, Dan E., and Reed Steiner. "Deliverance." *NCIS*. Season 6. DVD. Directed by Dennis Smith. Aired on February 10, 2009. Hollywood: Paramount Home Entertainment, 2009.

Glasberg, Gary. "Patriot Down." *NCIS*. Season 7. DVD. Directed by Dennis Smith. Aired on May 18, 2010. Hollywood: Paramount Home Entertainment, 2010.

Grant, Gil. "The Good Wives Club." *NCIS*. Season 2. DVD. Directed by Dennis Smith. Aired on October 5, 2004. Hollywood: Paramount Home Entertainment, 2006.

Karjane, Heather M., Bonnie S. Fischer, and Francis T. Cullen. *Campus Sexual Assault: How America's Institutions of Higher Education Respond*. RAINN, 2002. https://www.rainn.org/pdf-files-and-other-documents/Public-Policy/Legislative-Agenda/mso44.pdf.

Kelley, John C., and Jesse Stern. "Forced Entry." *NCIS*. Season 2. DVD. Directed by Dennis Smith. Aired on December 7, 2004. Hollywood: Paramount Home Entertainment, 2006.

Kondolojy, Amanda. "*NCIS* Renewed by CBS for 11th Season." *TV by the Numbers*, February 1, 2013. http://tvbythenumbers.zap2it.com/2013/02/01/ncis-renewed-by-cbs/167648.

Meroney, John. "The Leatherneck behind *JAG*." *American Enterprise* 9, no. 5 (Sept/Oct 1998): 796.

Military, Frank. "The Meat Puzzle." *NCIS*. Season 2. DVD. Directed by Thomas J. Wright. Aired on February 8, 2005. Hollywood: Paramount Home Entertainment, 2006.

Mitchell, Steven Long, Craig W. Van Sickle, Donald P. Bellisario, and Grant Gill. "Lt. Jane Doe." *NCIS*. Season 2. DVD. Directed by Dan Lerner. Aired on October 19, 2004. Hollywood: Paramount Home Entertainment, 2006.

Moran, Thomas L. "UnSEALed." *NCIS*. Season 1. DVD. Directed by Peter Ellis. Aired on April 6, 2004. Hollywood: Paramount Home Entertainment, 2006.

Moreno, Alfonso. "Caged." *NCIS.* Season 6. DVD. Directed by Leslie Libman. Aired on January 6, 2009. Hollywood: Paramount Home Entertainment, 2009.

RAINN (Rape, Abuse and Incest National Network). "Reporting Rates." Accessed May 14, 2013. http://www.rainn.org/get-information/statistics/reporting-rates .

Reuters. "Actress Betty White Named America's Most Appealing Celebrity." April 10, 2013. http://www.reuters.com/article/2013/04/10/entertainment-us-celebrites-idUSBRE9390WM20130410.

Schenck, George, and Frank Cardea. "Prime Suspect." *NCIS.* Season 10. DVD. Directed by James Whitmore Jr. Aired on March 5, 2013. Hollywood: Paramount Home Entertainment, 2013.

Stemple, Lara. "HBO's *Oz* and the Fight against Prisoner Rape: Chronicles from the Front Line." In *Third Wave Feminism and Television: Jane Puts It in a Box,* edited by Merri Lisa Johnson, 166–188. New York: I.B. Tauris, 2007.

United States Department of Defense. *2012 Workplace and Gender Relations Survey of Active Duty Members.* March 15, 2013. http://www.sapr.mil/public/docs/research/2012_Workplace_and_Gender_Relations_Survey_of_Active_Duty_Members-Survey_Note_and_Briefing.pdf.

Chapter Two

"Don't Tell Her She's Lucky"[1]

Teachable Moments on Criminal Minds

If *NCIS* would fit at one end of a spectrum rating prime-time CBS shows by how well characters respond to and learn from their experiences with rape and rape victims, *Criminal Minds* might be at the opposite end. While the rape narratives represented on *NCIS* are interchangeable in that they could be moved around within the chronology of the overall show, the same is not true of *Criminal Minds*. Rather than presenting characters with static understandings of rape and relating to rape victims, *Criminal Minds* shows many of its characters develop through the seasons, creating more understanding and empathy within the universe of the show and also, potentially, creating teachable moments for the show's viewers.

Criminal Minds first aired in 2005; it aired its tenth season in 2014–2015, but only the first eight seasons are under consideration here. The show's popularity, though, extends to its most recent season. The Season Ten premiere was the most-watched show on Wednesday, October 1, 2014, with around 11.5 million viewers.[2] *Criminal Minds* is about the FBI's Behavioral Analysis Unit (BAU), a team of profilers who travel the country supporting local police departments by offering their expertise and investigative skills geared mostly toward violent, serial crimes. This fictional version of the BAU is headed by Senior Supervisory Special Agent (SSA) Aaron Hotchner, but his role in the team doesn't have the same kind of influence as *NCIS*' Gibbs. The rest of the *Criminal Minds* team fills in a lot of the same roles as the other characters in *NCIS*: the playboy second-in-command (SSA Derek Morgan to *NCIS*' DiNozzo), the intelligent almost-sidekick (Dr. Spencer Reid to McGee), the tough woman with a mysterious past (SSA Emily Prentiss to Ziva), the technologically brilliant, quirky girl (tech analyst Penelope

27

Garcia to Abby), and the older, distinguished gentleman (SSA David Rossi to Ducky). The members of the *Criminal Minds* team work together differently than those of the *NCIS* team, but the similarities in their makeups are important in ways that highlight their approaches and responses to rape narratives.

The fact that the main characters on *Criminal Minds* are profilers creates a narrative space for reflection on rape as a comprehensive issue at the same time that episodes focus on specific occurrences of the crime. Because profiling determines what is likely to be true about a suspect due to his or her past behavior, the BAU team spends screen time considering the nature of the crimes and what those crimes might tell them about the people responsible, whom they refer to as unsubs, short for "unknown subjects." The show, then, becomes a guide for the audience to do the same. Viewers observe these federal agents as they parse what they can about the nature of a rapist from the specific evidence, and because all the pieces are laid out before them, viewers become complicit in the search for justice, often arriving at the inevitable conclusion before the agents themselves. This is part of what makes the formulaic police procedural enjoyable to audiences; viewers have an advantage over the law enforcement officers because they see more of the full picture, specifics that the investigators are not privy to. Viewers frequently see part of the crime as it is being committed in the show's universe, and there are other factors that permeate the fourth wall, such as recognizable guest stars and the amount of time remaining in an episode. If while watching the show, viewers feel like part of the team, there is an open narrative space for the team's considerations of the nature of rapists and rape itself to spur the same reflection for viewers.

By the numbers, *Criminal Minds'* first eight seasons accounted for 186 total episodes. Twenty-six of those included at least one rape narrative. In two fewer seasons than *NCIS*, *Criminal Minds* more than doubled the number of rape narratives. While the extra attention to rape may not be significant in itself, *Criminal Minds* also focuses more directly on rape narratives by providing multiple examples of episodes in which the central investigation is actually of rape for its own sake rather than as a stepping stone in part of another investigation—for instance, not rape/homicide or rape as part of a separate homicide investigation, as happens several times on *NCIS*.

In addition to its more direct focus, *Criminal Minds* creates rape narratives that allow Hotchner's BAU team to show empathy and understanding for individuals who have been raped by taking the time to educate each other and themselves and by drawing on their past experiences with rape investigations. Members of the BAU show their consideration and support by offering their understanding and by ensuring that people who have been raped are interviewed in environments that make them feel comfortable. These FBI agents develop bonds with victims, which sometimes last longer than an individual episode. There are no episodes in which this team believes a person who reports a rape is lying; it is always assumed that a crime really did occur. This may be due, in part, to the fact that the BAU is invited into ongoing investigations by local law enforcement, but even so, the premise of the show creates a narrative space in which the stories told by people who say they were raped are believed. Even in the single instance where a woman proves to have lied about her attack, she was given the benefit of the doubt by most of the BAU, and since it doesn't occur until Season Eight, the pattern of trusting the word of reporting rape victims is already well established. This episode will be discussed further later in this chapter.

Even though the premise of the show creates a space for rape narratives that is much different than that of *NCIS*, Hotchner's team, and even Hotchner himself, evolve as the seasons of *Criminal Minds* progress, for the most part becoming more understanding and aware of the needs of rape victims. This tone is set by the very first instance of a rape narrative on *Criminal Minds*, from Season One, Episode Four, "Plain Sight."[3] While viewing some fourteen hundred television episodes for this project overall, I noticed the number of times an investigator would refer to someone who had been raped as "lucky"—lucky not to have been killed or beaten or whatever other circumstances hadn't occurred.[4] Use of the word "lucky" diminishes the severity of rape, and on the majority of shows, if anyone talked back to an investigator who referred to someone who had been raped as lucky, it was the victim her or himself.

In this very first episode of *Criminal Minds* to deal with a rape narrative, viewers witness an exchange between male unit chief Aaron Hotchner and female SSA Elle Greenaway[5] at the scene of an attempted rape. In the course of their conversation, Hotchner refers to the victim, Marcia Gordon, as a "lucky woman."[6] While his intention was most likely to call attention to the fact that Mrs. Gordon's rape was attempted rather than completed and that she had survived her attack while another woman, Brenda Samms, had not, Elle does not appreciate his word choice. She corrects him: "She's probably not feeling so lucky right about now."[7] This exchange, and its presence in the first rape narrative presented in the series, sets up the rest of the episodes that follow as teachable moments, when viewers witness agents engaging in instructive and constructive dialogues about how to discuss and treat people who have been raped.

In addition to correcting Hotchner's speech, Elle's concern during this part of the episode is for Marcia Gordon's comfort. When Elle asks the local officer in charge if she can be the one to question Mrs. Gordon, he wants to know why. Her response is that Mrs. Gordon is surrounded by men—her husband and five officers. Elle takes Mrs. Gordon outside for some air and offers the woman time to collect her thoughts.

Mrs. Gordon: You don't want to question me?

Elle: Not until you are ready.[8]

Even though it is her job to get what information she can, Elle's primary concern seems to be Mrs. Gordon's comfort. This approach is rewarded, as Mrs. Gordon responds to Elle's offer to give the woman a moment alone with her account of what happened: "When we were fighting, I kept staring him right in the eyes. I thought, if he's going to kill me, he's going to have to look at me while he does."[9] While Mrs. Gordon's attack ends up being unrelated to the series of rape/homicides that BAU has been called to San Diego to investigate, these exchanges regarding what happened to her establish the fact that treating victims with respect and understanding will lead to results.

The early instructive moment between Elle and Hotchner comes back in Season Two, Episode Five, "The Aftermath,"[10] when Hotchner steps into the role of teacher. Outside a victim's home, one of the local officers in Dayton, Ohio, tells Hotchner, "She's lucky. [Her injuries are] relatively minor."[11] Hotchner's response to the officer echoes Elle's advice from Season One: "Do me a favor. Don't tell her she's lucky."[12] In addition to showing the chain reaction of education of specific characters as *Criminal Minds* progresses, considering these two moments side by side also addresses the idea held in some parts of society that rape victims should be considered somehow lucky because they weren't killed or more badly hurt. When Hotchner, as unit chief, plays the role of student in Season One and of teacher in Season Two, viewers have a model of a team leader who evolves in his thinking about this specific type of crime, at the same time calling attention to the careless way some people—either fictional or real—talk and think about it.

Hotchner plays the role of teacher again in Season Six, Episode Seven, "Middle Man," when the BAU travels to Indiana to work a rape case with the local sheriff's department. Women who worked as strippers are being murdered after being held and repeatedly raped for several days, and the sheriff says, "Sometimes it seems like they're asking for it."

Hotchner: Nobody asks for this, Sheriff.

Sheriff: Not consciously anyway. Shall we go in [to interrogation, where a missing woman's father is waiting]?

Hotchner: I think I'll speak to him alone.

Sheriff: Look, I call it like I see it.

Hotchner: These women are victims of heinous crimes. I won't have you judging them in front of their families.

Sheriff: And I won't have you telling me how to run my show. The governor may have requested your help, but this is my case.

Hotchner: This is not a show. It is your case. And you can watch from the outside. [13]

Viewers will recognize this scene as an important break from Hotchner's typical interactions with local law enforcement. As team leader, his job is to reassure the locals that the FBI is there to assist, not take over. While he might suggest that is still the case here, Hotchner is pulling rank and will not allow the sheriff to participate in the interview. The strength of his reaction asks viewers to pay close attention to this educational moment, when Hotchner is determined to make it very clear to the sheriff and to viewers that the strippers and prostitutes the sheriff refers to are not asking for anything and should be treated with the respect due to all people who have been victims of rape.

The sheriff's words, and the ways those words contribute to rape culture, become even more significant when it becomes clear to viewers that the middle man referred to in the title of this episode is the sheriff's son. The lesson about careful speech and consideration for rape victims that viewers first saw Hotchner learn from Elle comes back at least these two times, showing the significance of one of the series' first rape narratives even years later.

Early episodes that include rape narratives also have other effects on the way *Criminal Minds* addresses the issue. In addition to the teachable moment mentioned earlier, "The Aftermath" from Season Two addresses issues of consent and the insensitivity faced by people who have been raped after they report being attacked. In this episode, a rapist began his attacks raping a series of young women who attended a Bible college in Dayton followed by another series of women, this time in their mid-thirties and seeking treatment at a specific fertility clinic. The connection the BAU discovers between these different groups of women is that they all filled out surveys processed by the same data company, and when they checked a particular box on those forms, the rapist, who worked for the company, interpreted that response as consent. It would be nearly impossible for viewers to follow that logic, which calls at least a small amount of attention to the fact that none of these women could rationally be interpreted as having been somehow "asking for it." Because "The Aftermath" is still a fairly early episode in the scope of the show, the clear lack of consent in this case might help solidify viewers' interpretations of what will and will not count as consent in later rape narratives.

Also in this episode, viewers hear the voices of two of the women who were raped by this man, one from the college and one from the fertility clinic. The show jumps back and forth between two scenes that show a subset of the

BAU with each of the women. Jennifer "J.J." Jareau,[14] Morgan, and local detective Maggie Callahan interview college student Cheryl Cosgrove, while Elle, Hotchner, and Reid are present at the hospital while Alicia Jordan is undergoing a rape exam. The way these two scenes are spliced together blends them and their content; it isn't difficult for viewers to apply what each woman is saying to the experience of the other.

The lack of consent involved in this case is further highlighted by the fact that Cheryl says she was a virgin when she was attacked. She also calls attention to the ways she did not feel supported immediately after the attack, something J.J. tries to make up for in the following exchange:

> **Cheryl:** The police all act like just because he didn't kill you, he didn't somehow end your life. [. . .] When I went to the doctor, he said that my injuries were minor.
>
> **J.J.:** And you think if they were worse it would somehow be better?
>
> **Cheryl:** I don't know.
>
> **J.J.:** Look at me. If someone hands over a wallet at gunpoint, everyone thinks that's the smart thing to do. You did what you had to do to survive. Don't let anyone tell you different.[15]

This conversation takes place at some remove from Cheryl Cosgrove's rape (at least a month has passed), but the timing seems more fluid since it is interwoven so closely with Alicia Jordan's rape exam. And the lesson J.J. imparts here isn't just for Cheryl, either. While the episode sets Cheryl up as a supremely sympathetic victim, everything J.J. says to her also applies to all the other victims tied to her, including Alicia and the other victims of this particular rapist, and perhaps even more broadly since the two groups of women do not have all that much else in common, as viewers learn from the rest of the episode.

The same things that tie Cheryl to the others also work for Alicia's experiences. Viewers watch as Alicia rolls over onto one side, as the hospital gown she is wearing is moved aside, and they hear her crying as she is examined even though it is happening offscreen. The scene turns viewers into voyeurs as it unfolds, to which Alicia herself calls further attention as she speaks with Elle, Hotchner, and Reid. "Every time I think it's over," Alicia says, "someone else wants to photograph me or touch me or ask me to relive it."[16] Viewers know this to be true even beyond what Alicia has experienced to this point because they see Cheryl being reinterviewed at nearly the same time—being forced to relive her trauma—and they see how Alicia's experience is representative of what Cheryl most likely went through as well.

"The Aftermath" is also an important episode in the progression of Elle Greenaway's character; it is one of her last appearances on the show. At a certain point during their interview, Alicia begins to cry, and Elle steps in to end the interview, which puts her in the position, again, of looking out for the best interest of the victim. Shortly thereafter, Elle puts herself at risk and goes undercover as a potential target for the rapist. Having just returned to the field after being shot and nearly killed at the end of Season One, Elle mishandles her assignment, moves on him too soon, and there isn't enough evidence to make a case against the suspect. They have no choice but to let him go.

Elle is furious, an emotional response that has been building throughout the course of the episode, and the moment she confronts the suspect in the dark parking lot outside his home, viewers know something bad is going to happen. Later, Elle will claim that she went to the suspect's house to speak to him, and it will be labeled a good shoot, in self-defense. That is only because Elle lies to the local police, claiming that the suspect pulled a gun, which wasn't the case at all. While their conversation may have turned toward threats at the end—when the suspect tells Elle, "Thank you, you've just made a lot of women very happy,"[17] his words are easily construed as threatening given the context—Elle was not in immediate danger.

Elle was the BAU's sex-crimes specialist. She was the one who stepped in with that initial teachable moment, the one who was most concerned with the comfort of the traumatized, and the one who was able to convince them to talk to her. Much of what *Criminal Minds* does right in terms of addressing rape narratives stems from the groundwork she laid. But when it comes to this particular case, Elle is unable to handle herself. She kills the suspect, who was certainly guilty, but what she did was take revenge rather than seek justice. There may be some who see nothing wrong with that or who don't make the distinction, but the fact that she turns in her badge and gun at the end of the next episode, as a direct result of the response to her shooting, suggests that the broader narrative does even if Elle doesn't.[18]

The act of violence Elle commits against that rapist in Ohio doesn't exactly come out of nowhere. It was foreshadowed by the events in Season One, Episode Nineteen, "Machismo,"[19] showing that even though the outcome might not have been ideal, Elle Greenaway was a character affected and influenced by her experiences within *Criminal Minds*' rape narratives. In this episode, the BAU travels to Mexico by special invitation to help investigate a series of murders that are eventually linked to a series of rapes. Based on the sexual nature of the homicides—in which the unsub attacked women's genitals with a knife—the BAU profilers determined that he most likely evolved from a peeping tom to a rapist to a murderer, escalating at each point due to some stressor that effected his ability to continue on with the "lesser" crime.

This story line uses the issue of underreporting to subtly blame the victims: There are times when it seems like the local police and even Elle suggest that the women's choice not to report leads to the continued, escalated attacks. The unsub in "Machismo" won't stop until he is stopped, the agents say, and a rapist who has nothing to fear because his crimes aren't being reported to the police isn't likely to stop. The detective responsible for inviting the BAU to Mexico talks about how he knew what was going on in his town but couldn't do anything because no one who was attacked would talk to him. While there might be some merit to such statements, presenting the issue in this manner diverts some of the blame from the rapist to the women who have been raped.

When Elle accompanies the detective to interview Milagros Villanueva, one of the women who was attacked, she refuses to accept any of that blame. "Most of the time, nobody cares what happens to women," Milagros says.[20] Elle encourages Milagros to trust her, and as a result of that conversation, Milagros arrives at the police station later on in the episode with several of the other women who were attacked by the same man. She acts as their spokeswoman: "Here we are. Prove this will finally do some good."[21] The distrust these women harbor toward the local authorities reflects the difficulties rape victims face when reporting the crimes committed against them in the real world—encountering officers of the law or the court who don't believe their stories or who can't or won't prosecute. While Elle convinces this group of victims in "Machismo" to temporarily place their trust in the police, it is clear that they have no faith in their police force when it comes to believing their individual stories and voices. Instead, they find strength in numbers since more voices add weight to their combined experience, and it is harder to dismiss a victim's story if there are many women telling the same one.

Their faith in the police doesn't last long. Once the pattern behind the crimes becomes clear—the rapist is killing the mothers of all the women he raped in the order he raped their daughters—the women take the matter of justice into their own hands. They band together not to kill the man who attacked them but to castrate him. When the authorities arrive, the man is lying on the ground bleeding and the women responsible step into the camera frame as a unit, defiant. Back at the police station, when the detective asks whether the women will be charged with a crime, his boss, the female district attorney general, responds: "Charged? Why? They were only protecting their homes."[22] By sanctioning the women's actions, the district attorney general gives these women the right to extract their own revenge. This act of violence foreshadows the violent, extrajudicial revenge Elle will take against the rapist in "The Aftermath," which takes place several months later in the *Criminal Minds* universe.

The differences between the two incidents, which include the outcome (castration versus death), the responsible parties (victims versus a law enforcement officer), and the location (the episode "Machismo" works hard to remind viewers that the kind of "justice" that is sanctioned by authorities in this episode is just fine on the other side of the border, whereas Elle's shooting takes place in Ohio), are important. Even though Elle's shooting is also officially sanctioned—the Dayton police call it a clear case of self-defense—viewers know that the version of events she told them was a lie. They know what really happened in that parking lot, and not only are Elle's actions problematic for legal and ethical reasons, but watching her extract that kind of "justice," which she may be using her recent past experiences to justify, complicates her overall effect on how members of the BAU treat rape narratives. Her near-immediate departure from the show is one of the things that keeps her actions from negating all the good she did for rape victims—once the character is out of sight, the ways she complicated the narrative lose much of their impact.

These two rape-revenge narratives are distanced from the remaining characters—the first by physical distance and the border between the United States and Mexico and the second by Elle's departure from the BAU. Another clear example of a rape-revenge narrative is in Season Seven, Episode Twelve, "Unknown Subject."[23] This episode is complex: At first it appears that women who had been raped by an unsub nicknamed the Piano Man[24] were being revictimized by their attacker. The BAU team eventually determines that the women are being raped a second time by a second unsub—an orderly from the hospital where they were all treated after their attacks. The narrative also plays on issues with reporting; Rossi himself states, "Eighty percent of women who are raped never report it. Understandable [that these women] wouldn't want to report it a second time. That's how he is getting away with it."[25] This becomes a teachable moment for the audience by reiterating the necessity of reporting rape when it occurs, particularly with Hotchner's response: "He's banking on their silence."[26] Hotchner's claim here almost turns the decision not to report a rape into an act of collusion.

One thing that this episode does very well is make it clear that rape is not the victim's fault. Too often, women are held responsible for adopting certain behaviors that are meant to protect them from being raped. In this episode, these women who are being raped a second time took a variety of precautions that were supposed to allow them to ward off attackers: they took self-defense classes and began carrying weapons; one of them began keeping salt next to her sink to induce vomiting if she were ever drugged again. These women took many different precautions, but in the end, the second rapes still happened. While the moment is horrifying for the characters and viewers who empathize with the characters, the ineffectiveness of these precautions argues that the only person whose actions cause rape is the rapist. It is not, nor should it be, a woman's responsibility to avoid being raped; making the changes that a victim-blaming society expects made no difference during these second assaults.

While the BAU is searching for these rapists, the police have warned all the victims of the second possible threat. Regina Lampert, one of the women originally raped by the Piano Man, recognizes the piano player at the bar where she works as her rapist and abducts him. This man used a date-rape drug to subdue his victims, bound them with piano wire that left scars on their wrists and across their chests, and held them captive for twelve hours. Regina uses similar tactics—she uses a stun gun to render the man unconscious and takes him back to her house, where she uses piano wire to tie him up while he is seated at a piano. After an extended scene in which Regina recounts the story of what happened to her, the man attempts to gaslight Regina, to convince her that she misremembers and that they did in fact have consensual sex at some point after she was raped: "I never did anything to you you didn't want," he said, and "Every Wednesday night, every week, she'd let a different guy pick her up. One night she was so trashed, I couldn't understand what she was saying. It was 'your place.' And when we got there, she told me not to ask her about them. That's when I saw the scars."[27] Even as he presents what might be a plausible alternate chain of events, perhaps enough to cause some doubt for viewers, this man raises important questions of consent. In his version of the story, Regina wasn't capable of clearly articulating her desires. Critical viewers may wonder if even the altered version of events would exonerate this man who, it seems, took advantage of a woman in a clearly intoxicated state. If she was too drunk to clearly articulate consent, would she be considered capable of giving it?

The episode culminates in a confrontation at Regina's house. Regina holds the man at gunpoint, and it is up to Prentiss to talk her down. What Prentiss does is lie. She tells Regina that if she pulls the trigger, she will kill an innocent man. Defeated, Regina lets the man walk out her door, where he is immediately arrested as the Piano Man rapist. Unlike the group of victims in "Machismo," Regina Lampert is brought into the station. She refuses to give her statement to anyone other than Prentiss.

Regina: Why didn't you let me pull the trigger?

Prentiss: Because you would be in prison.

Regina: As opposed to where I am right now? Meanwhile, he gets a lawyer and a fair trial.

Prentiss: He will never see the light of day. Ever.

Regina: Can you guarantee that? You know when they talk about victims getting revictimized by the system? They mean you.

Prentiss: I know it's hard . . .

Regina [interrupting]: No, you don't. You have no idea what it's like when the monster from your nightmares comes back for you.

While she may be correct in that Prentiss never confides in anyone that she was raped, there is a moment when Regina recognizes that some of what she said rang true with Prentiss—the part about the nightmare. Prentiss' own past involves an undercover assignment through Interpol where she posed as the lover of an arms dealer, who escaped from prison in Season Six and came after Prentiss. She killed him, something Regina picks up on—not the specifics but the general idea. So while Regina's monster is still living out in the world, Prentiss' is dead by her own hand—where Prentiss had a choice, Regina didn't. While I don't intend to argue that she should have been allowed to kill the man who raped her, Regina is a victim and deserves the truth and control over her choices. The connection drawn between what Regina did, what happened to her, and Prentiss' past creates a narrative space that connects Prentiss to this woman more directly than she connected even with the other women who had been raped by the Piano Man earlier in the episode.

Many members of the BAU team have specific episodes when they identify closely with the victims. J.J. has such an episode when three girls from her hometown soccer team go missing.[28] Rossi has one when the children of a murdered couple from one of his first cases are targeted.[29] But the person who seems to be affected most frequently is Penelope Garcia, the BAU's technical analyst. She rarely goes out in the field with the team, usually staying back at Quantico where she has access to her computers and can focus on the work that she does best. Garcia's work with support groups for families of victims of violent crimes comes up several times throughout the first eight seasons of *Criminal Minds*: first in the episode where she is shot after illegally prioritizing the cases of victims whose family members she counsels[30] and again in Season Seven, Episode Eight, "Hope."[31] Garcia uses the experience she has gained as a member of the BAU team to provide outreach to victims and their families after the immediate moment of their trauma has passed, which gives her opportunities to apply what she knows in ways that help address the trauma but also gives *Criminal Minds* opportunities to address the ways that the crimes the BAU investigates create continued suffering and trauma. In "Hope," that continued trauma is compounded by new trauma when the surviving family member who participated in one of Garcia's support groups becomes the victim of a new, related trauma.

On the anniversary of her daughter Hope's disappearance, Monica goes missing when, after a meeting of Garcia's support group, she discovers a flyer with Hope's picture on it under her windshield wiper. Viewers watch as she agrees to leave with the man, who eventually admits that he was the one who abducted eight-year-old Hope seven years earlier. He leads Monica to believe that her daughter is still alive, but after discovering she had become pregnant as a result of her rape, Hope killed herself. That is why the man joined Garcia's support group—to mourn the death of his pregnant "wife." That is also why the man abducts Monica; it is his hope that if he impregnates her, they will be able to re-create Hope.

In this episode, viewers see the man enter the room where Monica is being held and watch as he overpowers her, throwing her down on the bed, which viewers see as a reflection in a mirror. The reflection offers a slight removal from the actual assault; viewers aren't watching it but instead a reflection of it. Whatever measure of comfort that might offer is negated by the knowledge that this is the same man who raped and impregnated Monica's young daughter.

It is because of Garcia's friendship with Monica that the BAU is even involved in this case. When she discovers her friend missing after the meeting, Garcia immediately calls Morgan for help, and she is at the house during the final confrontation between Monica and the rapist. Monica fought to regain control when she could, scratching the man's face when she had the chance, burning him with hot tea, but it is during that final confrontation, when she shoots the man who abducted and raped her daughter and then raped her as well, that she is able to take back control of the situation. As problematic as it may be that Monica was essentially allowed to kill him,[32] Garcia was present for that final moment just as she had been for a significant portion of the trauma Monica had suffered through to that point. This connection to Garcia is important not just because it was the reason for the BAU's involvement in the first place but also because it strengthens a bond between Monica and the viewers, who care about her more than they might have otherwise partly because she is a mother who lost her young daughter in a horrific way and partly because she is important to Garcia, who is important to viewers. Due to this connection and the previously discussed examples of revenge narratives, viewers are ready to forgive Monica her vigilantism with little to no effort.

This isn't the only time Garcia played a significant role in a rape-revenge narrative. In Season Six, Episode Eight, "Reflection of Desire,"[33] it is revealed that Garcia has a secret from the rest of the BAU team: she has a role in a play. The crimes the BAU investigates in this episode are a series of murders that include a ritual wherein the unsub dresses his victims up like glamorous '50s movie stars. Throughout the episode, the investigation is interspersed with stark scenes of Garcia sitting at a vanity, talking to herself in a mirror. She is wearing a black wig and uses red lipstick, first on her lips and then to draw a heart on the mirror itself. Then she monologues: "In all of us lives a dark side. In the end, it's as natural as the air we breathe. I was eighteen when I faced a man who chose to embrace his dark side, and by doing so, he took my humanity. Every day since, I had put on a mask to hide what now suffocates me. The truth. And nothing speaks louder than the truth."[34] Garcia is playing a character in a play, and the rape narrative in this episode of *Criminal Minds* is fictional even within the universe of the show. As the BAU gets closer to the murderer they are chasing, the content of the play Garcia is acting in is slowly revealed in a way that might allow viewers to believe, at least for a time, that they are actually getting a glimpse into Garcia's history. Instead, there is a level of metafictional remove between *Criminal Minds* viewers and the rape narrative, but Garcia does still put herself into a position where she plays the role of a rape victim. Speaking to an unidentified man, Garcia's character explains: "Nine girls you raped and butchered. You took from them what you took from me. But I survived. You should have killed me." And then the character Garcia is playing shoots and kills the man who raped her.

When Morgan asks her why she would choose such a play, Garcia explains that she "gets to vent."[35] In her job as technical analyst of the BAU, Garcia is typically less directly involved in the quest for justice, but both "Hope" and "Reflection of Desire" show how she searches for justice for victims outside the confines of her job. By working with support groups and counseling victims, she is able to use the knowledge of the terrible things people do to one another that she gains at her job to help people. And when she takes on the role of the unnamed rape victim turned murderer in the play, she literally forces the issue of justice and revenge for rape victims front and center through what she sees as an opportunity to vent some of the emotions she confronts while doing her job. These examples also work within the show as a whole as they present opportunities for Garcia to educate both other characters within the *Criminal Minds* universe and viewers.

Quite a few episodes of *Criminal Minds* deal with crimes committed against children and teenagers. The most important one for the purposes of this project is Season Two, Episode Twelve, "Profiler, Profiled,"[36] because viewers learn in this episode that Derek Morgan was sexually assaulted by his football coach when he was a teenager and never told anyone about it. Derek's personal experience with the kind of trauma rape victims face plays a role in Season Seven, Episode Eighteen, "Foundation,"[37] because it allows Derek to empathize with and create an emotional connection to a boy who had been held captive for years and was unresponsive to all other attempts to get him talking. Because viewers learn about Derek's past so early in the series, it is clear how his experience influences most of his interactions with rape victims. The other thing Derek's past achieves is the reminder that not all rape victims are female. Viewers know Derek Morgan as an adult and he was assaulted as a child, but there are enough connections spread across the first eight seasons of *Criminal Minds* to remind viewers that the man they see interviewing victims has been in that position himself.

In addition to including a history of sexual assault in the development of one of the show's main characters, Morgan's masculinity is one of the specific examples of the work *Criminal Minds* does to show viewers who the potential victims of rape and sexual assault really are. In Season Four, Episode Twenty, "Conflicted,"[38] the victims are college-age men. After a second victim, Dan Keller, who is described as a predatory male, is found asphyxiated and stuffed into a closet while on spring break, the BAU travels to South Padre Island, Texas. Prentiss is the first to say anything about the unexpected nature of this iteration of the college rape narrative: "Men being raped and murdered on spring break? That's a twist."[39] Her point here reflects the most likely take of viewers as well: it isn't the crime itself that is a surprise but the gender of the victims. Sexual violence against women on spring break is expected; college-age boys are supposed to be the perpetrators, not the victims.

In their initial discussion of the case, the BAU team assumes that even with male victims, the unsub is also most likely male. Prior to any discussion of this specific unsub's gender, the team uses masculine pronouns, referring to the unsub repeatedly as "he." This happens in a voice-over even as viewers see images of Dan Keller following a person who appears to be female into the hotel room where Dan's body is later found. The team then explicitly discusses their assumption that the rapist is, in fact, male:

> **J.J.:** Male raping male. Are we assuming our unsubs or victims could be gay?

> **Reid:** That's not necessarily true. In male rape, sexual preference typically has less to do with the crime than the power and dominance the attacker feels from the act itself.[40]

The emphasis on recognizing rape, even though this particular conversation focuses on male-male rape, as an act mostly about power and control rather than sex is important. And this focus is important for reasons the show considers when Garcia says that there have been "no reports of male rape anywhere in the area, which isn't a surprise since it's like one of the least reported crimes on the books."[41]

While *Criminal Minds* opens a narrative space for consideration of adult males who are the victims of rape, one thing the show does not do is give that demographic a voice. The male victims in "Conflicted" are college-age men, but they are killed and thus unable to talk about what happened to them. The majority of male victims are minors at the time of their assaults—a category that, of course, includes Morgan. While there are attempts to articulate the trauma of their experiences, the show doesn't present any instances of an adult male participating in the investigation of the crime committed against him. Adult male rape victims are acknowledged but silenced in the *Criminal Minds* universe: Morgan, as a trained investigator, does articulate parts of his trauma, but only at a fairly far remove from the actual experience, achieved through the passage of time. Another episode that gives viewers an opportunity to consider the experience of adult male rape victims is Season Eight, Episode Five, "The Good Earth."[42] In this episode, the female unsub abducts adult male victims and holds them captive in one of the outbuildings on her property. The focus of the episode, though, is not on the possible rape of the four men being held hostage by a female unsub but instead on the potential results. After the team decides that the unsub responsible for the disappearances of four men is a woman, they present their profile to the local police, suggesting that the unsub may be in search of an ideal specimen. The female sheriff asks, "Specimen? For what?" and it is J.J. who responds: "Possible breeding."[43] So even though it is clear that any sexual contact that would result in this possible breeding would be forcible, there is no discussion throughout the episode of the possibility of rape. While the narrative could have been more explicit in terms of discussing a possible rape, this episode does offer another potential examination of a rape narrative that addresses male victims and even female rapists—creating the opportunity for viewers to consider the fact that rape is not a crime defined by gender, even though many shows, including *NCIS*, and parts of society might consider it so.

This consideration of flexibility of gender in the roles of victims and perpetrators plays a significant role in "Conflicted," the episode with college-age male victims that has already been discussed in part. While the BAU is correct and the perpetrator of those rapes on spring break is a man named Adam Jackson, there was originally some suspicion that there might actually be multiple unsubs—specifically, a man and a woman working together as a team: a woman to draw in the alpha male victims and a male to commit the actual rape/homicides. What the team discovers, though, is that Adam suffers from dissociative identity disorder. Amanda, his other identity, developed in an effort to protect Adam from the abuse he sustained as a child, and it was Amanda who took control during the encounters with Dan Keller and William Browder, the other victim. A complicated example, this episode addresses gendered concerns in several ways—there are male victims, a female rapist (of sorts), but also issues of how bodies can and are controlled by socially constructed gender and also by mental illness and disorder.[44]

Both "Conflicted" and "The Good Earth" deal with rape narratives that hint at the possibility of female rapists, but neither makes it explicit that such a thing is possible. In "Conflicted," the rapist is biologically male, and in

"The Good Earth," it is never made clear that any rape actually occurs. There are three episodes, however, where male rapists do have female partners who encourage or help facilitate rape. In Season Two, Episode Three, "Perfect Storm," Laura Clemensen's parents receive a DVD that depicts their daughter being raped and brutalized. When another girl, Tiffany Spears, goes missing, the BAU travels to Jacksonville to assist in the investigation. While they are able to rescue her before she is killed, they do not arrive in time to keep her from being raped. In the course of their investigation, the BAU team first thinks two ex-cons are responsible for these crimes. While both men were complicit, what the end of the episode uncovers is that the real partnership is between one of the men and his wife, Amber, who is in fact the more dominant partner. This becomes clear once the BAU determines that, as a child, Amber was raped and beaten by her father and brother and abandoned by her mother, who refused to believe her daughter's story.

Once Jason Gideon puts these pieces together, the team uses the information to force Amber's husband to give away the location where Amber is holding Tiffany Spears, the cabin where she herself was assaulted. Morgan picks Tiffany up and carries her out of the cabin while Amber yells after them: "So you saved the little whore. But trust me, she'll never be the same."[45] This reminder creates an opportunity for viewers to see Amber in both roles—as a victim of incestuous sexual assault and as the perpetrator of similar violence against Tiffany Spears. While the trauma of what happened to her in the past isn't used to justify her current choices, Amber's background does ask viewers to consider the lasting effects sexually violent crimes can have on victims, a consideration that doesn't always become apparent in the episodic nature of police procedurals.

There are two additional episodes in which a man's wife is complicit in the rapes he commits, both in Season Five. Episode Five, "Cradle to Grave,"[46] shows women and girls who have been abducted caged in a basement and kept captive for as long as it takes them to produce sons. The episode begins with fairly sexualized visual images of a woman's bare legs and her upper chest and shoulders. She is screaming and panting, and then a baby begins to cry. Viewers are not aware of the circumstances of this birth when they first see these images, but it isn't long before they see the cage. The episode reveals that the couple responsible for these crimes holds multiple victims for years at a time, long enough to sober them up (as most are drug-addicted runaways) and for the husband to impregnate them. Minutes after they give birth to a son, the women are murdered and their bodies are dumped in the desert.

The repeated rapes of multiple women that would be necessary to populate the plot of this episode are only discussed briefly. Instead, "Cradle to Grave" focuses mainly on the children, who are being created as part of this couple's attempt to replace the baby they lost. The shift in emphasis makes sense to viewers, who are concerned about the fate of the girl children, but that concern is certainly not enough to completely overwhelm a consideration of the rape narrative and the wife's role in it even though it is certainly the husband responsible for impregnating their captives. This wife wants her child back, and she is incapable of sustaining a pregnancy herself due to cancer. That fact attempts to paint her in a sympathetic light, a trend that carries through all of the female unsubs considered in these rape narratives.

Episode Twenty, ". . . A Thousand Words,"[47] also proves to be about a wife who condoned the rapes her husband committed. The episode begins when a man calls 911 to report a dead body: his own. After the man commits suicide while still on the phone with the dispatcher, the BAU arrives to discover an elaborately set stage—so elaborate and meticulous in presenting all the details of the rapes he has committed that it leaves the BAU, Reid in particular, questioning what the unsub is attempting to keep hidden.

Viewers are first introduced to the man's wife in a misleading scene. Dressed in white and very pregnant, the woman is kneeling in her garden wearing headphones. Early in an episode of a show like *Criminal Minds*, a scene like this reads as an invitation for something to go wrong. It does, but not in the way that viewers expect. The man who sneaks up behind her is just a deliveryman; it is what he delivers, her husband's suicide note, that is the danger. And not to the man's wife but to Rebecca Daniels, the man's last victim, whom his wife is still holding captive and whom she now blames for her husband's suicide.

The deliberate misrepresentation of the wife foreshadows the victimization the BAU eventually discovers in her past: She met her husband while visiting her father in prison. Both men were incarcerated on rape charges, and she was her father's preferred victim. There are several reasons this background information is significant. The first is the way it attempts to blur the lines between victim and perpetrator and make the wife seem more sympathetic. With the odds stacked so heavily against her, it almost seems understandable that this woman, and also Amber from the Season Two episode "Perfect Storm," would find herself in a position of perpetuating the cycle of abuse she herself suffered. The second is the way it begins a discussion of recidivism in sexual predators. In this instance, the team calls attention to the fact that spending time in prison did not deter the primary unsub, the male rapist, from committing future crimes; instead, it taught him to escalate to murder. While investigating the unsub's tattoos, Rossi and Prentiss discover that he got at least one of his tattoos in prison. Rossi knows "why rapists become killers after they've been in prison." Prentiss is the one who lays it out explicitly: "They learn not to leave a witness."[48]

When the team eventually finds and rescues Rebecca Daniels, who has delivered her captor's baby and then finds herself chained to the floor with no options as the wife dies almost immediately after giving birth, there is little to no discussion of the sexual trauma she faced. However, a local detective who became emotionally invested in this case does ask Hotchner about her chances.

Detective: Is she going to be okay?

Hotchner: I wouldn't bet against anybody who survived what she did. [49]

This commentary is important because the episode itself seems to contradict it. While Rebecca Daniels and her female captor were not subjected to the same circumstances, viewers have still been presented with another example of a rape survivor who did not go on to be okay.

All of the episodes considered to this point include at least one rape narrative, and all of these rape narratives tell stories of attacks and assaults that really did occur in the *Criminal Minds* universe. There is only one instance when the show tells a story about a woman who lies about having been raped. By Season Eight, Episode Nineteen, "Pay It Forward," [50] the show has established a pattern of trusting women who report they were raped. There are several mitigating circumstances that cushion the conceit that this victim did in fact lie about what happened to her. First of all, it happens at a remove. First, because the rape Leanne Tipton reported happened twenty-five years in the past. Second, because the crimes the BAU is actually investigating are the decapitations of several members of the community in the small town of Bronson Springs, Colorado, including one that happened twenty-five years ago and was only discovered when the head of the victim was uncovered in a time capsule. The team is called in when three other community members turn up dead with their heads missing. It is determined that the murderer is attempting to avenge the supposed rape of Leanne Tipton, whom the unsub married after overhearing her statement to the police all those years ago. Tory, the husband and murderer, saw himself as Leanne's protector, and he killed Wade Burke, Leanne's supposed rapist, to avenge her and then the other three after they engaged in covering up the supposed rape.

When Leanne learns what her husband has done—after she finds the fresh heads in their deep freezer—she explains: "Tory, there's something about that night you don't know." [51] Viewers may suspect what she has to say, but before Leanne can confess to her lie, the scene switches to the police station where the BAU team is working. SSA Alex Blake, a new agent in Season Eight who fills the space left by Prentiss' departure, is a linguist, and when she enters the room, she has Leanne's witness statement from twenty-five years ago in her hand. "Leanne's statement about the rape is off," Blake says to the room. [52] She then breaks down the language Leanne used, pointing out places where Leanne undersold or oversold her claims as well as a place where her verb choice—"tried to take off my clothes" instead of actually "took off my clothes"—suggests that Leanne wasn't telling the truth.[53] It is Reid, though, who first suggests that Leanne made a false accusation. That it was the new agent to the team who brought forth this evidence that a rape victim might be lying seems important; it took a new set of eyes to shift the team's focus in that direction.

The most problematic thing about that accusation is that by the time the action switches back to the truck where Leanne is confessing her lie to her husband, she has already said the words. So even as Blake and Reid are accusing the woman of lying, she is confessing to her husband. By approaching the scene this way, the episode strips agency from Leanne instead of allowing her the opportunity to confess on-screen. Instead, viewers get her husband's reaction only.

Tory: No. You're lying.

Leanne: I was in love with Wade. And that night, we got into a fight.

Tory: No. That's not what happened. He raped you.

Leanne: My dad would have beaten me senseless if he found out about Wade. I was so scared. I made up a story. I'm so sorry.[54]

This apology, aimed at her husband, is clearly not enough to make up for the lasting effects of what has happened as a result of what she has done: while she had no direct involvement in the murders, her actions resulted in the deaths of four people. While only one of them (Wade) was innocent—since the other three did engage in what they thought was a cover-up—none of them deserved to die.

Of all the rape narratives considered from the *Criminal Minds* universe, this one has the latest airdate—April 10, 2013. The reason this is significant is that while *NCIS* presents a whole series of rape narratives with victims who lie or are accused of lying, it takes *Criminal Minds* nearly eight full seasons to do so. While it is difficult to pin down the number of false rape reports that are actually filed—given, especially, that rescinding a report does not always mean that a rape didn't occur—the percentage fluctuates depending on who is being asked, anywhere from 2% to 40%. According to Megan McArdle, writing for *Bloomberg*, "The number of false accusations is what statisticians call a 'dark number'—that is, there is a true number, but it is unknown, and perhaps unknowable."[55] By waiting so long to present such a narrative, and by first firmly establishing the ways in which the majority of BAU agents believe the word of rape victims to be credible, *Criminal Minds* takes an approach to false allegations of rape that, while it may be extreme—given the beheadings that occurred as a result of Leanne's lie—creates a more balanced picture of a subset of rape narratives that often get more than their fair share of attention.

It isn't just in this one way that *Criminal Minds* presents a more fully developed picture of rape narratives than *NCIS*. In addition to defaulting to the idea that people who have been raped can and should be treated as trustworthy, the show presents an array of different types of victims: both female and male victims, victims who are given agency and the capabilities to contribute in valuable ways to the investigations of the crimes committed against them, victims who are portrayed years after the trauma they have experienced and show how they are just like anyone else, looking for ways to move forward with their lives. The BAU team shows sensitivity and growth in the ways that they work with and question individuals who have been raped. They pay attention to the victims' comfort level and act as advocates and educators in regard to other law enforcement officials who might speak carelessly or, occasionally, hurtfully. *Criminal Minds* manages to, for the most part, avoid the kind of victim-blaming that is often prevalent in American society. The development of characters who experienced sexual assault as children includes one of the team's own, Derek Morgan, and the show also addresses the ways in which sexual assault affects the family members of victims. The agents in this show find themselves investing not just in seeking justice but in providing support for victims—sometimes over-zealously, as is the case with Elle Greenaway in "The Aftermath." Viewers see examples of main characters accompanying victims to the hospital or providing extended support, for instance, in Garcia's work with support groups, which is mentioned at several different points in the series.

There are flaws to be found in the way the show itself occasionally presents rape narratives, but it seems that those flaws might just be reflections of the real world. When dealing with unsubs who were abused as children, the show addresses the cycle of violence that perpetuates itself in the lives of those who were treated violently when they were young. This is particularly prominent with female perpetrators and female partners of perpetrators. There are times when guest characters use language that places blame on victims instead of where it belongs, but it is important to note that the majority of the times this happens, it becomes clear later in the episode that the character is guilty of rape or sexually violent crimes. Whenever a member of the BAU uses such language, it is in an attempt to obtain a confession or is quickly addressed and corrected in a way that proves to be educational.

The layered approach to law enforcement created in *Criminal Minds* opens the narratives on this show up to a variety of perspectives on rape, rape victims, and rape narratives. The views that carry the most weight with viewers, however, are likely the views of the recurring cast of main characters, which shifts a bit but, for the most part, remains consistent throughout the eight seasons of the show considered here. These characters create many teachable moments and use their past experiences to grow in terms of how they approach rape investigations and how they treat rape victims. While there is still some room for improvement in terms of creating narratives in which rape victims of a variety of genders are able to have a voice, overall, there is much to be learned from this version of the FBI's BAU.

NOTES

1. Edward Allen Bernero, "Plain Sight," *Criminal Minds*, season 1, episode 4, directed by Matt Earl Beesley, aired on October 12, 2005 (Hollywood: Paramount Home Entertainment, 2006), DVD.

2. Saba Hamedy, "TV Ratings: CBS Wins the Night with *Criminal Minds* and *Stalker*," *Los Angeles Times*, October 2, 2014, http://www.latimes.com/entertainment/envelope/cotown/la-et-ct-tv-ratings-criminal-minds-modern-family-20141002-story.html.

3. Bernero, "Plain Sight."

4. At least two of the other shows considered in this project use the adjective "lucky" when referring to women who have been raped. On *Rizzoli & Isles*, the episode "Sailor Man" from Season Two includes Maura Isles referring to how a victim is "lucky to be alive." Two of the episodes in which a detective from *Law and Order: SVU* refers to a victim as lucky in some way are Season Three, Episode Eight, "Inheritance," and Season Four, Episode One, "Chameleon."

5. SSA Emily Prentiss first appears in Season Two, Episode Nine, "The Last Word," and she is a recurring member of the cast until Season Nine, Episode Fourteen, "200." Prior to her arrival, SSA Elle Greenaway fulfills a very similar role in the BAU from the series premiere until Season Two, Episode Six, "The Boogeyman."

6. Bernero, "Plain Sight."

7. Ibid.

8. Ibid.

9. Ibid.

10. Chris Mundy, "The Aftermath," *Criminal Minds*, season 2, episode 5, directed by Tim Matheson, aired on October 18, 2006 (Hollywood: Paramount Home Entertainment, 2007), DVD.

11. Ibid.

12. Ibid.

13. Rick Dunkle, "Middle Man," *Criminal Minds*, season 6, episode 7, directed by Rob Spera, aired on November 3, 2010 (Hollywood: Paramount Home Entertainment, 2011), DVD.

14. At the beginning of *Criminal Minds*, J.J. serves as the BAU's liaison. She is responsible for sifting through the many requests received by the unit, determining which cases are most likely to pose a continued threat to the public, and dealing with the media. She leaves the BAU in Season Six but returns in Season Seven having completed the necessary training to become a profiler.

15. Mundy, "The Aftermath."

16. Ibid.

17. Ibid.

18. Elle's last words to Hotchner as she turns in her badge and her gun are "This isn't an admission of guilt." Andi Bushell, "The Boogeyman," *Criminal Minds*, season 2, episode 6, directed by Steve Boyum, aired on October 25, 2006 (Hollywood: Paramount Home Entertainment, 2007), DVD.

19. Aaron Zelman, "Machismo," *Criminal Minds*, season 1, episode 19, directed by Guy Norman Bee, aired on April 12, 2006 (Hollywood: Paramount Home Entertainment, 2006), DVD.

20. Ibid.

21. Ibid.

22. Ibid.

23. Breen Frazier, "Unknown Subject," *Criminal Minds*, season 7, episode 12, directed by Michael Lange, aired on January 25, 2012 (Hollywood: Paramount Home Entertainment, 2012), DVD.

24. The media's role in giving unsubs nicknames is a recurring point of contention for the BAU.

25. Frazier, "Unknown Subject."

26. Ibid.

27. Ibid.

28. Andrew Wilder, "North Mammon," *Criminal Minds*, season 2, episode 7, directed by Matt Earl Beesley, aired on November 1, 2006 (Hollywood: Paramount Home Entertainment, 2007), DVD.

29. Edward Allen Bernero, "Damaged," *Criminal Minds*, season 3, episode 14, directed by Edward Allen Bernero, aired on April 2, 2008 (Hollywood: Paramount Home Entertainment, 2008), DVD.

30. Chris Mundy, "Penelope," *Criminal Minds*, season 3, episode 9, directed by Félix Alcalá, aired on November 21, 2007 (Hollywood: Paramount Home Entertainment, 2008), DVD.

31. Kimberly Ann Harrison, "Hope," *Criminal Minds*, season 7, episode 8, directed by Michael Watkins, aired on November 16, 2011 (Hollywood: Paramount Home Entertainment, 2012), DVD.

32. In "Hope," it is unclear whether Monica Kingston is charged with any crime after the shooting. The last scene of the episode shows her releasing a cage of butterflies to memorialize her daughter with Garcia standing at her side.

33. Simon Mirren, "Reflection of Desire," *Criminal Minds*, season 6, episode 8, directed by Anna J. Foerster, aired on November 10, 2012 (Hollywood: Paramount Home Entertainment, 2011), DVD.

34. Ibid.

35. Ibid.

36. Edward Allen Bernero, "Profiler, Profiled," *Criminal Minds*, season 2, episode 12, directed by Glenn Kershaw, aired on December 13, 2006 (Hollywood: Paramount Home Entertainment, 2007), DVD.

37. Jim Clemente, "Foundation," *Criminal Minds*, season 7, episode 18, directed by Dermott Downs, aired on March 21, 2012 (Hollywood: Paramount Home Entertainment, 2012), DVD.

38. Rick Dunkle, "Conflicted," *Criminal Minds*, season 4, episode 20, directed by Jason Alexander, aired on April 8, 2009 (Hollywood: Paramount Home Entertainment, 2009), DVD.

39. Ibid.

40. Ibid.

41. Ibid.

42. Bruce Zimmerman, "Good Earth," *Criminal Minds*, season 8, episode 5, directed by John Terlesky, aired on October 31, 2012 (Hollywood: Paramount Home Entertainment, 2013), DVD.

43. Ibid.

44. An additional issue raised in "Conflicted" worth closer attention is how Adam's mental illness manifests in the episode, particularly given the fact that the episode ends with Reid attempting to reach Adam; Amanda has taken over Adam's body completely.

45. Erica Messer and Debra J. Fisher, "Perfect Storm," *Criminal Minds*, season 2, episode 3, directed by Félix Alcalá, aired on October 4, 2006 (Hollywood: Paramount Home Entertainment, 2007), DVD.

46. Breen Frazier, "Cradle to Grave," *Criminal Minds*, season 5, episode 5, directed by Rob Spera, aired on October 21, 2009 (Hollywood: Paramount Home Entertainment, 2010), DVD.

47. Edward Allen Bernero, ". . . A Thousand Words," *Criminal Minds*, season 5, episode 20, directed by Rosemary Rodriguez, aired on May 5, 2010 (Hollywood: Paramount Home Entertainment, 2010), DVD.

48. Ibid.

49. Ibid.
50. Bruce Zimmerman, "Pay It Forward," *Criminal Minds*, season 8, episode 19, directed by John Terlesky, aired on April 10, 2013 (Hollywood: Paramount Home Entertainment, 2013), DVD.
51. Ibid.
52. Ibid.
53. Ibid.
54. Ibid.
55. Megan McArdle, "How Many Rape Reports Are False?" *Bloomberg View*, September 19, 2014, http://www.bloombergview.com/articles/2014-09-19/how-many-rape-reports-are-false.

REFERENCES

Bernero, Edward Allen. "Damaged." *Criminal Minds.* Season 3. DVD. Directed by Edward Allen Bernero. Aired on April 2, 2008. Hollywood: Paramount Home Entertainment, 2008.
———. "Plain Sight." *Criminal Minds.* Season 1. DVD. Directed by Matt Earl Beesley. Aired on October 12, 2005. Hollywood: Paramount Home Entertainment, 2006.
———. "Profiler, Profiled." *Criminal Minds.* Season 2. DVD. Directed by Glenn Kershaw. Aired on December 13, 2006. Hollywood: Paramount Home Entertainment, 2007.
———. ". . . A Thousand Words." *Criminal Minds.* Season 5. DVD. Directed by Rosemary Rodriguez. Aired on May 5, 2010. Hollywood: Paramount Home Entertainment, 2010.
Bushell, Andi. "The Boogeyman." *Criminal Minds.* Season 2. DVD. Directed by Steve Boyum. Aired on October 25, 2006. Hollywood: Paramount Home Entertainment, 2007.
Clemente, Jim. "Foundation." *Criminal Minds.* Season 7. DVD. Directed by Dermott Downs. Aired on March 21, 2012. Hollywood: Paramount Home Entertainment, 2012.
Dunkle, Rick. "Conflicted." *Criminal Minds.* Season 4. DVD. Directed by Jason Alexander. Aired on April 8, 2009. Hollywood: Paramount Home Entertainment, 2009.
———. "Middle Man." *Criminal Minds.* Season 6. DVD. Directed by Rob Spera. Aired on November 3, 2010. Hollywood: Paramount Home Entertainment, 2011.
Frazier, Breen. "Cradle to Grave." *Criminal Minds.* Season 5. DVD. Directed by Rob Spera. Aired on October 21, 2009. Hollywood: Paramount Home Entertainment, 2010.
———. "Unknown Subject." *Criminal Minds.* Season 7. DVD. Directed by Michael Lange. Aired on January 25, 2012. Hollywood: Paramount Home Entertainment, 2012.
Hamedy, Saba. "TV Ratings: CBS Wins the Night with *Criminal Minds* and *Stalker*." *Los Angeles Times*, October 2, 2014. http://www.latimes.com/entertainment/envelope/cotown/la-et-ct-tv-ratings-criminal-minds-modern-family-20141002-story.html.
Harrison, Kimberly Ann. "Hope." *Criminal Minds.* Season 7. DVD. Directed by Michael Watkins. Aired on November 16, 2011. Hollywood: Paramount Home Entertainment, 2012.
McArdle, Megan. "How Many Rape Reports Are False?" *Bloomberg View*, September 19, 2014. http://www.bloombergview.com/articles/2014-09-19/how-many-rape-reports-are-false.
Messer, Erica, and Debra J. Fisher. "Perfect Storm." *Criminal Minds.* Season 2. DVD. Directed by Félix Alcalá. Aired on October 4, 2006. Hollywood: Paramount Home Entertainment, 2007.
Mirren, Simon. "Reflection of Desire." *Criminal Minds.* Season 6. DVD. Directed by Anna J. Foerster. Aired on November 10, 2010. Hollywood: Paramount Home Entertainment, 2011.
Mundy, Chris. "The Aftermath." *Criminal Minds.* Season 2. DVD. Directed by Tim Matheson. Aired on October 18, 2006. Hollywood: Paramount Home Entertainment, 2007.
———. "Penelope." *Criminal Minds.* Season 3. DVD. Directed by Félix Alcalá. Aired on November 21, 2007. Hollywood: Paramount Home Entertainment, 2008.
Wilder, Andrew. "North Mammon." *Criminal Minds.* Season 2. DVD. Directed by Matt Earl Beesley. Aired on November 1, 2006. Hollywood: Paramount Home Entertainment, 2007.
Zelman, Aaron. "Machismo." *Criminal Minds.* Season 1. DVD. Directed by Guy Norman Bee. Aired on April 12, 2006. Hollywood: Paramount Home Entertainment, 2006.

Zimmerman, Bruce. "Good Earth." *Criminal Minds.* Season 8. DVD. Directed by John Terlesky. Aired on October 31, 2012. Hollywood: Paramount Home Entertainment, 2013.

———. "Pay It Forward." *Criminal Minds.* Season 8. DVD. Directed by John Terlesky. Aired on April 10, 2013. Hollywood: Paramount Home Entertainment, 2013.

Chapter Three

"She's Evidence"[1]

Becoming a Victim and
Personal Experience with Rape on CSI

If *NCIS* mostly ignores or silences rape victims and narratives at one end of the spectrum and *Criminal Minds* creates many teachable moments about the same on the other, *CSI: Crime Scene Investigation* fits somewhere in between. Similar to both shows in several ways—ensemble cast, same network, operates along similar lines as a police procedural—*CSI* sets itself apart in terms of ratings. While *NCIS* became the most-watched scripted show in the United States in 2011, *CSI* was named the most-watched show in the world for the fifth time in seven years.[2] The show, and the rape narratives it told, reached more than sixty-three million people in as many as sixty-five different countries.[3] *CSI* takes the rape narratives told in this country beyond U.S. borders, and considering the messages those narratives send, becomes even more relevant when potential audiences are so large.

CSI's investigators are also scientists, referred to as both crime scene investigators and criminalists. Viewers see them in labs more often than interrogation, though these specific crime scene investigators do end up working rather closely with the Las Vegas Police Department in that area at times. They are also involved in the prosecution of crimes, appearing in court to present their findings about the physical evidence. But their job focuses mostly on gathering, examining, and interpreting the evidence. Gil Grissom, who serves as supervisor to the graveyard shift from Season One until Season Nine, repeatedly reminds his team and the audience that they are not cops, that the evidence will tell the story of what happened at any given crime scene. In fact, the facet of the show for which it is best known is the technology the CSIs use in the *CSI* universe, which is leaps and bounds ahead of the technology available to similar agencies in the real world. But whether or not the science is realistically portrayed is not the issue here.

The first thirteen seasons of *CSI* include a total of 295 episodes. Of those, forty-two include rape narratives that fall within the parameters set up for this project. Because the show is set in Las Vegas and as such is saturated with the "what happens in Vegas stays in Vegas" mentality, a lot of the crimes the CSIs investigate involve some aspect of sexuality, from sex work to bondage clubs to furdom conventions. There are episodes about sex trafficking, the sexual abuse of minors, and statutory rape. There are episodes in which what began as consensual sex escalates to violence and others in which distinguishing sex and sexual violence and rape becomes difficult. When considering the number of episodes that include at least one clear rape narrative, though, *CSI* has a similar ratio to *Criminal Minds*; both shows address rape narratives in about 14% of episodes within the seasons being considered here. These episodes include scenarios that give voices to victims of spousal rape and male victims, and *CSI* is the only one of these three CBS shows to bring Victims' Services into at least one narrative.

CSI's treatment of rape narratives can also be distinguished from most other shows by the number of main characters whose lives are directly affected by those narratives. *CSI* doesn't attempt to erase rape narratives, nor does it show the investigators learning as observers from a safe distance. Instead, quite a number of this show's characters have direct experiences with sexual violence.

NICK STOKES

The only main character who remains so in all thirteen seasons under consideration in this chapter, Nick Stokes was sexually assaulted by a babysitter when he was nine years old. He confides this information to his colleague, Catherine Willows, in Season Two, Episode Three, "Overload,"[4] when he has difficulty containing his emotional reactions to a case. While the moment of his confession is powerful, it is difficult for viewers to put Nick in the role of victim. He was assaulted as a child and viewers only come to know the adult version of Nick; the time that has passed and Nick's strong, adult body creates a distance from the assault. The particulars of his childhood abuse are never discussed and rarely even mentioned on the show, but Nick's reaction to sexually based crimes that involve kids from that point in the series on reminds viewers of his past and asks them to consider how such a past might influence his interaction with all sexual assault and rape victims. He is rarely shown actually interviewing or interacting with rape victims. At least, that is the case when the victims are female. This could be accounted for by the way his female colleagues—Sara Sidle and Catherine Willows in particular—step up to do the processing and interviewing. This seems especially reasonable given how the show frequently comments on the gender of the investigators, showing male officers of the law waiting for female colleagues to approach or question female victims.

The episode in which Nick takes charge on a rape case is Season Ten, Episode Six, "Death and the Maiden,"[5] which begins with a young man running from an attacker. When the second person catches the young man, viewers see him being thrown to the ground beside a Dumpster, which hides him from view but doesn't block his screams. When CSIs arrive, it is Nick who accompanies the victim to the hospital after his status is given to include multiple contusions and severe lacerations. When Nick enters Tommy Baker's hospital room, however, to process him—photograph his injuries, collect samples and his clothing—Tommy begins to yell, this time for Nick to get out and leave him alone.

Nick does. He returns to the crime scene, where Catherine has found various blood and semen samples. It isn't clear whether Catherine believes the semen is connected to this particular crime as the investigators refer to the crime scene as "hooker alley." It isn't until back at the lab that Nick tells Catherine about Tommy's reaction to Nick's presence in the hospital room. They also discuss their theory of the crime—even if they could connect the "manager" of the prostitute who made the 911 call to report Tommy's beating to the crime, they doubted he would testify. It isn't until DNA tech Wendy Simms finds a mixture of the victim's blood and an unknown male's semen that they consider rape. Catherine is the one to actually put the pieces together: "[Tommy] refused medical treatment. He went home and showered. And according to his brother, he wouldn't talk about what happened. If this were a woman, what would you think?" Nick's response: "I'd think she was raped."[6]

It might not have happened until Season Ten of the third show *Assault on the Small Screen* considers, but Tommy Baker is a living adult male rape victim. The fact that this is the same episode that includes the first visit any of the investigators make to Victims' Services is also significant. The show doesn't steer away from the fact that it hasn't included narratives with male rape victims before this point:

April Martin[7]: Men almost never report it. People think it's a prison thing, but it's just as likely to happen on the outside. This your first?

Nick: Yeah. That's why I'm here, looking for some insight.

April: Your victim was raped in an alley. In my experience, it means he probably didn't have a strong connection to his attacker. Either they didn't know each other or the connection was casual. And don't be surprised if Mr. Baker never admits he was raped. Odds are you'll probably close the case for lack of cooperation and then make fun of him around the office.[8]

In April Martin, viewers see a character who voices the realities of the situation, but her perspective is easily dismissed because anyone watching the show is more likely to side with Nick during the exchange that follows her comment about how men who report being raped are likely to be treated. This is especially true here because viewers are aware of Nick's history with sexual assault, which doesn't negate Martin's point but does make it unlikely that Nick would engage in such behavior.

The fact that it takes an investigator's first male victim to send one of the criminalists in the *CSI* universe to Victims' Services isn't surprising, but it is a bit unsettling. By Season Ten, viewers have seen many narratives involving women who were raped, and there have been zero corresponding visits to Victims' Services. This tells viewers two things: first, female rape victims are familiar to the criminalists. They don't need to seek out insights or additional help for cases with female victims; they are common enough that the characters know what to do in those situations. This leads to a second statement Nick's visit in this particular episode makes: Even criminalists in the *CSI* universe are familiar with rape as a women's issue rather than as a human issue.[9] If the person running away at the beginning of this episode had been female, investigators and viewers alike would have suspected a rape occurred much earlier, perhaps as early as that very first scene. On the other hand, if the victim had been a woman, viewers may not have had to guess about what happened behind that Dumpster; they probably would have seen more of the assault, whether it be the rapist covering the female victim with his body or beginning to remove either his or the woman's clothing. Those scenes are familiar within most rape narratives on *CSI*, but Tommy's attack was completely offscreen and so far under the radar that it takes a significant portion of the episode for the possibility that a rape occurred to even arise.

One thing not showing the attack does is remove any opportunity for imagery to sexualize the encounter. Neither Tommy nor his rapist is gay; what happened to Tommy was not about sex or desire. It was entirely about violence, dominance, and control, and it was portrayed that way. This is not always the case with rape narratives involving female victims. When the person being raped is a woman, there are all too often provocative shots of her body or confusing and misleading camerawork that can lead viewers to believe an act of sexual violence is somehow tender or romantic.

When Nick interviews Tommy and attempts to give him April Martin's business card, Tommy denies that he was raped. He does, however, confess to killing the person who attacked him—his girlfriend Jess's older brother.

Tommy would rather be labeled a murderer than a rape victim. Also of note, both Tommy's girlfriend and his brother confess to the murder as well. Tommy's brother Mark confesses to killing the rapist so no one would find out what happened: "Tommy never would have been able to live that down. The truth is, it would have been better if that bastard had just killed Tommy."[10] Troubling for so many reasons, this comment implies that it is impossible to overcome the trauma and shame not of being raped but of being labeled a victim. Both Tommy and his brother seem to share that view, at least to an extent.

Nick does not bring up his own history with sexual trauma when talking with Tommy at any point, but viewers most likely have it in mind as a reason why Nick steps into the role of empathetic confidant usually filled on *CSI* by one of the female criminalists. Viewers never hear exactly what happened to Tommy, but the episode makes it clear that he did eventually confess the whole story to Nick. While the audience sees a flashback to Tommy's attacker explicitly stating his motivation for the attack—"I'm going to ruin you like you ruined my sister"[11] —Nick hears that story from Tommy's perspective. What could have been an empowering moment to give men who have been raped a voice is muted by the fact that while Nick heard Tommy's story, viewers hear the literal voice of the rapist instead. What viewers hear from Tommy is mostly self-blame and recrimination about the effects of the attack, not the attack itself: "I can't even think about [Jess] now without seeing his face. God, I didn't even fight back. I just froze up. You know? Why couldn't I have at least fought back?"[12] Nick explains that what happened is not Tommy's fault and does not need to affect his relationship with Jess. In the end, though, Tommy leaves the interview room and walks right by Jess without saying a word to her, unable in that moment at least to address the reality of what happened to him.

This episode and Nick's own history with sexual assault does some work in the *CSI* universe to address the particular kind of shame male victims face. Without his history, Nick may not have been able to empathize with Tommy as easily, and whatever this particular episode doesn't do, one thing it does is attempt to open up the possibilities for what rape narratives look like and to whom they happen.

CATHERINE WILLOWS

As assistant night shift supervisor, Catherine Willows is Grissom's second-in-command. Before she became a criminalist, Catherine worked as a stripper, a detail that comes up fairly frequently as the show moves through Las Vegas. Catherine also used to be married to a man named Eddie who is accused of rape in Season One, Episode Six, "Who Are You?"[13] In this particular instance, only the second rape narrative on *CSI*,[14] the woman accusing Catherine's ex-husband is a stripper named April who lied about the rape. She was hoping for a large cash settlement since she wrongly believed that Eddie was a famous music producer. In addition to being troublesome because it contributes to the idea that false rape allegations are a rampant problem, this early rape narrative is problematic because one of the criminalists working the case is the accused's ex-wife. Catherine's personal investment in this case requires that Grissom reassign it to someone else, but Catherine does more than she should before handing over the file to another CSI. The fact that the victim turns out to be lying overshadows Catherine's inappropriate involvement, but this is the second of two rape narratives so far on the show that suggest corruption in the legal system investigating and prosecuting these rapes.

While they are divorced, Eddie's being accused of rape still has a direct effect on Catherine and her life because the former couple has a young daughter, Lindsey. If Catherine had been a part of putting together the case that could send her ex-husband, her daughter's father, to jail, there would have been direct and lasting ramifications in her life regardless of her personal feelings for the man. The fact that there are points later in the show when Catherine seems to still be in love with Eddie only adds to that personal connection to that particular rape narrative.

While there are rape-related cases in which Catherine becomes emotionally invested to varying degrees between Seasons One and Seven, the next rape narrative in which she is directly involved is when she becomes a possible victim in Season Seven, Episodes One and Two, "Built to Kill Part One" and "Built to Kill Part Two."[15] While it could be argued that everyone is a possible (or potential) rape victim, in this particular instance, the evidence suggests that possibility is a bit more likely than not. Catherine and Nick go to a bar where John Mayer is playing a concert. After dancing briefly, Catherine goes to the bar, and the bartender informs her that a man down the bar would like to buy her a drink. She declines, but as the scene grows fuzzy around Catherine, viewers realize her drink has been tampered with. At some point, Catherine is able to focus enough to notice Nick waving goodbye, leaving her on her own. While they don't know exactly what will happen, viewers do know it is something bad.

When Catherine wakes up, it is morning. Sunlight streams through holes in the curtains in a cheap motel room, and Catherine herself is naked, only half covered by a sheet. Her dress is on the floor with her purse. The first thing she does is check her wallet, which seems to be untouched. Wrapping herself in a blanket, Catherine goes to the window and looks outside, clearly trying to get a grasp on her surroundings. Once dressed, after staring at herself in the mirror for a long moment, Catherine dials the number for the crime lab. She hangs up as soon as someone answers. Instead, she gathers a variety of things from the room and her purse and begins to process the victim. She scrapes under her own fingernails, dropping the results into a shower cap. She wipes around the sink drain with tissues she then collects. She fumbles a bit as she unwraps a tampon and then hesitates for only a moment before inserting it—she uses it in place of a vaginal exam. During the whole process, Catherine is clearly and understandably upset. Viewers paying close attention may also be upset, not just because of what has happened to Catherine but also because of the way she is presented during this nontraditional rape exam: one of her breasts is nearly hanging out of her dress. While the character clearly has other things on her mind at that particular moment, the choice made by the show to expose the actress' body in that way as her character conducts her own rape exam is disconcerting.

The next scene builds on the viewers' discomfort: Catherine is in the shower after she has gathered all the evidence. The scene, which is shot from above, first shows Catherine's whole body under the water. Viewers witness her crying as water rains down on her, and while there is no direct view of her breasts or anything more than her shoulders and upper chest, the provocation is there. As this beautiful, naked woman cries in the shower over the likelihood that she has been raped, viewers become curious about just how much they are going to show, and the suggestion of her sexuality is reinforced by the next shot: a silhouette of naked Catherine through a barely opaque shower curtain. "Built to Kill Part One" ends with Catherine crying into her hands in the shower as viewers are presented with images that show how attractive she is.

This juxtaposition of Catherine's emotional response to her possible rape and the suggestive images of her naked body sexualize her experience. Even though the show and this character in particular tend to do a reasonable job of reminding viewers that rape is a crime not about sex but about violence, the way it is presented here includes various reminders of the fact that Catherine has a hot body and looks good naked. A shower scene after a rape isn't new. Sarah Projansky in *Watching Rape* explains that "the post-rape washing scene becomes a trope, a very brief moment outside the narrative flow that stands in for women's experiences with rape."[16] Even so, that the show chose to portray this woman naked in a suggestive way within moments of the audience's discovery of her possible rape seems like a second violation, one that remains unresolved even as the continuation of this episode resolves much else of what actually happened to Catherine.

"Built to Kill Part Two" opens with a recap of the earlier events. Viewers see Catherine's perception grow fuzzy at the bar, rewitness when she wakes in the motel and parts of the improvisation of the rape kit. She is shown in the shower again. As Catherine, with her hair still wet and wearing the previous night's dress, crosses the parking lot toward the motel's office, viewers see the memories that come back to her: she was being carried over the shoulder of a man. The motel clerk is no help when Catherine questions him. Part of his job, he says, is not to notice too much of what is going on around him. This exchange might lead viewers to contemplate all of the other assaults that could have occurred in that motel or similar motels because no one paid any attention to a drunk woman being carried around by a man. Habitual viewers of the show have seen a plethora of examples of the terrible things that can happen to women to whom no one pays much attention.

But Catherine's assault is different because viewers of the show know her and also because they are used to seeing her take charge. Catherine is a strong woman: Grissom's go-to, unapologetic about and unashamed of her past as a stripper, an intelligent and determined single mother. Viewers watching these events see Catherine's emotional detachment as she turns her own body into evidence, a series of samples to be collected. There is even more significance to those actions, though: The choice to collect the rape kit herself taints all of the evidence, which Sara Sidle, a fellow CSI, articulates when she arrives at the motel.

Sara: What's going on?

Catherine: I may have been roofied and raped. I woke up here.

Sara: What?

Catherine: I improvised my own rape kit. I've got pubic combings, nail scrapings, vaginal swab, urine sample . . .

Sara: Whoa, whoa, whoa. Did you call it in?

Catherine: I called you.

Sara: Catherine, doing it yourself is going to make anything you get inadmissible.

Catherine: Yeah, I know procedure. I didn't want an official investigation. I just want to know what happened.

Sara: Okay. All right.

Catherine: I gotta get this stuff to the lab. Room 229. It's right up there. Please print it? And keep it between us?[17]

Sara agrees. This exchange, and the implications of it, are troubling. The evidence Catherine collected herself is inadmissible, and she has taken a shower. There is no longer any chance of retrieving any evidence that could be used to prosecute if Catherine were to change her mind once her head was a bit clearer. That is in addition to the fact that this narrative created an opportunity to show the system work for one of its own, but Catherine chose not to put her trust in it. While that is most likely not because she doesn't have faith in the system—particularly since she works within it every day—there is the possibility to read her decision that way.

According to the Bureau of Justice Statistics, "On average, an estimated 211,200 rapes and sexual assaults went unreported to police each year between 2006 and 2010."[18] While Catherine's decision not to file an official report should be her own, the narrative of this episode presented an opportunity for a possible victim with intimate knowledge of the inner workings of the system to use it, and her choice not to take advantage of that opportunity doesn't instill viewers with much confidence in the system. This may be particularly true because Catherine does take advantage of her access to the system's resources. First, she calls Sara, a trained criminalist, to assist her in collecting evidence. She also has lab technicians Wendy Simms and David Hodges running the samples. But she doesn't make any of that official in any way that could do her some good if the conclusion of her investigation were different.

Other than Sara, Catherine tells no one of what she thinks could have happened to her until much later in the day. When she eventually tells Grissom, it is only because of the extenuating circumstances. Had she actually been raped or had the outcome of the situation not made it clear that the whole scenario was an elaborate setup aimed at revenge against Catherine's biological father, casino owner Sam Braun, would she have ever told Grissom at all? Viewers may suspect not after her defensive explanation to Grissom: "I should have told you, but I didn't want a sermon. I did my own rape kit. It came back negative."[19]

So Catherine was not raped. She certainly was assaulted, and the sense of violation she felt before learning the truth of what happened to her would have mirrored the feelings of a person who had woken up the same way and actually been raped. While Catherine can find solace in the fact that she wasn't physically violated in that way, the emotional response would likely be much the same as if she had—if for no other reason than it has been made extremely clear to her and to viewers that she easily could have been. Her decision not to follow protocol and the way in which she eventually reported what happened to her only to one female coworker and then much later her supervisor suggest shame at finding herself in the role of victim. This shame is misplaced, as Catherine herself would tell any number of other victims, and while a viewer can certainly understand that Catherine is entitled to whatever emotional response seems appropriate to her, the way she takes on the role of victim reinforces unfortunate and potentially dangerous attitudes toward reporting sex-based crimes to the proper authorities.

The lasting effects of this episode come up multiple times. In Season Eleven, Episode Nine, "Wild Life,"[20] Catherine is having a conversation with Detective Lou Vartan, a recurring character and Catherine's boyfriend at the time. In this episode, two women in Vegas on vacation claim not to remember what happened to them after a long night of partying and sex. A man one of the women accused of raping her fell from the balcony and died, which is the crime the CSIs are actually investigating. Vartan has doubts about the story the women are telling.[21]

> **Vartan:** They claim they don't remember any of it? Come on. Give me a break.
>
> **Catherine:** Give me a break. Do you know what it's like to wake up naked in a motel room with no memory of how you got there? Your head is throbbing, you're bruised, you're sore. You've got no idea of what you did or what was done to you.
>
> **Vartan:** But you do?
>
> **Catherine:** Well, yeah. A couple years ago, I went with a friend to a John Mayer concert and someone roofied my drink.
>
> **Vartan:** What? You were raped?
>
> **Catherine:** No, thank god. I wasn't. I thought I was but even worse than that was having no memory of it. There were just hours of my life, gone.
>
> **Vartan:** How come you . . . you never told me any of this?
>
> **Catherine:** It's not something I like to talk about.[22]

This exchange is significant for two reasons. The first is because it addresses the idea that Catherine's emotional response may not have been much different in the immediate aftermath of the event if she had actually been raped. She was focused on not knowing what could have happened; then at least what really did happen wasn't the point. Catherine's reluctance to talk about what happened to her also brings back the question of whether or not she was ashamed to find herself in the role of victim. Viewers may return as well to the question of why she chose not to report what happened the same way they may wonder why she chose not to confide in someone she is supposedly intimate with.

Nick's history with sexual assault was presented with the built-in distance of time. The potential of Catherine's rape was shown to viewers in a way that mirrored Catherine's own experience with it—waking up to the discovery and the gradual piecing together of all the necessary information about what occurred during the missing time. Her job as a criminalist often puts her in the role of lead CSI in rape and rape-related cases, and she proves herself to be mostly empathic and sympathetic to what victims experience, particularly after her own experience in Season Seven. Even so, her decision not to report what might have happened to her runs contrary to what the narrative could have accomplished if she had placed her trust in the system the way she frequently encourages other individuals who have been raped to do.

GLORIA PARKES AND RAYMOND LANGSTON

When Gil Grissom leaves *CSI* at the end of Season Nine, Catherine steps into his role as night shift supervisor, but CSI One Raymond Langston steps into Grissom's role as central character on the show. First introduced in Grissom's last episodes, Langston was a college professor who set up a teleconference for his class with Nate Haskell, also known as the Dick and Jane Killer. Langston's relationship with Haskell is complex, and the story line between the two men spans Langston's time in Las Vegas (Seasons Nine through Eleven). Known for attacking couples, killing the men immediately, then torturing the women for days before finally killing them as well, the Dick and Jane Killer is referred to as solely a killer for many episodes. It is possible, of course, that rape is implied when a serial killer like Haskell keeps just the women alive for days, but it isn't until Season Ten, Episode Twenty-Three, "Meat Jekyll,"[23] that Langston first mentions the fact that Haskell raped the first woman he abducted. Her name was Tiffany Cohen, and she and her boyfriend Joel Steiner were Haskell's first couple. There is no mention of Haskell as a rapist prior to this episode, though he has been a recurring character for more than a season by this point.[24]

The absence of any mention of rape from the rest of the murders Haskell has committed and its late addition to the story told about what kind of killer Haskell is should tell viewers that something significant is coming. That single rape, and the fact that Ray Langston was the one to speak it out loud, sets up the conclusion of the narrative constructed around these two characters: Season Eleven, Episode Twenty-Two, "In a Dark, Dark House,"[25] is the last episode either of the men appears in as well as the culmination of the rape narrative that began a year earlier.

As the final episode in a three-part season finale, "In a Dark, Dark House" begins once Langston tracks Haskell back to his childhood home after the murderer has kidnapped Gloria, Langston's ex-wife. While it is the fact that Haskell kidnapped, tortured, and raped Gloria that leads Langston to kill Haskell by throwing him from a second-story balcony, it is disconcerting how little of the rape narrative is actually about Gloria, the person who was

raped. She is certainly present throughout the episode, but from the opening
scene when Langston and Haskell face off in the bedroom (Gloria is there) to
one of the final scenes that takes place outside of her hospital room, Gloria
hardly speaks. Haskell is the one to tell Langston about what he has done to
her—telling Ray that he should ask her about it as she whimpers in the
background. She is unresponsive when Ray crouches before her and only
groans or grunts when he eventually leads her out of the house. When they
pass Haskell's body on the stairs, Ray uses his own body as a buffer, and
when Gloria hesitates to move forward, he puts his hands on her waist and
shoulder to guide her the rest of the way from the house.

When viewers do get to see through Gloria's perspective at the hospital,
everything is hazy; the picture is distorted as Ray and then Gloria are taken
into the trauma unit. Catherine comes in to process Gloria, and in a montage,
viewers see her combing Gloria's hair and scraping underneath her fingernails. Gloria is still almost completely unresponsive, which may raise questions about who consented to the sexual assault examination kit in the first
place. The scene flashes back and forth between Catherine collecting evidence from Gloria's body and Sara Sidle and Greg Sanders, another CSI,
processing the scene back in Nate Haskell's childhood bedroom. Viewers
watch Greg examine the bed and discover the hooks Haskell used on Gloria
to hold her limbs in place. But the words for what happened to her never
come out of her mouth. Instead, the facts are presented through the evidence
Greg and Sara collect and the report Catherine writes after her examination.
The words "sexual assault" and "forceful penetration" can be seen on the
page after Catherine is shown rolling back the blankets on Gloria's hospital
bed and encouraging her to spread her legs. There are flashbacks to the
bedroom, what viewers most likely interpret as Gloria's memories as Sara
and Greg discover the various instruments Haskell used to torture her. There
is a scene where Gloria attempts to pull herself free from the hooks he has
threaded through her flesh—and it is at this point that Gloria speaks her first
words of the episode: She says "oh God" as she attempts to tug the wire
anchoring those hooks through her arms from the wall.[26]

When Catherine is done collecting the necessary evidence, she speaks to
Gloria: "You're going to make it through this, Gloria. You survived. He's
dead, and you're not. You beat him."[27] Gloria does not respond or react to
Catherine's words. The doctor, while speaking with Ray, confirms that Gloria has yet to speak about what happened to her. The doctor also explains that
Gloria seems to be suffering from "acute traumatic stress. [She is] [a]lert but
not making eye contact, not communicating."[28] It is at this point that Gloria's
mother arrives at the hospital, interrupting the doctor and asking for Ray to
be removed from the hospital. As he is no longer Gloria's husband, he has no
rights to the information the doctor has been sharing with him, which becomes another kind of violation. Not only are Gloria and Ray no longer

married, but Haskell murdered Gloria's new husband, Phil, before he abducted her. The decisions Ray has been making for her weren't his to make, and while it makes rational sense that Gloria's mother would take over as the decision maker and as Gloria's voice, the fact is that this stress disorder took Gloria's ability to speak for herself. She is a grown adult victim of a horrific crime, she is closely connected to one of the main characters, and she is not given the opportunity within the narrative to speak or make decisions for herself.

In addition to this silencing, another troubling part of this episode is the access Langston has to the report Catherine has put together on Gloria's rape. Due to his personal involvement, Ray is not working Gloria's case. As such, he has no right to the information contained within that report unless Gloria decides to share it with him. That choice is taken out of Gloria's control, though, when Catherine allows Ray access to the report. Viewers see it as well, as the camera focuses in on phrases like "lacerations and trauma consistent with sexual assault," "trauma indicated sexual assault," "various foreign instruments," and "forceful penetration."[29] As Ray reads, viewers see a brief flashback to Gloria in the house with Haskell, attempting to hold back any verbal response to her torture. The juxtaposition might suggest that these are two things she may have chosen to withhold, as would certainly be her right.

That Gloria would be unable to put what she experienced into words is understandable and would be even if the specifics of what happened to her were less horrific than the torture viewers know she must have endured. At issue here isn't so much that Gloria doesn't speak but that so many step in to speak for her. First Ray and then her mother take control of all decision making for her. While some of that is necessary in the immediate moment after she is taken out of that house, it is troubling that the story line takes and keeps the victim's voice—perhaps particularly because this woman is so closely connected to Ray, and through Ray, to the rest of the CSIs. The only words she says throughout the entire episode, other than the flashback to when she says "oh God" in the house, come when Catherine enters the hospital room again hoping to question her. Gloria's mother asks Catherine not to make her daughter relive her trauma, and instead of asking the questions she most likely would have with any other victim, Catherine acquiesces and asks only how Gloria is feeling.

In some ways, Catherine's effort to be nice dismisses the importance of Gloria's role as the victim. Haskell is dead, and there is enough physical evidence to prove what he did to Gloria, but it seems unlikely that Catherine would have foregone questioning the victim in just about any other circumstance. Taking Gloria's statement, making it a part of the police record of what occurred in Haskell's house, carries weight and serves to acknowledge the trauma she went through. Perhaps it came later and just wasn't shown, but there is no way for viewers to know whether or not that is actually the case. So instead of having an opportunity to tell her story—whether or not she did, perhaps she should have been asked—Gloria's only response is to the question Catherine actually asks. How is she feeling? "I'm tired," Gloria says.[30] She repeats herself once, and that is all. The entire rest of the episode, someone or something else speaks for her. Haskell has his last word about what happened to her when he tells Ray that "there's still a little piece of me in her too"[31] as Gloria cries in the background. Gloria's mother's last word is about how her daughter "can't speak for herself yet"[32] as she and Ray have a heart-to-heart in front of a large window through which viewers see Gloria sleeping, again in the background. Ray has his last word about what it was that saved Gloria's life in the final scene of the episode.

When Ray discovers the chalk drawing of musical notes Gloria left across the floorboards in a closet where she was held by Haskell, the scene flashes back to Gloria and Ray's first date. Gloria's career as a concert cellist played a significant role in her interactions with Haskell that led to her abduction, but in this scene, viewers see Gloria playing her cello as Ray looks on. When she is done playing, she speaks: "'The Swan' by Saint-Saëns. It's not really the story for a first date, but, um, that piece of music saved my life."[33] So Gloria, through the combination of Ray's discovery in Haskell's house and that flashback, has a small voice, one that allows her to speak directly to someone who knows her well enough to recognize the significance of the message. The issue, though, remains that she could have been given agency through the narrative to express her own trauma and the role that song played in saving her then and now rather than having Ray interpret that message for viewers.

Ray interprets Gloria's message and its meaning. He takes control of making decisions for her that he has no right to make. He accepts Gloria's mother's blame for what happened to Gloria, for bringing her to Haskell's attention. Gloria doesn't have the opportunity to make her voice heard and is often relegated to the background. Ray, on the other hand, is the main character. Viewers are more invested in him and are also aware of the complicated nature of his feelings for his ex-wife after an earlier episode when he had little choice but to give his blessing as she prepared to marry someone else, a man now dead by Haskell's hand. For all that this rape narrative is clearly Gloria's, she fades into the background of the story being told about her ex-husband. That the two stories come together in the end—Ray Langston will return to Baltimore with Gloria and her mother to be with her after her assault—doesn't change the fact that his interaction and relationship with Haskell overshadows and even silences hers.

SARA SIDLE

While Sara Sidle doesn't have the same kind of direct experience with rape or sexual assault that Nick, Catherine, and Ray have, she settles into the role of strongest and most vocal advocate for rape victims as early as the first season of *CSI*, and she has a habit of getting emotionally invested in her cases to the point that her colleagues, Grissom in particular, worry about the effects this may have on both Sara and the cases.

In Season One, Sara is the one to explain how a rape exam works and how the clock metaphor used throughout the rest of the series works: "Some bruising is normal when sex occurs. Injuries at eleven, twelve, or one o'clock indicate consensual sex. Injuries around the dinner hour, five, six, seven, indicate forced entry. The woman hasn't done anything to help her partner and thus sustained serious bruising."[34] Both guest stars on the show and viewers learn valuable information about the nature of rape investigations, and they learn it from Sara.

In Season One, Episode Sixteen, "Too Tough to Die,"[35] Sara makes a personal connection with a rape victim who was found unconscious and half-dressed on the side of the road. At first, Sara is reluctant to accompany her to the hospital, but when Grissom insists—"evidence won't stay on the body long at the ER," he tells her[36]—Sara goes. After sending the uniformed officer out of the room, Sara watches the woman's face and talks to her as she conducts the rape exam. She takes the time to warm the speculum with her hands, compares the vaginal exam she is about to conduct to her own yearly exam, connecting to the victim even though the woman is comatose.

The ways Sara's approach to this (and future victims) differs from Grissom's in particular is made clear in a later scene. Still speaking to the victim, whom she begins to call Jane, short for Jane Doe, Sara says, "This never should have happened to you. But I promise I will find out who did this." Grissom overhears her. "She's evidence, Sara," he says after a brief conversation about the rape exam.[37] Sara refuses to leave it at that, though. In order to find the woman's real identity, Sara manually searches missing persons reports through the night. Pamela Adler is not just evidence to Sara, and she isn't just another victim.

When Grissom tries again, this time in the lab, to warn Sara against getting too close to the victims, Sara responds, "She's special to me. I can't help it."[38] And when a belt loop Pamela pulled from her attacker's jeans leads the CSIs to her rapist, Sara returns to the hospital to share the news. She doesn't notice Pamela's husband in the room until after she has told Pamela the outcome: "We caught him. If you hadn't pulled that belt loop, we might not have gotten him. You did good."[39] After Tom, Pamela's husband, explains to Sara that Pamela has stabilized and won't die, he asks her to come see them some time in the new facility to which Pamela will be moved.

"Definitely," Sara says, and viewers find out in Season Nine, Episode Two, "The Happy Place,"[40] that she kept her word.

Another episode that highlights the way Sara is viewed by her colleagues as the go-to for rape victims is Season Four, Episode Twenty-Three, "Bloodlines."[41] In this episode, both Sara and Catherine are present for Linley Parker's rape kit at the hospital. When the evidence is ready, Sara volunteers to take it back to the lab, and Catherine is surprised. "You don't want to take the statement?" she asks.[42] Sara's response is to ask whether Catherine minds doing it. While Catherine has no problem taking the statement, her surprise makes it clear that she expected that Sara would want to talk to the victim and that her choice not to is uncharacteristic.

Grissom reinforces this point when he notices Sara watching Linley work with a sketch artist from the hallway at the lab in a later scene. Sara's investment in victims, particularly rape victims, is clearly an issue of concern for her supervisor. He suggests she might want to take a vacation. Her response: "I'm still on the case. I just didn't do the interview for once in my life. When was the last time you took a vacation? Never, right?"[43] Both Catherine's and Grissom's concern as well as Sara's defensive reaction call attention to the fact that there is something off about her behavior.

In Season Seven, Episode Eighteen, "Empty Eyes,"[44] Sara holds Cammie Brookston's hand as she dies. Cammie was not raped, but she was murdered by the same man who raped and/or murdered all five of her roommates. For obvious reasons, Sara's emotions are deeply involved in this case, but when Nick asks if she is okay, Sara says, "We usually show up too late to meet the victims."[45] While that is true for most murder victims, it certainly isn't for quite a few of the rape narratives.

But in this rape narrative, Cammie's isn't the only hand Sara holds. She meets the victim again, this time a man who has been stabbed with the same knife that killed Cammie and the others. Sara climbs into the ambulance with the man, holds his hand, and talks with him the same way she did with Cammie. After they arrive at the hospital, Sara begins to process her stabbing victim. Viewers become aware only just ahead of Sara that something is off about the man; the way he stares at Sara as she works is disconcerting. Seconds later, she discovers that his fingerprints are obscured by calluses and he has a port-wine stain on his shoulder, something Cammie had tried to tell her about but that didn't made sense to Sara until she saw it. The way the tension builds in this scene between the way the man is watching Sara and the lack of attention she is paying to him suggests the possibility of physical danger. The episode ends a short while later, but not before the rapist explains why he killed Rebecca Mayford: "I saw this girl I liked at the bar. I followed her home. I knew she wanted to party. I chose her. Girls act sometimes like they don't want what they want. Because they want you to take it. They like that. But this girl. She was flirting with me. And I just gave her the party of her life."[46] Coming from the mouth of a rapist, these words don't mean much other than to add to the shame Sara feels about letting her emotional connection to this case overwhelm her objectivity and the concern viewers feel for her safety. If all it took for him to fixate on Rebecca was to be in the same bar, how might he be feeling about Sara, who has shown him so much attention?

Though both Nick and Cammie's ex-boyfriend tell Sara it was a good thing she was there to hold Cammie's hand as she died, the events that follow suggest that Sara gets too close to the victims: The final scene of the episode is a conversation between Sara and Grissom. "I held his hand," she says. "Just like I held hers. I lost perspective."[47] As she draws the connections viewers have already drawn, she calls into question not just her actions in response to the stabbing victim who turned out to be the rapist, but to Cammie as well, calling for the kind of distance that Grissom is much better at maintaining.

These episodes in which Sara's emotional responses in rape narratives accumulate, and while dealing with rape victims isn't the only or even the explicit reason for Sara's decision to leave Las Vegas in Season Eight, in Episode Six, "Who and What,"[48] the team is called out to a house where a woman was raped and killed while her husband watched. Sara leaves the house abruptly, and when Grissom follows her to see if she is all right, she clearly isn't and gets in the car to leave the scene. Burned out, at least partly due to these rape cases, Sara leaves Vegas and doesn't return for good until Season Eleven.

Sara's interest in serving as an advocate for rape victims is presented as if it were a flaw. While the case could be made that her interest in advocating actually does interfere with her job—gathering and interpreting the physical evidence—the fact that her emotional responses to victims are often policed by her male colleagues or sometimes put her in potentially dangerous situations creates a hostile environment for that kind of sympathy. It suggests to viewers that within the *CSI* universe, it is better to remain detached from victims the way Grissom does—treating their bodies as sites for evidence collection. Sara's desire for interpersonal connections with victims could serve as a way to disrupt that idea and turn rape victims' bodies back into human beings that deserve to be recognized and respected as such.

In the first thirteen seasons of *CSI*, there are rape narratives that silence victims and ones that teach lessons about rape. There are all different kinds of victims, and more than any other show considered in *Assault on the Small Screen*, there are main characters whose lives are directly affected by rape or sexual assault. For all the ways in which the rape narratives presented in *CSI* might perpetuate certain rape myths—a disproportionate amount of false allegations, victim-blaming, and the like—one thing *CSI* does is attempt to take some of the narrative remove away from sexual assault. While it isn't the only show that has a main character who experiences sexual assault—Derek Morgan from *Criminal Minds* and Olivia Benson from *Law and Order: Special Victims Unit* just to name two—this show reminds viewers more often than most others that anyone can become a victim of sexual assault. Neither Nick's nor Catherine's experiences were related to their jobs. Gloria's rape was due to her connection to Ray and his connection to Haskell through his job, but that began even before he became a CSI. Sara's experience with rape came entirely through her job but worked in such a way that it contributed to a lifestyle change; she leaves town and goes to Costa Rica for research. The experiences of these four characters are some of the most significant portrayals of rape narratives on the show.

The attitudes and representations of rape on *CSI* are as complex and convoluted as the plots of the episodes. The criminalists at the LVPD always catch the rapist but not always right away. They provide support for victims, but for some more than others. They have personal experiences with rape that most likely shape how they respond to crimes of that nature, and above all else, they focus on what stories the physical evidence can tell.

NOTES

1. Elizabeth Devine, "Too Tough to Die," *CSI*, season 1, episode 16, directed by Richard J. Lewis, aired on March 1, 2001 (Hollywood: Paramount Home Entertainment, 2003), DVD.

2. Sara Bibel, "*CSI: Crime Scene Investigation* Is the Most-Watched Show in the World," *TV by Numbers*, June 14, 2012, http://tvbynumbers.zap2it.com/2012/06/14/csi-crime-scene-investigation-is-the-most-watched-show-in-the-world-2/138212.

3. Ibid.

4. Josh Berman, "Overload," *CSI*, season 2, episode 3, directed by Richard J. Lewis, aired on October 11, 2001 (Hollywood: Paramount Home Entertainment, 2003), DVD.

5. Jacqueline Hoyt, "Death and the Maiden," *CSI*, season 10, episode 6, directed by Brad Tanenbaum, aired on November 5, 2009 (Hollywood: Paramount Home Entertainment, 2010), DVD.

6. Ibid.

7. April Martin is the Victims' Services professional Nick Stokes seeks out.

8. Hoyt, "Death and the Maiden."

9. Data gathered for a Department of Justice report from 2000 determined that one in every thirty-three men had been a victim of rape. This is compared to one in every six women. United States Department of Justice, *Full Report of the Prevalence, Incidence, and Consequences of Violence against Women*, November 2000, http://www.ncjrs.gov/pdffiles1/nij/183781.pdf.

10. Hoyt, "Death and the Maiden."

11. Ibid.

12. Ibid.

13. Carol Mendelsohn and Josh Berman, "Who Are You?" *CSI*, season 1, episode 6, directed by Danny Cannon, aired on November 10, 2000 (Hollywood: Paramount Home Entertainment, 2003), DVD.

14. In Season One, Episode Four, "Pledging Mr. Johnson," the secondary narrative throughout the episode is about a judge who is blackmailing CSI Warrick Brown to tamper with the evidence in a rape trial. Warrick does not do so and instead wears a wire so that the judge can be arrested and prosecuted for the attempt. Josh Berman and Anthony E. Zuiker, "Pledging Mr.

Johnson," *CSI*, season 1, episode 4, directed by Richard J. Lewis, aired on October 27, 2000 (Hollywood: Paramount Home Entertainment, 2003), DVD.

15. Sarah Goldfinger, David Rambo, and Naren Shankar, "Built to Kill Part One," *CSI*, season 7, episode 1, directed by Kenneth Fink, aired on September 21, 2006 (Hollywood: Paramount Home Entertainment, 2007), DVD; David Rambo, Sarah Goldfinger, and Naren Shankar, "Built to Kill Part Two," *CSI*, season 7, episode 2, directed by Kenneth Fink, aired on September 28, 2006 (Hollywood: Paramount Home Entertainment, 2007), DVD.

16. Sarah Projansky, *Watching Rape: Film and Television in Postfeminist Culture* (New York: New York University Press, 2001), 109.

17. Rambo, Goldfinger, and Shankar, "Built to Kill Part Two."

18. Bureau of Justice Statistics, *Nearly 3.4 Million Violent Crimes per Year Went Unreported to Police from 2006 to 2010*, August 9, 2012, http://www.bjs.gov/content/pub/press/vnrp0610pr.cfm.

19. Rambo, Goldfinger, and Shankar, "Built to Kill Part Two."

20. Treena Hancock and Melissa R. Byer, "Wild Life," *CSI*, season 11, episode 9, directed by Charles Haid, aired on November 18, 2010 (Hollywood: Paramount Home Entertainment, 2011), DVD.

21. Vartan's doubts are validated when the woman admits that she was having consensual sex with the man who died when he fell off the balcony; she just didn't want to be caught in the act of cheating on her husband.

22. Hancock and Byer, "Wild Life."

23. Naren Shankar and Evan Dunsky, "Meat Jekyll," *CSI*, season 10, episode 23, directed by Alec Smight, aired on May 20, 2010 (Hollywood: Paramount Home Entertainment, 2010), DVD.

24. Haskell first appears in Season Nine, Episode Nine, "19 Down." His last appearance is Season Eleven, Episode Twenty-Two, "In a Dark, Dark House." He appears in nine episodes total and his name comes up in a variety of others during that time.

25. Tom Mularz, "In a Dark, Dark House," *CSI*, season 11, episode 22, directed by Jeffrey Hunt, aired on May 12, 2011 (Hollywood: Paramount Home Entertainment, 2011), DVD.

26. Ibid.
27. Ibid.
28. Ibid.
29. Ibid.
30. Ibid.
31. Ibid.
32. Ibid.
33. Ibid.

34. Andrew Lipsitz and Ann Donahue, "To Halve and to Hold," *CSI*, season 1, episode 14, directed by Lou Antonio, aired on February 15, 2001 (Hollywood: Paramount Home Entertainment, 2003), DVD.

35. Devine, "Too Tough to Die."
36. Ibid.
37. Ibid.
38. Ibid.
39. Ibid.

40. Sarah Goldfinger, "The Happy Place," *CSI*, season 9, episode 2, directed by Nathan Hope, aired on October 16, 2008 (Hollywood: Paramount Home Entertainment, 2009), DVD.

41. Sarah Goldfinger et al., "Bloodlines," *CSI*, season 4, episode 23, directed by Kenneth Fink, aired on May 20, 2004 (Hollywood: Paramount Home Entertainment, 2004), DVD.

42. Ibid.
43. Ibid.

44. Allen MacDonald, "Empty Eyes," *CSI*, season 7, episode 18, directed by Michael Slovis, aired on March 29, 2007 (Hollywood: Paramount Home Entertainment, 2008), DVD.

45. Ibid.
46. Ibid.
47. Ibid.

48. Carol Mendelsohn et al., "Who and What," *CSI*, season 8, episode 6, directed by Kenneth Fink and Danny Cannon, aired on November 8, 2009 (Hollywood: Paramount Home Entertainment, 2010), DVD.

REFERENCES

Berman, Josh. "Overload." *CSI*. Season 2. DVD. Directed by Richard J. Lewis. Aired on October 11, 2001. Hollywood: Paramount Home Entertainment, 2003.

Berman, Josh, and Anthony E. Zuiker. "Pledging Mr. Johnson." *CSI*. Season 1. DVD. Directed by Richard J. Lewis. Aired on October 27, 2000. Hollywood: Paramount Home Entertainment, 2003.

Bibel, Sara. "*CSI: Crime Scene Investigation* Is the Most-Watched Show in the World." *TV by Numbers*, June 14, 2012. http://tvbynumbers.zap2it.com/2012/06/14/csi-crime-scene-investigation-is-the-most-watched-show-in-the-world-2/138212.

Bureau of Justice Statistics. *Nearly 3.4 Million Violent Crimes per Year Went Unreported to Police from 2006 to 2010*. August 9, 2012. http://www.bjs.gov/content/pub/press/vnrp0610pr.cfm.

Devine, Elizabeth. "Too Tough to Die." *CSI*. Season 1. DVD. Directed by Richard J. Lewis. Aired on March 1, 2001. Hollywood: Paramount Home Entertainment, 2003.

Goldfinger, Sarah. "The Happy Place." *CSI*. Season 9. DVD. Directed by Nathan Hope. Aired on October 16, 2008. Hollywood: Paramount Home Entertainment, 2009.

Goldfinger, Sarah, David Rambo, and Naren Shankar. "Built to Kill (Part 1)." *CSI*. Season 7. DVD. Directed by Kenneth Fink. Aired on September 21, 2006. Hollywood: Paramount Home Entertainment, 2007.

Goldfinger, Sarah, Eli Talbert, Carol Mendelsohn, and Naren Shankar. "Bloodlines." *CSI*. Season 4. DVD. Directed by Kenneth Fink. Aired on May 20, 2004. Hollywood: Paramount Home Entertainment, 2004.

Hancock, Treena, and Melissa R. Byer. "Wild Life." *CSI*. Season 11. Directed by Charles Haid. Aired on November 18, 2010. Hollywood: Paramount Home Entertainment, 2011.

Hoyt, Jacqueline. "Death and the Maiden." *CSI*. Season 10. DVD. Directed by Brad Tanenbaum. Aired on November 5, 2009. Hollywood: Paramount Home Entertainment, 2010.

Lipsitz, Andrew, and Ann Donahue. "To Halve and to Hold." *CSI*. Season 1. DVD. Directed by Lou Antonio. Aired on February 15, 2001. Hollywood: Paramount Home Entertainment, 2003.

MacDonald, Allen. "Empty Eyes." *CSI*. Season 7. DVD. Directed by Michael Slovis. Aired on March 29, 2007. Hollywood: Paramount Home Entertainment, 2008.

Mendelsohn, Carol, and Josh Berman. "Who Are You?" *CSI*. Season 1. DVD. Directed by Danny Cannon. Aired on November 10, 2000. Hollywood: Paramount Home Entertainment, 2003.

Mendelsohn, Carol, Naren Shankar, Richard Catalani, and Danny Cannon. "Who and What." *CSI*. Season 8. DVD. Directed by Kenneth Fink and Danny Cannon. Aired on November 8, 2009. Hollywood: Paramount Home Entertainment, 2010.

Mularz, Tom. "In a Dark, Dark House." *CSI*. Season 11. DVD. Directed by Jeffrey Hunt. Aired on May 12, 2011. Hollywood: Paramount Home Entertainment, 2011.

Projansky, Sarah. *Watching Rape: Film and Television in Postfeminist Culture*. New York: New York University Press, 2001.

Rambo, David, Sarah Goldfinger, and Naren Shankar. "Built to Kill (Part 2)." *CSI*. Season 7. DVD. Directed by Kenneth Fink. Aired on September 28, 2006. Hollywood: Paramount Home Entertainment, 2007.

Shankar, Naren, and Evan Dunsky. "Meat Jekyll." *CSI*. Season 10. DVD. Directed by Alec Smight. Aired on May 20, 2010. Hollywood: Paramount Home Entertainment, 2010.

United States Department of Justice. *Full Report of the Prevalence, Incidence, and Consequences of Violence against Women*. November 2000. http://www.ncjrs.gov/pdffiles1/nij/183781.pdf.

Chapter Four

"Does Anyone Think Rape Isn't a Major Crime?"[1]

Female Cops and Rape Narratives on
The Closer *and* Rizzoli & Isles

The shows *The Closer* and *Rizzoli & Isles* both have main characters who are female police officers. In these cases, the female law enforcement officers are the central, titular characters of their shows, and it is through their perspectives that most of the narratives are filtered. According to a report by the Bureau of Justice Statistics, "Women accounted for about 15% of the total sworn law enforcement officers in large local police departments" in 2007.[2] These two shows take place in Los Angeles and Boston, respectively, and the real-world number fits the representations they create: one or two women working on a team made up of mostly men. *The Closer*'s Brenda Leigh Johnson and *Rizzoli & Isles*' Jane Rizzoli present femininity in two very different ways, but each of these women is a successful law enforcement officer and investigates rapes and sexual assaults frequently. Having female main characters shifts the perspective of typical police procedurals, which are commonly male-centric, and also changes the way these shows handle rape narratives.

In addition to their female-based focus, these two shows represent a shift in broadcast format from those previously considered in this project. While *NCIS*, *Criminal Minds*, and *CSI* are all major network (CBS) shows, *The Closer* and *Rizzoli & Isles* aired on a basic cable network TNT. Although TNT has had quite a bit of success with its staggered, off-season programming, it is rarely able to compete with the major networks in terms of ratings numbers. These shows do have more freedom when covering controversial or difficult topics because they are not held to the same standards as network shows. *The Closer*, for instance, "helped redefine the power balance between basic cable and broadcast networks," according to Paul Levinson, a media professor from Fordham University.[3] He cites the division of Emmy nominations—split equally between broadcast and cable in 2010[4]—as evidence supporting the point. Also in 2010, *The Closer* and *Rizzoli & Isles* were breaking ratings records as ad-supported cable's two biggest series of all time; *The Closer* season finale drew 7.2 million viewers and *Rizzoli & Isles* drew 6.6 million.[5] *The Closer* premiered in 2005, and in 2010, *Rizzoli & Isles* premiered in the next time slot. The shows aired back-to-back for two years with *Rizzoli & Isles* building off of *The Closer*'s success in more ways than one.

As two shows about successful female police officers and the team of people they work with, both shows address rape narratives repeatedly. *The Closer* has twenty-seven episodes that present rape narratives, which is nearly 25% of the total 109 episodes. In its first four seasons, *Rizzoli & Isles* has sixteen episodes with rape narratives, which is nearly 28% of the total fifty-six episodes. Percentage-wise, the two shows deal with rape narratives nearly the same amount. Additionally, while both shows present individual episodes that address various rape narratives, they also include at least one multi-episode, multiseason arc that pits the main female police officer against a rapist and puts her into situations that risk both her safety and her sanity.

THE CLOSER

When Deputy Chief Brenda Leigh Johnson joins the Los Angeles Police Department, she does so as the head of a newly created Priority Homicide Division.[6] As a CIA-trained interrogator, Brenda's job is to get a confession that will lead directly to a conviction, and throughout the show she has a near perfect record of doing just that. Because she came to the LAPD at the rank of deputy chief, viewers assume she has already had a successful career in law enforcement, particularly once they learn that she is the highest-ranking female officer in the department from the first day she arrives. Her team of six other detectives includes one other woman until Season Four when, after a romantic entanglement within the unit goes south, Detective Irene Daniels transfers. The men assigned to Brenda's unit are, at least at first, resentful of her authority. While those feelings may be partly due to the fact that she is new to the department and comes in outranking them all, the mockery she endures in Season One tends to focus on the ways Brenda presents her femininity. Because even though she is a deputy chief at the LAPD and most police departments are predominantly masculine, Brenda is also a Southern lady. The show places a heavy emphasis on her romantic and home life as well as her health and opportunities for career advancement in later seasons that would have given the LAPD its first female captain.

The show begins to address Brenda's position as a female officer in the series premiere when she is the first to notice that the original name of her new unit—Priority Murder Squad—is abbreviated to PMS on the stationery. Brenda's Southern manners and feminine style of dress, which often includes high heels and a skirt, are also emphasized on the show as early as Season One, Episode One, "Pilot,"[7] when, as part of an investigation, Brenda visits a victim's hair stylist, manicurist, and personal shopper. She also frequently plays on the tendency of others to underestimate her and her small stature in the interrogation room. The fact that Brenda's gender performance is weighed almost as heavily as her skills in the interrogation room in that first episode sets viewers up to pay close attention to how she carries herself and how she is treated as a high-ranking female officer.

The fact that Brenda is so unapologetically feminine and also the central character of *The Closer*—she works as part of a team, but she is the boss and thus separate from them—influences the way the show handles and addresses rape narratives. When Brenda's unit is renamed Major Crimes in Season Four, Episode Nine, "Tijuana Brass,"[8] Brenda outmaneuvers Chief William Pope, her boss, and Commander Taylor, with whom she works closely, to expand the reach of her unit beyond homicides. In that conversation, which takes place in front of a member of the press, Brenda aligns rape with the other major crimes that receive priority attention from her squad. Brenda explains the restructuring of her unit to the reporter and to viewers: "Major Crimes puts my division in charge not only of homicide but also the larger fraud cases and kidnappings and rapes." The reporter asks for clarification: "Rape and kidnapping?" In her response, Brenda is daring either Pope or Taylor to argue: "Well, yes, those are major crimes, aren't they? I mean does anyone think rape isn't a major crime?"[9] If anyone had before, Brenda's question, and the way it is framed, shames them into silence and thus creates a clear understanding that, yes, in the show's universe and from Brenda's perspective, rape is a major crime and takes priority.

A close look at the first and last rape narratives from *The Closer* that directly involve Brenda herself will provide a fairly representative look at the show's overall approach to rape narratives. In Season One, Episode Six, "Fantasy Date,"[10] Carla Simmons, the victim in a rape/homicide, is the daughter of a congresswoman. When informed of the circumstances of her daughter's death, the congresswoman, a former district attorney, explains that Carla "is not the kind of girl people want to hurt. She doesn't have stalkers."[11] This statement suggests that there are certain kinds of girls people do want to hurt and perhaps that there might be certain kinds of girls, different in some unspecified way from her daughter, who deserve to be brutalized, raped, and murdered. While viewers would have trouble holding that kind of suggestion against a mother who just found out that her daughter had been killed, the constructed nature of any dialogue in the script of the show is worth paying attention to. It is the script that makes that suggestion, not just the character of Congresswoman Simmons.

If that were the only such suggestion, it wouldn't hold much weight—however, the congresswoman's background as a prosecutor may lend it additional veracity. The episode, though, furthers this idea when viewers learn more about Carla's supposed online life. Brenda first uncovers it while interviewing Carla's ex-boyfriend. Brenda poses as a secretary and leads the ex-boyfriend to guess that Carla is the rape victim he is there to discuss. He does not know that Carla is dead, and his questions turn to asking if Carla has suggested that he was involved in her attack.

Brenda: Oh, no, sir. No one is accusing you of anything.

Ex: You know, I warned her. When we broke up? I told her that if she wanted to do that weird stuff . . .

Brenda: Weird stuff? Maybe I should write that down.[. . .] I've heard a lot of weird things around here. You can tell me. I have probably heard worse.

Ex: It's just, um, you know. Drugs. And, um, role-playing. She wanted to experiment sexually. [12]

And maybe that is the kind of girl Congresswoman Simmons had in mind, the kind to whom things like rape and murder were supposed to happen, but that kind of thinking is dangerous. It suggests that sexually violent crimes should only happen to a certain kind of woman and that certain kinds of women deserve such treatment.

Other parts of the episode work against this idea. After her conversation with the ex-boyfriend, Brenda returns to Carla's house alone. There is a uniformed officer standing guard, but Brenda dismisses him. While conducting a thorough search of Carla's home, Brenda discovers a stash of drugs. She is considering them when viewers see a large, bare-chested, masked figure sneaking up behind her. Brenda is taken by surprise, gets tossed around the room by a man who is much larger than she is, and fights back even after her assailant has duct-taped her mouth shut. She head-butts him, and he punches her in the face. The man reaches between their bodies after he has pinned Brenda to the bed, and when he starts to lift her skirt she is able to pull her gun and press it against his stomach. She then arrests him for breaking and entering, attempted rape, and assaulting a police officer.

Brenda is also not the kind of girl people want to hurt, at least not, presumably, in the eyes of Congresswoman Simmons or the viewers. She is the heroine of the story, the one who solves the crime. She is strong and capable and armed. She is the police officer. Yet she is nearly raped. Audiences see the aftereffects of her assault in the teary and bedraggled version of typically brash Brenda bandaging her own head wound while looking in the bathroom mirror back at the police station. She moves haltingly, as if sore, and pulls her sweater off her arms to inspect the bruises she sustained when she was assaulted. Viewers further witness her vulnerability in the moment when she reaches out to FBI agent Fritz Howard, with whom she is involved in a romantic relationship. She apologizes for waking him but doesn't quite manage to contain a sob. Witnessing Brenda in that vulnerable moment—which even so early in the series viewers recognize as out of character—serves as a reminder to viewers that rape can, or can nearly, happen to anyone. Rape isn't something that only happens to a certain kind of person.

A short while later, Brenda watches as Sergeant David Gabriel, who is often Brenda's go-to, interrogates the man who attacked her. When she first enters the electronics room, the rest of her team pays her a little too much attention, under which Brenda bristles: "Don't make such a fuss, okay? It's not like I got shot or anything."[13] Though she is dismissive of the significance of her attack, her body language does some work, if not quite enough, to counteract the damage her words might do to the overall serious and careful weight *The Closer* gives rape narratives—she keeps her body completely wrapped up in an oversized sweater and her arms crossed against her torso in a defensive, protective manner.

The results of Gabriel's interrogation of Brenda's assailant are familiar within the context of a rape narrative, but with a twist. In response to Gabriel's questioning, the attacker says, "And tell me this. If you ask to be raped, then how can you be surprised [. . .] and when I say the woman who did this to my face was asking for it, I mean really asking for it."[14] Gabriel's facial expression makes it clear that he has heard that excuse before, but he asks for clarification anyhow. And the man provides it: "Look in my bag, you'll see it. She had a personal on the Jones List. Directions, her address [. . .] I was responding to her, that's all. She was literally asking for it."[15] But it wasn't Carla who was attacked; it was Brenda. And it wasn't Carla who posted the personal ad on the website, either. And the young man responsible for Carla's death wasn't entirely a rapist or a murderer; he had also responded to the ad he believed Carla had placed, and her death was almost an accident. She fell and struck her head against a piece of furniture while trying to fend off his attack. But whether that specific attacker or the man who attacked Brenda was a rapist, Carla was in fact raped and killed.

The ad in which Carla supposedly was "asking for it" was placed by her ex-boyfriend. After he struck her during a fight, Carla dumped him. In retaliation, he posted the ad in her name, with her address and directions for how to gain entry into her home in hopes that "if she knew what real violence was like, she'd see what [he] did was really nothing. It was just supposed to be rape."[16] Even as the man responsible for Carla's rape and murder and Brenda's attack is dismissive of the crime, Brenda and Gabriel are able to turn his admission into a case for first-degree murder. This particular outcome for the case does three things: First, it directly addresses and fights back against the idea that women who are raped are in some way asking for it. As previously mentioned, regardless of what the men who attacked Carla (or Brenda while mistaking her for Carla) thought, what happened to her was rape. Second, it underscores the fact that rape, at its core, is about power and control, not about sex. Carla's ex-boyfriend attempted to use rape as a weapon—to gain control over Carla, who wanted nothing to do with him.

Additionally, while *The Closer* is not the first show to put its main character at risk of sexual assault, inserting Brenda into such a position so early—and still long enough after the premiere that viewers have come to care about and root for her—is important to the show's overall approach to rape narratives. In an episode that pays direct attention to questioning what kind of girl ends up in that situation, the fact that Carla was set up and the fact that Brenda herself was at risk shows viewers that in *The Closer* universe, rape is a crime that can happen to anyone, regardless of lifestyle, job title, or training.

The final rape narrative in *The Closer* culminates in the series finale, but it begins in Season Four, Episode Thirteen, "Power of Attorney."[17] This is the episode when Brenda first meets Phillip Stroh.[18] A defense attorney, Stroh specializes in representing sex offenders, and at first, he calls attention to himself in seemingly innocuous ways: He stumbles into the "murder room," as Brenda's team calls their office space, and he is zealous in his commitment to his clients. In this particular case, he works out a deal for his client; the man had a partner who was the one to actually kill Jessica Goodall and rape Lauren Clark, Rebecca Howe, and four others. In exchange for a lighter sentence, the client will name his partner. When he does, he names Stroh.

As defense attorney, Stroh is in a position to access evidence and to tamper with witness identifications. He is able to insulate himself from his client's claim, and he knows that Brenda has no evidence to substantiate it. In their final confrontation in this episode, Brenda makes Stroh a promise: "I will hunt relentlessly to tie you to these crimes until the day you die."[19] This is the point where she becomes personally and in some ways directly involved in this rape narrative. She means it, she will follow through, and it will cost her her career with the LAPD and nearly her life.

The idea of Stroh returns in Season Five, Episode Eight, "Elysian Fields,"[20] when viewers learn that Brenda has nightmares featuring Stroh and sleeps with his file next to her bed. It is also revealed that she has had Gabriel pulling the files of all the sex offenders Stroh defended in the last three years, with no results. "Well," she says, "let's try five, shall we?"[21] Brenda's investigation into Stroh is little more than an aside in this episode, but it serves as a reminder that her promise to him has yet to be fulfilled.

In the seventh season of *The Closer*, Brenda's career is at risk due to a lawsuit that only tangentially involves Stroh. Both Episodes Ten, "Fresh Pursuit,"[22] and Twelve, "You Have the Right to Remain Jolly,"[23] mention that Brenda has been harassing Stroh for over two years. In "You Have the Right to Remain Jolly," she admits that she has sent Stroh flowers from Jessica Goodall, a woman he killed, every year on the anniversary of her death. This particular gesture is interesting in the way that it shows Brenda working to give Jessica back the voice Stroh silenced, but it is equally, if not more, problematic because she is an officer of the law and her actions certainly constitute harassment. Regardless of what she believes or even knows to be true, she can only act on what she can prove, and her personal investment in this rape narrative isn't actually serving the best interests of Stroh's victims, who still have not gotten the justice they deserve.

It is hard to know whether Brenda's overzealous pursuit of Stroh is really for the victims' benefit anymore. This is especially true in Season Seven, Episode Sixteen, "Hostile Witness,"[24] when Brenda brings Natalie Gilbert, a homeless and mentally ill woman who was raped, home with her and attempts to force her to remember the rape. After facing Stroh in court and accusing him on the record of being a rapist and partnering with his new client, the speech Brenda gives is borderline threatening: "You're perfectly safe here tonight. I'm only concerned with what happens later, when you're out on your own and the LAPD isn't around. Of course, if you could identify the guy, we could pick him up, end this ongoing threat against your life. But as it stands now, he's going to come after you again."[25] Midway through this speech, Fritz, who is now Brenda's husband, comes home and overhears what his wife is telling Natalie.

Fritz: Do you really think it's fair to drag that poor girl through her rape again when it's clear she doesn't want to think about it?

Brenda: Do you think it's fair that the guy who did that to her is running around free? I'm trying to find him and put him in prison.

Fritz: No, you're not. You're trying to nail Stroh.

Brenda: It's the same thing.

Fritz: Is it?[26]

Fritz is right to question her, and not just because of her methods here. With Brenda, the ends always seem to justify the means, and the heart of the entire lawsuit against her is that it shouldn't work like that. This message seems to be emphasized by the rape narrative in this episode because when Brenda and Fritz get Natalie to agree to return to where she was raped, the person she identifies as her attacker and the partner of Stroh's client isn't Stroh at all; it's the bartender. The event is traumatic for Natalie, who breaks down when she recognizes her rapist, and Brenda isn't any closer to tying Stroh to any rapes. The outcome of this episode may lead viewers to wonder what else Brenda could have missed while reviewing all those rape cases if she has only been looking for evidence that ties back to Stroh.

The last episode of the series is Season Seven, Episode Twenty-One, "The Last Word."[27] In this episode, Brenda believes she sees Stroh on a security camera following a woman who is later murdered, and she has a witness who can identify Stroh after catching him in the act of burying Karen Ocidi's body, which led to the discovery of several other bodies in the same area—all women who had been strangled, raped, and buried naked.

After an interview with Stroh that leads nowhere, Brenda asks his opinion as someone who works so closely with sex offenders. Stroh's responses are creepy, whether Brenda and viewers are convinced he is a rapist.

Stroh: Obviously he enjoys killing women during sexual intercourse.

Brenda: It's not sex. It's rape.

Stroh: Potato, po-tah-to. Let's not get all bogged down in political correctness.[28]

Even that brief part of their exchange presents a solid understanding of the tone Stroh uses while talking with Brenda—taunting and supremely confident. After Brenda carries out a borderline ethical plan she created with the district attorney, she brings her witness, a teenaged boy named Rusty, home with her. Fritz is gone, having traveled to D.C. for one night to see if he can grease some wheels to move the Stroh case forward.

After this series of events, the confrontation with Stroh and Fritz's absence in particular, viewers are likely not surprised when Stroh is standing in Brenda's kitchen after she discovers the torn screen on her bathroom window—a familiar detail from crime scenes including that of Jessica Goodall's murder. With some help from Rusty, Brenda is able to fight off Stroh, and she shoots him. She considers whether to just let him die before calling 911. Stroh offers to tell her everything, but Brenda is no longer interested.

While it seems likely that at least some of what Stroh has done will come out now, the fact that Brenda responds to his offer the way she does—"You know what? I don't want to hear it"[29]—really does suggest that she wasn't chasing Stroh in order to get justice for his victims. He is smart and familiar enough with the system that he will know what not to say when it comes to a trial, and viewers have seen Brenda force herself to sit through horrific confessions before[30] in order to discover the truth of what happened to the victims of violent crimes.

But this was Brenda's last case. She kept her promise to Stroh, and she is ready to let go of that particular rape narrative. Throughout her years with the LAPD, Brenda has used some questionable tactics, such as threats of prison rape in Season One, Episode Eight, "Batter Up,"[31] and Season Four, Episode Three, "Cherry Bomb."[32] She also basically forces victims to talk to her in "Cherry Bomb" as well as in Season Five, Episode Thirteen, "The Life,"[33] and "Hostile Witness" from Season Seven. Those are just the examples of rape narratives. Decisions Brenda has made have led to deaths—usually of killers, but still. The ways in which she pushes too far are couched in the context of her role as a deputy chief for the LAPD and the assumption that she is on the side of justice. She manages, for most of the show, to strike an acceptable balance between serving justice and punishing perpetrators, but later in the series, she is less successful at maintaining that balance. Her focus on serving and protecting victims lessens as the seasons pass, and by the final episode, when she nearly becomes a victim again herself, her decision to leave the LAPD makes sense to viewers. Much is left unknown with Stroh—what he might have done to her given the chance, what will happen when or if he goes to trial—but Brenda has decided to take back the control she has given over to her hunt for him.

RIZZOLI & ISLES

Based on novels by Tess Gerritsen, *Rizzoli & Isles* is a buddy cop show with two female leads. Boston homicide detective Jane Rizzoli works closely with her best friend, medical examiner Maura Isles, and quite a bit of the show focuses on their friendship in addition to the cases they are working. Both women are presented as the best and brightest in their respective fields through a series of artifacts featured in the show's opening credits as well as comments made throughout the course of the series. Viewers learn that Jane is the youngest detective in Boston Police Department history, and Maura is the chief medical examiner for the Commonwealth of Massachusetts. Both women have been very successful in fields in which many of their colleagues are men. While many of the show's remaining characters are men, the focal point of this series is the perspectives of these two successful women.

Jane and Maura's close relationship also leads to two different presentations of femininity. Maura serves as Jane's ultrafeminine antithesis—Maura is more interested in fashion and cooking and caretaking than Jane, who has a bloody nose from playing basketball with her brother Frankie when viewers first meet her. Jane's interests are more stereotypically masculine, as is her wardrobe. Playing on the buddy-cop genre, these two women are a bit of an odd couple, but their commitment to their work and their different approaches and perspectives greatly influence the way their show addresses rape narratives.

The first four seasons of *Rizzoli & Isles* have eighteen episodes that contain rape narratives. Because the show is still on the air, a broad look at how the series as a whole handles this particular type of story line isn't possible, but any discussion of rape narratives in Jane Rizzoli's world would begin with the series premiere. Season One, Episode One, "See One, Do One, Teach One"[34] begins with a close-up shot of a woman in a nightgown. A longer look at the scene shows a man seated nearby. He is tied down. The woman is crying and then screaming as another man circles around her until he reaches out to tear away the nightgown. Viewers don't see anything more of the scene, but the fade-out is scored by the woman's scream.

The next scene is Jane and Frankie in the driveway playing basketball. When Jane's nose ends up bloody, Angela Rizzoli, Jane and Frankie's mom, reprimands Jane for her injury, absolving Frankie of any blame. Innocuous in and of itself, the scene is a little disconcerting when juxtaposed with the opening scene: A terrified victim attacked in what viewers discover is her own home then another domestic scene where the victim (this time of an accident) is blamed for violence that happened to her.

Underscoring the juxtaposition, Jane is still bleeding when she is called to the scene. Gail Yeager is missing, and her husband, Martin, is dead. The evidence leads Jane and her former partner Vince Korsak to the same conclusion: The crime fits the pattern of serial killer and rapist Charles Hoyt,[35] also known as the Surgeon. The connection to Hoyt hits Rizzoli pretty hard, and viewers begin to learn why in a flashback. They see another woman laid out on a mattress in a basement, and Jane coming down the stairs only to be hit over the head and knocked unconscious. That is as much as viewers see at this point.

The person who attacked the Yeagers cannot be Hoyt; he is in prison. Jane and her new partner, Barry Frost, go visit him there to determine what he knows about the Yeagers. This is when viewers see the rest of what happened to Jane. She is pinned to the floor in that basement with scalpels Hoyt drove through her palms, with the man hovering over her, touching her body. In the course of an interrogation, the detectives don't learn anything from Hoyt, but viewers do. He talks about Jane's body, referring to when he touched her: "I love your neck. And your breasts. They're very firm."[36] Later in the episode, after he escapes from custody, Hoyt makes another reference to Jane's body, in a note attached to flowers he leaves outside her apartment: "Prickly on the outside, succulent on the inside—just like you."[37]

As the episode progresses, one thing that becomes clear is that Hoyt has an apprentice who killed Martin Yeager and kidnapped Gail. He also killed and then continued to have sex with her remains. One thing that does not become entirely clear is whether Hoyt raped Jane Rizzoli. The way he talks about her body suggests that he did, but the brief flashbacks viewers see show her fully clothed. She never says she was raped, but she was clearly traumatized by her experience with Hoyt. The physical pain she endured and even just the threat that she could easily have been raped as she was held captive by a rapist could be enough to account for that, but the possibility is introduced and the extent of what Jane endured could have been made more clear.

That clarity would have been appreciated even more so because the series premiere is not the only time viewers see Charles Hoyt. In Season One, Episode Eight, "I'm Your Boogie Man,"[38] Hoyt returns in Jane's dreams, and when she wakes up, she discovers a flare burning in the street outside her apartment building. While it is just like the flare she used to burn his face while escaping him in the series premiere, Hoyt didn't send the message directly. He will come back again later on, but in this episode, Hoyt has a second apprentice, a woman this time. After he killed her husband in front of her, Hoyt held Emily Stern in a basement for six months, repeatedly beating and likely raping her the entire time. She begins dating Frankie as a way to get to Jane.

Lola, the woman Frankie thinks Emily Stern is, is the product of the psychological problems that can arise from continued abuse. Evidence shows that even before Hoyt, Emily Stern was an abused wife. While all that happened to Emily Stern is not covered by the idea of "rape," it was one of the traumas she experienced, and through her connection to Hoyt, she plays an important role in that narrative. The fact that Frankie is forced to kill her in Jane's apartment means that even though the man himself is imprisoned, he can still gain access to Jane—both through her own subconscious and in a real, physical way that poses an immediate threat to her life. The way this threat finds its way into Jane's home reminds viewers that as long as Charles Hoyt is alive, Jane is constantly at risk.

In some ways, the Charles Hoyt rape narrative culminates in Season Two, Episode Ten, "Remember Me."[39] While investigating the death of a man who was in the process of being released from prison, Jane finds herself in the same infirmary where Charles Hoyt is being treated for his pancreatic cancer. Jane is the only one who is convinced that the two things are connected, and when it is revealed that one of the prison guards has become Hoyt's third apprentice, she is proven correct. After a confrontation in the infirmary in which Maura is knocked unconscious and Jane is tied up with zip ties, the two women come out on top, physically fine if not emotionally: Jane stabs Hoyt, killing him and declaring "I win" as she does.[40] Jane sur-

vives, and since Hoyt doesn't, he can no longer create new situations in
which Jane will find herself physically vulnerable, thus concluding at least
one aspect of the rape narrative.

Since the show is not over, though, neither is the narrative. The best
reminder of the effects Hoyt will continue to have on Jane is a conversation
that takes place earlier in the episode between Jane's past and current partners. Since he cannot ask Jane about the specifics of her interactions with
Hoyt, Frost asks Korsak.

Frost: Why doesn't she ever talk to me about it?

Korsak: What Hoyt did to her, you can't talk about. Just leave it alone,
Frost.

Frost: You were with her when it happened. She's my partner too, Korsak. You see what it does to her. I can't help her if she won't talk to me.

Korsak: The only thing that's going to help her is to shovel dirt on that
bastard's grave.[41]

The specifics of Jane's past with Hoyt aren't ignored here. In fact, it is the
opposite, as the dialogue calls viewers' attention to the fact that Frost isn't
the only one who doesn't know the full story of what happened—they don't
know either. Jane's male colleagues care about her and her well-being, but
by asking Korsak instead of Jane herself, Frost allows Jane's silence on the
topic to continue. And it is clear from his advice to Frost that she doesn't
speak to Korsak about what she experienced either. Viewers don't see her
talking to anyone about the trauma caused by her interactions with Hoyt even
though they know she feels it. It is as if by calling attention to the unknown
and saying that there's nothing more to talk about, the show is attempting to
move on from or even erase rape from Hoyt's narrative. This episode with
his last appearance refers to him as a killer and a torturer, but rape is never
mentioned among the crimes he has committed, just as it is never made
entirely clear what happened to Jane, whose refusal to talk about it fits with
the ways in which her personality is masculinized.

The reality is, though, that even though Hoyt is dead, he continues to
affect Jane's life. *Rizzoli & Isles* makes this clear in Season Four, Episode
Nine, "No One Mourns the Wicked,"[42] when Jane finds herself watching
interviews of Hoyt in order to solve another crime. He has a lasting impact
both on her character and on how viewers relate to her.

In other rape narratives throughout the show, Jane's response to victims
changes. In Season Two, Episode Three, "Sailor Man,"[43] she uses the endearments "sweetie" and "baby" while talking to Kim Tretorn, a rape victim
moments from death. This is shortly after she and Maura stood over the

woman, who was strapped to a gurney, and discussed, over the unconscious woman's body, how she was lucky to be alive and how it was the near-freezing temperatures outside that saved her but there's no way of knowing what kind of life she'll have. They are still standing outside, and the woman they are discussing is lying between them, capable of hearing everything they are saying though not conscious to do so. The moment turns her body into a prop, just part of the scenery, but in the end, Kim Tretorn wakes up long enough to give Jane the clues she needs to apprehend the rapist—a man impersonating a sailor during Boston's Fleet Week. She's a prop but gets enough of a voice to keep the investigation moving forward, and Jane crosses personal boundaries by using endearments to refer to the dying woman.

Phillip Stroh is in prison. Charles Hoyt is dead. Because *The Closer* has ended, viewers have a complete picture of Brenda Leigh Johnson's involvement with rape narratives. Even when Stroh's trial comes up in *The Closer* spin-off *Major Crimes*, Brenda does not return. Though Hoyt is dead, Jane Rizzoli still works for the Boston Police Department in the *Rizzoli & Isles* universe. She is still coming across new cases in episodes that continue to present rape narratives, and her experiences with Hoyt are likely still influencing her character even when viewers don't hear anything that directly says so. His actions are a part of who she is from the beginning of the television show.

Brenda had had direct involvement in a rape narrative before Stroh. Season One, Episode Six called attention to her potential to become a victim. In the five episodes prior to that, viewers had a chance to get to know her a bit, to come to care about her as a person before being asked to consider her in the role of victim. The same is not true for Jane. Her interaction with Hoyt is one of the first things viewers learn about her and is part of the reason viewers come to care for her; it is always part of who she is for as long as television viewers know her.[44]

The Closer and *Rizzoli & Isles* are both successful shows about successful female police officers. Brenda Leigh Johnson and Jane Rizzoli both have direct personal experience with rape narratives that influences their lives moving forward: after Stroh, Brenda leaves the LAPD, and after Hoyt, Jane continues to deal with the trauma she experienced because of him. While Brenda's departure from her department signaled the end of her show, Jane's story isn't over yet.

NOTES

1. James Duff and Mike Berchem, "Tijuana Brass," *The Closer*, season 4, episode 9, directed by Anthony Hemingway, aired on September 8, 2008 (Burbank, CA: Warner Home Video, 2009), DVD.

2. Lynn Langton, *Women in Law Enforcement, 1987–2008* (United States Department of Justice, June 2010), http://www.bjs.gov/content/pub/pdf/wle8708.pdf.

3. Gloria Goodale, "*The Closer* Opened Doors for Women—and for Basic Cable," *Christian Science Monitor*, July 12, 2010, http://www.csmonitor.com/USA/2010/0712/The-Closer-opened-doors-for-women-and-for-basic-cable.

4. Kyra Sedgwick, the actress who plays Brenda Leigh Johnson, was nominated five times for Primetime Emmys for Outstanding Lead Actress in a Drama Series. She won in 2010.

5. Bill Gorman, "TNT's *The Closer* and *Rizzoli & Isles* Close Out Summer with More Big Numbers," *TV by the Numbers*, September 14, 2012, http://tvbythenumbers.zap2it.com/2010/09/14/tnt's-the-closer-and-rizzoli-isles-close-out-record-setting-summer-as-ad-supported-cable's-top-two-series/63239/.

6. As will be discussed shortly, Brenda's new squad is first named the Priority Murder Squad but quickly changes to Priority Homicide. In Season Four, Episode Nine, "Tijuana Brass," the name of the unit changes again to Major Crimes.

7. James Duff, "Pilot," *The Closer*, season 1, episode 1, directed by Michael M. Robin, aired on June 13, 2005 (Burbank, CA: Warner Home Video, 2006), DVD.

8. Duff and Berchem, "Tijuana Brass."

9. Ibid.

10. Roger Wolfson, "Fantasy Date," *The Closer*, season 1, episode 6, directed by Greg Yaitanes, aired on July 18, 2005 (Burbank, CA: Warner Home Video, 2006), DVD.

11. Ibid.

12. Ibid.

13. Ibid.

14. Ibid.

15. Ibid.

16. Ibid.

17. Michael Alaimo, "Power of Attorney," *The Closer*, season 4, episode 13, directed by Rick Wallace, aired on February 9, 2009 (Burbank, CA: Warner Home Video, 2009), DVD.

18. Billy Burke, the actor who plays Phillip Stroh on *The Closer*, also plays a recurring role in several seasons of *Rizzoli & Isles*. In that show, though, his character is an FBI agent.

19. Alaimo, "Power of Attorney."

20. Michael Alaimo, "Elysian Fields," *The Closer*, season 5, episode 8, directed by Nicole Kassell, aired on July 27, 2009 (Burbank, CA: Warner Home Video, 2010), DVD.

21. Ibid.

22. Adam Belanoff, "Fresh Pursuit," *The Closer*, season 7, episode 10, directed by Michael M. Robin, aired on September 12, 2011 (Burbank, CA: Warner Home Video, 2012), DVD.

23. James Duff and Michael Alaimo, "You Have the Right to Remain Jolly," *The Closer*, season 7, episode 12, directed by Rick Wallace, aired on December 5, 2011 (Burbank, CA: Warner Home Video, 2012), DVD.

24. Steven Kane, "Hostile Witness," *The Closer*, season 7, episode 16, directed by Steve Robin, aired on July 9, 2012 (Burbank, CA: Warner Home Video, 2012), DVD.

25. Ibid.

26. Ibid.

27. James Duff and Mike Berchem, "The Last Word," *The Closer*, season 7, episode 21, directed by Michael M. Robin, aired on August 13, 2012 (Burbank, CA: Warner Home Video, 2012), DVD.

28. Ibid.

29. Ibid.

30. See Season Five, Episode Twelve, "Waivers of Extradition," in which Brenda interviews a serial killer for at least seven hours to hear him tell the stories behind all of his "souvenirs" in order to determine the names and locations of all his victims. Adam Belanoff, "Waivers of Extradition," *The Closer*, season 5, episode 12, directed by Kevin Bacon, aired on August 24, 2009 (Burbank, CA: Warner Home Video, 2010), DVD.

31. James Duff, "Batter Up," *The Closer*, season 1, episode 8, directed by Arvin Brown, aired on August 1, 2005 (Burbank, CA: Warner Home Video, 2006), DVD.

32. Michael Alaimo, "Cherry Bomb," *The Closer*, season 4, episode 3, directed by Rick Wallace, aired on July 28, 2008 (Burbank, CA: Warner Home Video, 2009), DVD.

33. Hunt Baldwin and John Coveny, "The Life," *The Closer*, season 5, episode 13, directed by Steve Robin, aired on December 7, 2009 (Burbank, CA: Warner Home Video, 2010), DVD.

34. Janet Tamaro, "See One, Do One, Teach One," *Rizzoli & Isles*, season 1, episode 1, directed by Michael M. Robin, aired on July 12, 2010 (Burbank, CA: Warner Home Video, 2011), DVD.

35. Michael Massee, the actor who plays Charles Hoyt on *Rizzoli & Isles*, also plays a serial rapist/killer on *Criminal Minds*, a dirty cop on *CSI*, and a man who kidnaps girls and holds them captive for years on *Law and Order: Special Victims Unit*.

36. Tamaro, "See One, Do One, Teach One."

37. Ibid.

38. Janet Tamaro, "I'm Your Boogie Man," *Rizzoli & Isles*, season 1, episode 8, directed by Mark Haber, aired on August 30, 2010 (Burbank, CA: Warner Home Video, 2011), DVD.

39. David J. North and Janet Tamaro, "Remember Me," *Rizzoli & Isles*, season 2, episode 10, directed by Randy Zisk, aired on September 12, 2011 (Burbank, CA: Warner Home Video, 2012), DVD.

40. Ibid.

41. Ibid.

42. Ken Hanes, Lisa Marie Petersen, and Janet Tamaro, "No One Mourns the Wicked," *Rizzoli & Isles*, season 4, episode 9, directed by Steve Robin, aired on August 20, 2013 (Burbank, CA: Warner Home Video, 2014), DVD.

43. Joel Fields, "Sailor Man," *Rizzoli & Isles*, season 2, episode 3, directed by Michael Zinberg, aired on August 1, 2011 (Burbank, CA: Warner Home Video, 2012), DVD.

44. I cannot speak to whether the same is true of the version of Jane Rizzoli that exists in Tess Gerritsen's novels in which the characters originated.

REFERENCES

Alaimo, Michael. "Cherry Bomb." *The Closer.* Season 4. DVD. Directed by Rick Wallace. Aired on July 28, 2008. Burbank, CA: Warner Home Video, 2009.

———. "Elysian Fields." *The Closer.* Season 5. DVD. Directed by Nicole Kassell. Aired on July 27, 2009. Burbank, CA: Warner Home Video, 2010.

———. "Power of Attorney." *The Closer.* Season 4. DVD. Directed by Rick Wallace. Aired on February 9, 2009. Burbank, CA: Warner Home Video, 2009.

Baldwin, Hunt, and John Coveny. "The Life." *The Closer.* Season 5. DVD. Directed by Steve Robin. Aired on December 7, 2009. Burbank, CA: Warner Home Video, 2010.

Belanoff, Adam. "Fresh Pursuit." *The Closer.* Season 7. DVD. Directed by Michael M. Robin. Aired on September 12, 2011. Burbank, CA: Warner Home Video, 2012.

———. "Waivers of Extradition." *The Closer.* Season 5. DVD. Directed by Kevin Bacon. Aired on August 24, 2009. Burbank, CA: Warner Home Video, 2010.

Duff, James. "Batter Up." *The Closer.* Season 1. DVD. Directed by Arvin Brown. Aired on August 1, 2005. Burbank, CA: Warner Home Video, 2006.

———. "Pilot." *The Closer.* Season 1. DVD. Directed by Michael M. Robin. Aired on June 13, 2005. Burbank, CA: Warner Home Video, 2006.

Duff, James, and Michael Alaimo. "You Have the Right to Remain Jolly." *The Closer.* Season 7. DVD. Directed by Rick Wallace. Aired on December 5, 2011. Burbank, CA: Warner Home Video, 2012.

Duff, James, and Mike Berchem. "The Last Word." *The Closer.* Season 7. DVD. Directed by Michael M. Robin. Aired on August 13, 2012. Burbank, CA: Warner Home Video, 2012.

———. "Tijuana Brass." *The Closer.* Season 4. Directed by Anthony Hemingway. Aired on September 8, 2008. Burbank, CA: Warner Home Video, 2009.

Fields, Joel. "Sailor Man." *Rizzoli & Isles.* Season 2. DVD. Directed by Michael Zinberg. Aired on August 1, 2011. Burbank, CA: Warner Home Video, 2012.

Goodale, Gloria. "*The Closer* Opened Doors for Women—and for Basic Cable." *Christian Science Monitor*, July 12, 2010. http://www.csmonitor.com/USA/2010/0712/The-Closer-opened-doors-for-women-and-for-basic-cable.

Gorman, Bill. "TNT's *The Closer* and *Rizzoli & Isles* Close Out Summer with More Big Numbers." *TV by the Numbers*, September 14, 2012. http://tvbythenumbers.zap2it.com/2010/09/14/tnt's-the-closer-and-rizzoli-isles-close-out-record-setting-summer-as-ad-supported-cable's-top-two-series/63239/.

Hanes, Ken, Lisa Marie Petersen, and Janet Tamaro. "No One Mourns the Wicked." *Rizzoli & Isles.* Season 4. DVD. Directed by Steve Robin. Aired on August 20, 2013. Burbank, CA: Warner Home Video, 2014.

Kane, Steven. "Hostile Witness." *The Closer.* Season 7. DVD. Directed by Steve Robin. Aired on July 9, 2012. Burbank, CA: Warner Home Video, 2012.

Langton, Lynn. *Women in Law Enforcement, 1987–2008.* United States Department of Justice. June 2010. http://www.bjs.gov/content/pub/pdf/wle8708.pdf.

North, David J., and Janet Tamaro. "Remember Me." *Rizzoli & Isles.* Season 2. DVD. Directed by Randy Zisk. Aired on September 12, 2011. Burbank, CA: Warner Home Video, 2012.

Tamaro, Janet. "I'm Your Boogie Man." *Rizzoli & Isles.* Season 1. DVD. Directed by Mark Haber. Aired on August 30, 2010. Burbank, CA: Warner Home Video, 2011.

———. "See One, Do One, Teach One." *Rizzoli & Isles.* Season 1. DVD. Directed by Michael M. Robin. Aired on July 12, 2010. Burbank, CA: Warner Home Video, 2011.

Wolfson, Roger. "Fantasy Date." *The Closer.* Season 1. DVD. Directed by Greg Yaitanes. Aired on July 18, 2005. Burbank, CA: Warner Home Video, 2006.

Chapter Five

"As Damaged as Me" [1]

Rape, Revenge, and Dexter's Women

Dexter Morgan is a blood spatter analyst for the Miami Metro Police Department. He is a brother and a father, a son and a husband, a friend. Most everyone who knows him would describe him as a solid guy, dependable, good at his work. Maybe a little reserved, he is a likable, normal guy. If news crews ever had reason to interview all his friends and coworkers, they would be stunned by what lurks under all those roles Dexter plays so well: a serial killer.

After debuting in 2006, *Dexter* aired on Showtime for eight seasons, ending in 2013. Titular character Dexter Morgan was an unapologetic serial killer for the show's duration. Based on novels and a character created by author Jeff Lindsay, this series is different from others considered in this project because it aired primarily on a premium channel [2] and as such was held to different standards when it came to sexual and violent content. Because of this, viewers saw more of Dexter than they otherwise would have: more of his body, his sex life, and more of the violence he commits against the individuals who end up strapped down to the table in the kill rooms he constructs.

While Dexter is a serial killer—and it is one of the first things viewers learn about him—his kills are governed by a code established for Dexter by his adoptive father, Harry Morgan, a former homicide detective with the Miami Metro Police Department. The code consists of a series of rules that lay out not just how Dexter kills but also whom he kills: murderers who have fallen through the cracks of the justice system but who Dexter can prove, often through less-than-legal methods, are guilty. The first rule of the code, mentioned repeatedly throughout the course of the series, is "Don't get caught." Viewers don't begrudge Dexter this self-serving primary goal, however; according to Ashley Donnelly in her article "The New American Hero: Dexter, Serial Killer for the Masses," "Dexter has given [viewers] license to empower the voice within us all that cries out for brutal, bloody, visceral justice."[3] Viewers don't want him to get caught, then, because he shows them something within themselves that may not find another outlet. And he doesn't just operate in this way for viewers; Dexter also extends the same license to characters within the show's universe.

Dexter has received some criticism regarding its content and morality from advocacy groups like the Parents Television Council, but that criticism has not stopped the show from becoming the most successful of Showtime's original programs. The series' eighth and final season attracted a "weekly average of 6.4 million viewers across all platforms," and the series finale, which aired on September 22, 2013, "was the show's highest rated telecast ever, and the largest viewership for an original episode in Showtime history."[4] The show's fifth season, which proves particularly important to the discussion in this chapter, aired in 2010 and was Showtime's best-rated season premiere in fifteen years.[5]

Of the ninety-six episodes that comprise the full series of *Dexter*, twenty-five of them include rape narratives (26%). Dexter's violence, though, is clearly differentiated from familiar narratives that combine or at least link violence and sexuality, a point clearly explained by Victoria L. Smith: "The writers of the show clearly want to distance Dexter from the 'run of the mill' male serial killer who takes sadistic pleasure in sexually violating and mutilating his victims' bodies, particularly women's. He is not driven by sick sexual lusts, only sick, but 'just,' violence."[6] Dexter's victims are more likely to be men than women, and in fact there are several occasions when the reason a man has ended up on Dexter's kill table is because he is a rapist.[7]

While there are features of the episodic police procedural at work in *Dexter*, seasons of the show also work through more developed story arcs than more traditional police procedurals. Each season explores at least one overarching conflict, and that style of developing narrative arcs influences how this chapter will approach a discussion of rape narratives.

Over the course of the show, Dexter loves three women. In the beginning of the show, Dexter is dating Rita Bennett, whom he marries at the end of Season Three. Rita is killed in the Season Four finale. Following Rita's death, Dexter has a complicated relationship with Lumen Pierce after she witnesses him kill the man who was holding her captive at the time of his death. Their relationship ends in the Season Five finale. In Season Seven, Dexter meets and eventually falls in love with Hannah McKay, another serial killer, whom Dexter originally intended to kill. All three of these women are blonde and lovely. They have all survived traumatic events that have scarred them and shaped them. All three—Rita, Lumen, and Hannah—were raped prior to their relationships with Dexter. Their desires for revenge after their sexual traumas directly impact their interactions with Dexter and drive the narratives forward.

RITA MORGAN (NEE BENNETT)

When viewers first meet Rita, in Season One, Episode One, "Dexter,"[8] Dexter introduces her in a voice-over. He explains her history: "Deb [Dexter's sister, a Miami Metro police officer] saved her life on a domestic dispute call, introduced us, and we've been dating for six months now. She's perfect, because Rita is, in her own way, as damaged as me."[9] He continues: "Rita's ex-hubby, the crack addict, repeatedly raped her, knocked her around. Ever since then, she's been completely uninterested in sex. That works for me."[10] Dexter explains that when he dates women, the relationship usually goes well until sex is introduced into the equation since it is difficult for him to hide the truth about his nature during such intimate moments—most women notice he doesn't engage emotionally in what he is doing with them in bed.

This immediate portrayal of Rita as a victim of repeated spousal rape and domestic abuse is significant in several ways. First, Rita's status as a victim colors everything viewers will ever think about her as a character. Second, since it comes so early in the opening episode of the series, it contributes to viewers' initial impressions of Dexter. Not only does he use his girlfriend as a prop in his masquerade to appear normal, but she is recovering from repeated, intimate trauma. Third, Dexter admits that her trauma actually works to his benefit; it makes it easier for him to appear normal as her attention isn't entirely focused on him. While he doesn't come out and say it directly, it seems as if it was the story of her trauma that attracted him to her in the first place—which aligns with the interest he shows in other rape victims later on in the series.

It is clear that Dexter is not a good guy—through the kind of voice-over that becomes commonplace for the series, he introduces himself as a serial killer even before viewers learn the realities of his relationship with Rita. The combination of these two ideas—Rita's trauma and the way Dexter is constantly hiding his true self from everyone but the audience—takes the form of Dexter's frequent, internal interrogations of his responses to Rita and her emotions and responses to him as he makes a show of being supportive of Rita's healing. While his consideration could appear kind if he were trying to avoid possibly triggering her, his in-depth consideration of her reactions serves his purpose of trying to manipulate her instead. Even so, what she has suffered at the hands of her ex-husband is important in terms of the way the show considers what is expected of and by survivors after such trauma.

In addition to the timing of the revelation of Rita's victim status, what Dexter actually has to say about it is important as well. By creating a comparison between their respective damage—by claiming that Rita is just as damaged as he is himself—Dexter plants seeds for several important ideas that develop throughout the rest of the show. First, Dexter is drawing a comparison between his own sociopathic tendencies and Rita's victimization. In the series premiere, viewers don't have the context to look at that claim through the lens of Dexter's history: the fact that he witnessed his mother's brutal murder as a very small child, yet he was old enough to recognize the significance of what he saw. Regardless of the events of his past, however, Dexter is comparing growing up to become a serial killer with being raped and brutalized by a spouse. While it would be difficult to argue that Dexter and Rita are not damaged individuals, suggesting that the two different kinds of damage are comparable is disingenuous. While Dexter's damage leads to his being in total control of himself and the bodies of others, what Dexter refers to as Rita's damage is the result of her losing all control over herself and her body until she reported her husband's abuse and had him arrested. Calling her "damaged" might be accurate; however, the comparison between surviving years of domestic violence and spousal rape and growing up to be a serial killer is troubling because it isn't until much later that viewers have all the information necessary to understand, as Stephanie Green puts it in her article "Desiring *Dexter*: The Pangs and Pleasures of Serial Killer Body Technique," that "Dexter is 'enhanced' by trauma"[11] he experienced as a child when he witnessed his mother's murder. Viewing Dexter's own trauma, and his response to it, through that lens may create room to view Rita, and the other women to be discussed in this chapter, as enhanced by their trauma as well.

Viewers may be introduced to Rita as a victim who lacks agency, but even in the first episode of *Dexter*, she is putting herself back together and healing. Her abusive husband, Paul, is in prison and she put him there. As far as she knows, she has the perfect boyfriend. She has two kids who, at that point, are little more than stray moments of adorable on a show that might otherwise be too gruesome to bear. She struggles at times with overcoming her trauma—for instance, in the premiere episode, Dexter gets sexually aggressive with her, putting his hand on her thigh and then reaching up toward her crotch rather abruptly; she reacts by getting up and leaving the car. She later apologizes to Dexter,[12] which is uncomfortable, as it did seem that he was pressuring her in spite of her understandable aversion to sex at that time. After that incident, Dexter and Rita's relationship slowly grows more physically intimate, first with her performing oral sex on him and eventually with the two of them having sex in Season One, Episode Eight, "Shrink Wrap."[13] The gradual development of their sexual relationship is met with Dexter's anxiety over the idea that if Rita recovers from her trauma enough to have sex with him, it will mean the end of their relationship. When it comes to Rita herself, though, her gradual interest in physical intimacy shows viewers an example of a rape victim reclaiming her sexual agency. While what motivates Dexter is fairly awful (per usual), Rita's healing is an important representation of life for a rape victim after the trauma has occurred.

Viewers see Rita's progress in other areas of her life as well. When her husband is released from prison, she immediately lays down ground rules, and she works to retain control over her children and herself when Paul tries to charm her back into his cycle of abuse. She manages this on her own for several episodes; however, the narrative arc of the show removes some of her regained agency in Season One, Episode Nine, "Father Knows Best,"[14] when Paul forces his way into Rita's house while their children, Astor and Cody, are sleeping. In order to keep the kids from harm, Rita attempts to appease him by luring him to the bedroom when it becomes clear to viewers that Paul intends to have sex with her whether she consents to it or not.

But even though it looks like Rita is about to be victimized again, she regains control with the help of a baseball bat she keeps under the bed. She uses the bat to subdue Paul and then removes herself and her children from the house. This is just the first specific instance on *Dexter* in which violence serves as the response to rape or attempted rape, and in this case, viewers are cheering Rita on.

After this incident, Dexter steps in to protect Rita and the kids. While Rita seeks a revenge of sorts for what Paul has done to her, she works within the confines of the justice system. Thus, what Rita wants is really justice for the crimes committed against her. Dexter works outside of the criminal justice system. In order to remove Paul from Rita's life, as well as his own, Dexter stages a scene in Season One, Episode Ten, "Seeing Red,"[15] so that the police find Paul in a motel room high on drugs and in violation of his parole.

While it might seem like Paul was lucky, insofar as the serial killer interested in removing him from Rita's life didn't just kill him, Paul is only in jail long enough to tell Rita about his suspicions that Dexter framed him before he is killed while in custody. Rita didn't want revenge; she wanted justice. It was Dexter who wanted, and got, revenge for the abuse she suffered, which is just one way to prove that Rita isn't as damaged as Dexter thinks she is.

Though her status as a rape survivor is one of the first things viewers learn about Rita, it only plays a significant role in the first season of *Dexter*. Afterward, story lines involving Rita focus on how her relationship with Dexter interferes with his Dark Passenger—the name he gives his urge to kill.

While it doesn't directly involve Rita, there is a significant rape narrative in Season Two that does affect her. After discovering the role Dexter played in sending Paul back to prison, Rita sends Dexter to Narcotics Anonymous to address his addiction, supposedly to heroin. While he draws some connections between his Dark Passenger and the others' drug addictions, what Dexter actually finds at NA meetings is Lila Tournay. They have a brief sexual relationship, but though Lila loves Dexter, Dexter chooses Rita. In an attempt to convince him to be with her instead, Lila files a false rape report against Angel Batista, a coworker of Dexter's who is the closest thing Dexter has to a friend.

Viewers know this report is false; they see Lila set up and carry out the details of her plan to frame Batista, which includes buying Rohypnol, telling Batista she likes rough sex, and drugging herself. They also see, in a troubling scene, the way Deb attempts to intimidate Lila into dropping the charges without the benefit of knowledge viewers have.[16] Season Two ends with a confrontation between Dexter and Lila that puts Rita's kids at risk, but in the end, Dexter saves them, the charges against Batista are dropped, and eventually Dexter kills Lila and his relationship with Rita continues to grow. They marry in Season Three, and by Season Four, they have a new baby (in addition to Rita's two children). Dexter works to find a precarious sort of balance between his two lives throughout Season Four, which has devastating effects when Trinity, a serial killer Dexter was reluctant to kill before learning more about him, kills Rita.

LUMEN PIERCE

The only thing Rita wanted as a resolution to her rape narrative was the justice available to her through the law. Lila attempted to manipulate the law to extract a kind of revenge. Viewers hear about Rita's rape narrative and see only a glimpse of it, but they believe it is real. Then there is Lumen Ann Pierce in Season Five, perhaps the most significant character from *Dexter* when discussing representations of rape and rape narratives. Lumen's rape narrative gives viewers none of the distance they had from what happened to Rita before the show began and a bit of Lila's desire for revenge.

To understand Lumen's narrative arc throughout Season Five, it is first necessary to understand how she and Dexter came to meet. Season Five, Episode One, "My Bad,"[17] picks up immediately after Dexter discovers Rita's body and shows the days following her death, when Dexter finds himself a single father of three and unable to function. In order to get back to himself, in Episode Two, "Hello, Bandit,"[18] Dexter decides to kill Boyd Fowler, who is the last stop for women abducted, held hostage, raped, and tortured by a group of five men led by Jordan Chase, a famous motivational speaker. Dexter knows none of that when he selects Boyd.

After several false starts attributed to Dexter's state of mind immediately following Rita's death, Dexter is forced to strap Boyd Fowler down to the kill table he improvises in Boyd's house in Episode Three, "Practically Perfect."[19] Something else Dexter doesn't know is that Boyd is holding a woman captive in the same house where Dexter kills him. Lumen, who would have been the thirteenth woman Boyd murdered, witnessed everything about Dexter's kill.

Boyd's previous twelve victims all ended up in barrels he dumped into a swamp—a detail that will become significant throughout the majority of the rest of Season Five of *Dexter*. Boyd's dying threat to Dexter—"You don't know what you are getting into"[20]—is certainly apt: without meaning to, Dexter has saved a life. Indirectly, he has done this before, by stopping future murders either through his work at Miami Metro or through his extracurricular activities, but this time, Dexter has saved a very specific life, and he must now figure out how to proceed with Lumen right there in front of him. She has suffered a lot already: abducted, raped, and tortured, all at the hands of the group of men who passed women around until the women reached Boyd, whose job was to kill them and dispose of their bodies.

When Dexter discovers Lumen in Boyd's house, she is half naked and filthy. She has open wounds across her back from a whipping, and she is either incapable of or unwilling to speak. Her trauma is not recent—it is ongoing. She has no way of knowing that Dexter won't hurt her, that he isn't just another member of the group responsible for her torture to this point. While she knows her captor is dead, she can't know that Dexter has no intention of killing her, and the threat to her life, the threat of additional rape or torture, is still very real to Lumen. When she has the chance, Lumen attacks Dexter in an attempt to escape him, and he is forced to physically subdue her. While viewers know Dexter has no interest in raping or otherwise harming her, it is clear in the moment that Lumen does not believe Dexter's repeated promises that he will not hurt her. And she has no reason to.

In order to convince Lumen that she will be safe with him, Dexter takes her to the swamp where Boyd dumped the first twelve bodies. He shows her what happened to one of the other women who had been in her position and not only gives her a knife but essentially allows her to attack him with it. This act of violence foreshadows what is yet to come for Lumen: Since Dexter's involvement in her freedom and Boyd's death precludes her from reporting what happened to her to the police, she has to ask Dexter for help in seeking revenge against the other men in the group.

Eventually, Dexter and Lumen become partners with a common goal. But neither has a particularly good reason to trust the other beyond the fact that they don't have much choice. In Episode Five, "First Blood,"[21] in fact, Dexter tries to convince Lumen to return to Minnesota, where she came from.

Dexter: If you stay in Miami, you'll never get past this.

Lumen: If you had something horrible happen to you, would you just forget about it and move on?

Dexter: I would want to.

Lumen: What if you couldn't? If you really want to help me get past this, help me find those guys and kill them. [22]

Given that it was his inability to forget and move on after Rita's death that put Dexter in this position, viewers recognize the similarities between Dexter's lifestyle and Lumen's request for assistance. Even so, he tries harder to convince her to go back to her old life.

Dexter: Going after those men won't help you get past this. It'll only make things worse.

Lumen: How could it get worse?

Dexter: It'll bring up something inside you that you don't want to know is there. Trust me. [23]

By the end of "First Blood," Dexter is convinced that Lumen has agreed to return to Minneapolis. He has also decided to avenge her and hunt down the other men responsible for what happened to her as she asked him to. This decision comes after an exchange in which first Dexter and then Lumen both almost kill the wrong man—a man who Lumen was certain was involved but could not have been, due to the electronic monitoring device he is wearing as a part of his parole. After this incident, Lumen agrees to leave Miami. Dexter even takes her to the airport.

In a disturbing scene that takes place shortly after Dexter and Lumen say their goodbyes, viewers watch Lumen as she goes through airport security. After she is sent back through the metal detector she set off twice, she is directed to step up onto a mat where she will be hand-searched.

When the female TSA agent first puts her hands on Lumen's body, viewers clearly see Lumen flinch. When the TSA agent tells Lumen to spread her legs, viewers hear what Lumen hears—the overlay of a man's voice repeating the same direction. The camerawork mirrors Lumen's disorientation in that moment, focusing on the faces of male passersby who seem to be paying too close attention to Lumen and to Lumen's body. The TSA agent continues her search, unaware of Lumen's reaction even though she is nearly hyperventilating. Viewers watch as the agent's hands move over Lumen's body, aware of what she is most likely reliving as she begins to gasp for air and fights to hold back tears.

The scene is incredibly invasive and captures the ways in which Lumen feels exposed. Being forced to relive that experience, to feel those specific emotions again, is most likely what drives Lumen to turn around and leave the airport, to stay in Miami. The forced physicality of that scene in the airport seems to lead to a decision on Lumen's part: she will have her revenge with or without Dexter's help.

In Episode Six, "Everything Is Illumenated,"[24] Lumen takes her first steps toward revenge. After showing her dress after a shower—which includes applying false eyelashes and a black wig as well as stowing a gun in her purse—the scene shifts to Dexter, who is back to his old habits: hunting down a man who kills other men after meeting them online and luring them in with the promise of sex in public restrooms. Partway through his pre-killing ritual, Dexter's phone rings. Lumen calls twice; Dexter silences both calls. Then she sends him a picture of a bloody man. He calls her back immediately. Lumen explains that she had returned to the club where she was first taken, in disguise, to see if any of the same men approached her. She was certain one had, and she convinced him to leave with her. Then she shot him. She thought he was dead, but when Dexter arrives to assist with body disposal, he is gone, leaving a bloody trail behind. Dexter and Lumen try to pin down the details while they search for the man.

Dexter: What's his name?

Lumen: I don't know.

Dexter: Did you check his wallet?

Lumen: No.

Dexter: Did you take his cell phone? He could have already called the cops, you know.

Lumen: I'm new to this!

Dexter: You don't even know who you shot!

Lumen: I shot one of the creeps who raped me!

Dexter: You don't even have any proof!

Lumen: I'm the proof! My memory! My experience!

Dexter: Hardly reliable tools.

Lumen: Fuck you.[25]

This exchange proves most important once it is revealed that Lumen was correct in her identification of Dan Manzel as one of the men responsible for what was done to her. Where rape narratives—this one included—frequently portray victims as unreliable or unstable, this episode represents a shift in Dexter's willingness to believe Lumen's account. But not right away.

The man Lumen shot attempts to play off of the trope of "unreliable woman" when he actually calls Lumen crazy. Until Dexter obtains the proof he requires that the man was involved from the rapist himself (Dan uses Lumen's cell phone to call one of his coconspirators to warn him "that last fucking bitch is alive"[26]), he refuses to believe she was right. Lumen's testimony wasn't enough this time, but with the corroboration from the rapist, it will be next time. So even though the end result of the episode is to bolster Lumen's credibility in the future, it only does so through the admission of the rapist, which gives his word more weight than hers—a trend that translates into many other rape narratives both fictional and in real life.

This episode also results in a tentative partnership between Dexter and Lumen. When Dexter asks Lumen how many more men were involved, both Lumen and viewers interpret the question as a commitment to helping Lumen get her revenge. Now viewers will have the opportunity to settle in and watch as Lumen's character continues to develop and evolve over the course of the rest of the season.

In Episode Seven, "Circle Us,"[27] viewers learn more about Lumen's background and the way she behaves on a regular day. Up to this point, Lumen has been thrown from one retraumatizing experience to the next. This episode opens with a voice-over of Dexter explaining that Lumen has been ensconced in his house for over a month. The exchanges between the two characters take on a quality that suggests routine, referring to a multitude of previous conversations they have had in the time that has passed since the previous episode. Lumen goes over the details of what she experienced—"I would be tied to a chair, blindfolded. Sometimes I wouldn't even know he was there until I'd hear this watch by my ear"[28]—as part of the work they are doing to find the other men involved.

And they have small disagreements. When Dexter objects to Lumen's use of the pronoun "we," she fights back.

Lumen: We're doing this together.

Dexter: Lumen, what I do, I do alone. I don't need a partner. I said I'd help you, but—

Lumen: Fine. Forget it.

Dexter: Forget it?

Lumen: There's no point to it then.

Dexter: You want these men brought to justice?

Lumen: Yeah. And I can't go to the cops because of you. So you're gonna have to be a little flexible here. I want to be a part of this. [29]

By demanding inclusion, Lumen assumes an active role in the retribution she seeks. That is what makes the revenge worth it in her mind—not that it happens, but that she is a part of it. The point raises the question of whether or not legal channels would have even been an acceptable substitute for Lumen, given how much less active her participation would have been and how much less control she would have had over the direction of the investigation. She would have had to hand over all of her information and control to the police and the prosecutors.

In order to maintain Lumen's control, she and Dexter work at cross-purposes with the police at Miami Metro. While they have different reasons than most rape victims for not reporting what happened to Lumen—it is mostly Dexter, not Lumen, whom they are protecting—they become part of the trend of rape as an underreported crime, and they actively stand in the way of law enforcement achieving its objectives. While Lumen and Dexter work toward the only kind of justice available to her, Deb and Miami Metro are on the case as well. While most of the department was willing to place all the blame for the Barrel Girls case (as it was called) on Boyd Fowler, Deb discovers that the DNA report proved there was more than one rapist. She has the case reopened, which leads to the discovery of a series of DVDs made by the rapists in Episode Ten, "In the Beginning."

As the DVDs are watched and logged into evidence, not only do the detectives and technicians discuss the disturbing nature of the images, but they print off still screens of each of the women for the murder board—a white board in the police station used to display the most important information about a case in a single place. Viewers see each of their faces, with the exception of #13 (as the DVDs are numbered), whom viewers know to be Lumen. Because Dexter tampers with the evidence, though, viewers are not given a clear picture of Lumen herself in any of those shots—nor does Miami Metro identify her as one of the women. It isn't difficult, though, for a viewer in possession of all the information Miami Metro doesn't have to picture Lumen in the place of those other women.

At no time is this made clearer than when Dexter takes the DVD he has stolen from evidence back to his apartment, where Lumen waits. He gives her the DVD and explains what is on it.

Lumen: Did everyone watch it?

Dexter: No! I managed to get it out of evidence in time.

Lumen: Did you . . . did you watch it?

Dexter: Only enough to make sure I had the right one. Are you sure you want to keep it?

Lumen: Number thirteen. That's what I was to them.[30]

Lumen's control breaks at this point, and the tears she has been containing fall. She collects herself after a brief moment and thanks Dexter for obtaining the DVD for her. By stepping in before anyone could see her face and eventually identify her, Dexter has allowed Lumen to retain whatever amount of control she currently feels she has gained over the men who hurt her. He has also given her control over the images that represent her complete lack of control over her own body during the time of her captivity, though not before watching some of it, even if it was just the smallest portion.

The next scene shows Dexter sitting alone in his dark bedroom listening as Lumen watches the DVD in the other room. It is clear that he can hear the sound from the DVD—Lumen's screams and the voices of the men carry to where he sits in the darkness while she is shown illuminated in the light from the screen. Viewers can't see what is happening on the DVD, but they can fill in the gaps with the images from the murder board at the police department. And watching Lumen as she watches what was done to her is perhaps more disturbing than the actual images would be.

The shot focuses in closely on Lumen's facial expression, moving in tighter and tighter until viewers can see the light of the DVD reflected in her eyes. By forcing viewers to literally see the scene through Lumen's eyes—in Lumen's eyes—there is no chance for the type of sexualization for the purpose of titillation that often comes across in rape scenes portrayed on television. Rather, viewers are forced to focus on the violent imagery of the twelve women whose pictures are posted on the murder board and the expression on Lumen's face as she watches what happened to her body.

This season of *Dexter* never once directly shows Lumen as a victim. Though she doesn't recognize it at the time, when she first encounters Dexter and first appears on the show, she is actually being rescued. Every subsequent time Lumen is seen in a risky situation, it is because she has put herself in a position that allows her to participate in obtaining revenge. Viewers see her suffering after the fact, a reminder of the ways in which this kind of trauma has lasting effects on victims, but from the time Dexter first sees Lumen to the time they say goodbye in the series finale, she is in the process of recovering from what happened to her. And for most of it, she is in control and actively seeking revenge.

On a show that has conditioned its viewers to sympathize with Dexter, partly through his vigilantism and partly due to "an intricately and carefully constructed space for the character and his violence—a space that is created through, and as an effect of, his difference from the more conspicuously monstrous men around him,"[31] it is even easier to sympathize with Lumen, whom viewers see as still in the thrall of her trauma. If Dexter was enhanced by what he experienced as a child, as Stephanie Green suggested,[32] then Lumen is similarly enhanced—and viewers watch as she builds the necessary skills to seek a vigilante kind of justice not just against any rapists who fall through the cracks in the justice system, but against the specific men who raped her.

Lumen doesn't earn this sympathy only from viewers, either. Deb, who watches the DVDs multiple times searching for evidence, is clearly distraught over this case and what she has seen: "Watching it actually happen is worse than any fucking crime scene. What these women went through, I don't know, maybe it's a fucking blessing they're dead. No one could go through something like this and have a life again."[33] Viewers know what kind of life a person could have after experiencing what Deb has been watching on those DVDs: Lumen's life with Dexter, which is just about to change.

Toward the end of "In the Beginning," Lumen kills for the first time. Of the five rapists, three of them are already dead—all by Dexter's hand, though Lumen was present for each. The role of spectator shifts with this fourth killing from Lumen to Dexter, and viewers see Lumen take back full agency in her quest for revenge when she kills Alex Tilden. This shift is further illustrated when Lumen also takes control over her relationship with Dexter once they return to his apartment: she initiates sex with Dexter. As Dexter's voice-over tells the audience about how he had always been taught to avoid human connection, Lumen leads him to the bedroom, strips off her shirt, and then pulls Dexter's over his head. This leads to touching, then kissing. At first, Dexter is hesitant. Lumen kisses him on the mouth; he responds by kissing her forehead. But he does eventually pick her up off the floor when she wraps her legs around his waist.

While it is clear that there is an intimate connection between these two characters, the physical intimacy doesn't read like an act of love due to the timing. Lumen has just regained a bit more control of herself because one fewer of her rapists exists out in the world. And she is responsible for that. The sex she has with Dexter, and even the silent moment afterward when they are both naked in bed staring into each other's eyes, seems more like another step toward her revenge—she can choose to have and enjoy sex again. She can choose to have a life beyond what was done to her.

So while Deb cannot or does not picture the life Lumen is creating for herself after what she has been through, there are plenty of other things that Deb gets right. She was first to consider a vigilante when it became clear that the department's rape suspects were going missing. She is the one who determines that the vigilante might just be the thirteenth, unidentified victim and a partner. She also understands that the partner must be someone who cares very much for the woman, whoever she might be. Regardless of the legality of what they are doing, Deb finds the relationship between the two vigilantes romantic: "I need someone I can trust one hundred percent," she tells Dexter in Episode Eleven, "Hop a Freighter." "She has someone in her life, a guy who's helping her, someone that would do anything and everything for her."[34] Viewers know how right she is and how close—literally—she is to both the thirteenth victim and the partner.

Deb's investigation leads her to Jordan Chase. He eventually leads her to the camp where the five rapists met as children, the same camp to which they brought the women they raped and tortured. We will return to Deb shortly. As the group's leader, Jordan never did the dirty work himself; instead, he encouraged the others to take advantage of women while he watched. The more viewers learn about Jordan and the role he played in what happened to Lumen, the more significance his initial message—to which viewers were first exposed in Boyd Fowler's house—carries. Jordan is a motivational speaker, and his philosophy centers around the idea that people should "just take" whatever they want: "Do you want to have control of your life? You have that power. You just have to learn how to use it. [. . .] The world does not put limitations on what you can have. But if you want something, take it."[35] At first, it was Boyd taking what he wanted with all of the sinister undertones that carried. Then it was Dexter, and now it is Lumen.

Because when Jordan captures Lumen after all of his partners are dead, Dexter and Lumen are ready for him. Jordan takes Lumen to the abandoned camp, and Dexter follows. After surprising Jordan, using a knife to pin one of his feet to the floor, Dexter releases Lumen and the two set up a kill room for Jordan. When it is time for Jordan to die, though, Dexter hands Lumen the knife, recalling perhaps the first time he handed her a knife before they became partners.

Dexter: You should be the one to do it.

Lumen: Is that okay with you?

Dexter: He's yours.[36]

While she may be deferential—or just considerate—of Dexter, Lumen refuses to give any of her control away to Jordan. She refuses him the right to call her by her first name, refuses to acknowledge his claim to credit for what she has become, and refuses him the right to even speak, cutting him off mid-sentence by plunging the knife into his chest. His last words—"I watched you so carefully the last time you were here. YOU used to just cower and cry"[37]—are crucial because in this moment of ultimate revenge, Lumen refuses him the opportunity to turn her back into a victim.

Instead of seeing Jordan Chase's memory of Lumen as a victim, viewers see the moment in which Lumen takes back what was taken from her. Seeing Lumen regain that control, knowing that it was what she had been working toward all season, is a triumphant moment. It is shortly thereafter that Deb arrives.

Because of a mostly opaque plastic sheet that hangs in the middle of the room, Deb comes across Chase's body yet is separated from Dexter and Lumen. She can make out the shape of them, but she cannot see enough to identify them. "I know who you are," she says. "Number thirteen. And I know what they did to you. I've seen the tapes. I watched them over and over. It's a miracle you survived. A fucking miracle. And you, whoever you are, you know that too. [. . .] Maybe it's true some people deserve to die, but I'm a cop, and I don't make that fucking decision. So I'm gonna call this in. In an hour, this place will be swarming with police. If I were you, I'd be gone by then."[38] Then she turns around and leaves, giving Dexter and Lumen enough time to get away with Jordan's body.

At the same time that Deb is letting Lumen and Dexter go, allowing them to get away with the revenge they have taken against Jordan Chase, this particular part of Lumen's narrative is interesting insofar as it speaks to the ways the police fail rape victims throughout the course of the show. It is to be expected that Deb only works cases that involve murder because she is a homicide detective, but at its heart, the overall narrative presents another example of a time when a living rape victim cannot find the help she needs in the police. Even Deb seems aware of the limitations of the police when she catches up with these vigilantes but gives them the time and opportunity to vanish without identifying themselves. With Chase dead, it is too late for the police to do anything other than punish Lumen and Dexter, but in this particular instance, Deb condones Lumen's style of revenge by allowing her to not just escape but also take Chase's body, the only remaining evidence that supports Deb's theory that vigilantes are killing these rapists. Her decision grants Lumen another aspect of control over her life; not only will it keep her out of prison, but the lack of evidence means no one will be coming after her either.

By the end of the season, the half-naked and filthy woman whom viewers first met immediately after her trauma is seated at the bow of Dexter's boat, grinning, with the whole city of Miami lit up behind her. She has achieved the revenge she was looking for, has taken back control of her body and her life, and it isn't really a surprise to viewers when she tells Dexter she has to leave. While she may have strong feelings for Dexter, she has just regained control over herself and does not feel the same urge that he does to give up control to a Dark Passenger (as Dexter refers to his own desire to kill). So it isn't just Dexter concerned with allowing Lumen her revenge and giving her back control—it's also Deb, and even the narrative of the show itself working to put Lumen in charge of what comes next for her.

HANNAH MCKAY

Dexter first meets Hannah McKay in Season Seven, Episode Three, "Buck the System."[39] Initially, he investigates her as a potential victim, to the point that he ends up with her strapped down to a kill table in Episode Six, "Do the Wrong Thing."[40] According to Harry's code, she is the perfect candidate, but Dexter cannot bring himself to kill her, and instead, they end up having sex after he cuts her free of the plastic wrap he used to tie her down. Like Lumen, Hannah recognizes who Dexter is from the very beginning of their relationship; unlike Lumen, the people whom Hannah has killed (for she is a killer too) weren't all guilty of committing crimes against her.

Dexter's relationship with Hannah is, in some ways, the most natural for him. The first time Dexter freely tells a woman that he loves her in the whole show is with Hannah, and up until the final episode of the series, he is ready to leave his life in Miami behind and move with Hannah and Harrison (his son) to Argentina. While that is interesting, it is not the reason we are focused on Hannah here. Or at least not yet.

There are two separate ways in which rape narratives play into Hannah McKay's story. The first regards a counselor at a halfway house where Hannah lived as a teenager. After he "put his hands on" both Hannah and a friend of hers, she "shut him down for good"[41] with rat poison. This was not Hannah's last kill, and not all of her kills were driven by the same kind of revenge motive that is reminiscent of Lumen's story line. What is particularly important about this development in viewers' understanding of Hannah, though, is that her sexual assault happened well before Dexter and Hannah ever met. Unlike Lumen, for whom Dexter began to have romantic feelings only after he began training her to kill, Hannah is already a fully formed killer when they meet. She has already settled into her role as "enhanced by trauma," and in such a way that she is able to take care of matters herself.

The second example of a rape narrative involving Hannah is in Season Eight when she returns to Miami with a controlling, wealthy husband. In Season Eight, Episode Seven, "Dress Code,"[42] Hannah first denies and then admits that she is still in love with Dexter. She asks him to kill her husband but ends up doing it herself after he returns to their boat, fully aware that she has seen Dexter, and throws her down on the bed, ready to sexually assault her. He doesn't get the chance, though, before Hannah kills him in their struggle. Dexter helps her dispose of the body, but again, Hannah took care of the killing all on her own. She took her own revenge.

In the series premiere, Dexter confesses: "I don't have feelings about anything, but if I could have feelings at all, I'd have them for Deb."[43] Over the course of eight seasons, Dexter comes to have feelings not only for Deb but also for three children and three different women. While Rita's role in his life begins as little more than a cover for his Dark Passenger, what he feels for her grows throughout the first four seasons of the show—up until Rita's death. Even his affair with Lila ends up strengthening his relationship with Rita, as Dexter learns just how attached he is to Rita and her kids. Part of what drew Dexter to Rita specifically was the ways he saw her as damaged— the result of the domestic violence and sexual abuse she suffered in her previous marriage. As their relationship grows, viewers watch Rita become a stronger person, partly because of her relationship with Dexter but also because of the actions she takes to seek justice after what her ex-husband did to her.

But Dexter never actually tells Rita that he loves her, responding to her declarations with "you too." After Rita's death, Dexter meets and maybe falls in love with Lumen. With her, Dexter doesn't have to hide who he really is; they met over one of his kills. She knows the darkness in him. And while their relationship certainly began out of obligation—Dexter couldn't let her go to the police to tell them what she saw and experienced—it grows into something much more by the end of Season Five when Dexter is making plans in anticipation of sharing his life with Lumen. The bond between them—he doesn't directly say he loves her, but he is convinced he does when Deb suggests that the vigilante's partner must love her—develops as Lumen recovers from her trauma. They first have sex after Lumen kills for the first time, and Lumen lives in Dexter's house, they share responsibilities for his kids, and they work daily toward a common goal. Dexter is ready to make a future with Lumen until she calls it off; when she says she has to leave Miami, Dexter throws a plate against the wall and cries while she comforts him. Lumen wanted justice but settled for revenge; the ways in which she is damaged are healed by the process she and Dexter go through together.

And then there is Hannah. While Lumen killed alongside Dexter for a short time, with him there to guide her, Hannah was "enhanced by trauma" before Dexter even met her. While something inside Dexter drives him to kill and Hannah kills more out of necessity, there is a repeated and calculated nature to her actions that wasn't true of Lumen. Hannah knows the truth about Dexter because he almost killed her—stopping himself from stabbing her through the heart to have sex with her instead. Hannah is in love with

Dexter even knowing exactly what he is; he falls in love with her as well, and in a way viewers haven't seen before. Dexter doesn't need to step in and save Hannah from the men who sexually assaulted her; he shows up afterward to help her pull it off, but he didn't create the circumstances. Hannah extracts her own revenge.

All three of these women who love Dexter survived repeated rape or sexual assault. Individually, they are vulnerable and strong, ferocious when they need to be, and capable of overcoming trauma that could be crushing. Collectively, they become representative of the emotional growth of *Dexter*'s main character. As viewers see them progressively take on more direct and personal responsibility for revenge, they do some of the same kinds of work as "contemporary serial killers and superheroes [like Dexter and Christopher Nolan's Batman who are] signs of American culture's anxiety about what gets to count as justice and what gets to count as revenge, and what is acceptable in a world where the 'correct' moral and ethical behavior lies firmly mired in a grey zone."[44] Rita's actions aren't gray like Lumen's and Hannah's might be in the scope of the *Dexter* universe, but the rape narratives with these three women at their center work against the all-too-familiar trope of the broken rape survivor.

NOTES

1. James Manos Jr., "Dexter," *Dexter*, season 1, episode 1, directed by Michael Cuesta, aired on October 1, 2006 (New York: Showtime Networks, 2007), DVD.

2. Edited heavily for content and to fit new time constraints (episodes of *Dexter* run nearly fifty-five minutes versus the typical network drama's forty-four), the show's first season aired on CBS in 2008 as an attempt to mitigate the damage to the network's lineup caused by the Writers Guild of America strike. Eric Goldman, "*Dexter*'s CBS Debut Date Announced," *IGN*, January 7, 2008, http://www.ign.com/articles/2008/01/07/dexters-cbs-debut-date-announced.

3. Ashley M. Donnelly, "The New American Hero: Dexter, Serial Killer for the Masses," *Journal of Popular Culture* 45, no. 1 (2012): 24.

4. Greg Braxton, "*Dexter* Finale Breaks Ratings Record for Showtime," *Los Angeles Times*, September 23, 2013, http://articles.latimes.com/2013/sep/23/entertainment/la-et-st-dexter-finale-breaks-ratings-record-for-showtime-20130923.

5. Bill Gorman, "*Dexter* Returns to Its Highest Rated Premiere Ever, Up Double Digits," *TV by the Numbers*, September 27, 2010, http://tvbythenumbers.zap2it.com/2010/09/27/dexter-returns-to-its-highest-rated-premiere-ever-up-double-digits/65350.

6. Victoria L. Smith, "Our Serial Killers, Our Superheroes, and Ourselves: Showtime's *Dexter*," *Quarterly Review of Film and Video* 28, no. 5 (2011): 392. doi:10.1080/10509200902820688.

7. Manos Jr., "Dexter."

8. Ibid.

9. Ibid.

10. Ibid.

11. Stephanie Green, "Desiring *Dexter*: The Pangs and Pleasures of Serial Killer Body Technique," *Continuum: Journal of Media and Cultural Studies* 24, no. 4 (2012): 580. doi:10.1080/10304312.2012.698037.

12. Coincidentally, Rita calls Dexter to apologize while he is working on "a little project"— disposing of the body of a rapist he just killed.

13. Lauren Gussis, "Shrink Wrap," *Dexter*, season 1, episode 8, directed by Tony Goldwyn, aired on November 19, 2006 (New York: Showtime Networks, 2007), DVD.

14. Melissa Rosenberg, "Father Knows Best," *Dexter*, season 1, episode 9, directed by Adam Davidson, aired on November 26, 2006 (New York: Showtime Networks, 2007), DVD.

15. Kevin R. Maynard, "Seeing Red," *Dexter*, season 1, episode 10, directed by Michael Cuesta, aired on December 3, 2006 (New York: Showtime Networks, 2007), DVD.

16. Scott Buck and Tim Schlattmann, "Left Turn Ahead," *Dexter*, season 2, episode 11, directed by Marcos Siega, aired on December 9, 2007 (New York: Showtime Networks, 2008), DVD.

17. Chip Johannessen, "My Bad," *Dexter*, season 5, episode 1, directed by Steve Shill, aired on September 26, 2010 (New York: Showtime Networks, 2011), DVD.

18. Scott Buck, "Hello, Bandit," *Dexter*, season 5, episode 2, directed by John Dahl, aired on October 3, 2010 (New York: Showtime Networks, 2011), DVD.

19. Manny Coto, "Practically Perfect," *Dexter*, season 5, episode 3, directed by Ernest Dickerson, aired on October 10, 2010 (New York: Showtime Networks, 2011), DVD.

20. Ibid.

21. Tim Schlattmann, "First Blood," *Dexter*, season 5, episode 5, directed by Romeo Tirone, aired on October 24, 2010 (New York: Showtime Networks, 2011), DVD.

22. Ibid.

23. Ibid.

24. Wendy West, "Everything Is Illumenated," *Dexter*, season 5, episode 6, directed by Steve Shill, aired on October 31, 2010 (New York: Showtime Networks, 2011), DVD.

25. Ibid.

26. Ibid.

27. Scott Buck, "Circle Us," *Dexter*, season 5, episode 7, directed by John Dahl, aired on November 7, 2010 (New York: Showtime Networks, 2011), DVD.

28. Ibid.

29. Ibid.

30. Scott Reynolds, "In the Beginning," *Dexter*, season 5, episode 10, directed by Keith Gordon, aired on November 28, 2010 (New York: Showtime Networks, 2011), DVD.

31. Lisa Arellano, "The Heroic Monster: *Dexter*, Masculinity, and Violence," *Television and New Media* 20, no. 10 (2012): 5, 6. doi:10:1177/1527476412450192.

32. Green, "Desiring *Dexter*," 580.

33. Reynolds, "In the Beginning."

34. Karen Campbell, Scott Buck, and Tim Schlattmann, "Hop a Freighter," *Dexter*, season 5, episode 11, directed by John Dahl, aired on December 5, 2010 (New York: Showtime Networks, 2011), DVD.

35. Johannessen, "My Bad."

36. Chip Johannessen and Manny Coto, "The Big One," *Dexter*, season 5, episode 12, directed by Steve Shill, aired on December 12, 2010 (New York: Showtime Networks, 2011), DVD.

37. Ibid.

38. Ibid.

39. Jace Richdale, "Buck the System," *Dexter*, season 7, episode 3, directed by Stefan Schwartz, aired on October 14, 2012 (New York: Showtime Networks, 2013), DVD.

40. Lauren Gussis, "Do the Wrong Thing," *Dexter*, season 7, episode 6, directed by Alik Sakharov, aired on November 4, 2012 (New York: Showtime Networks, 2013), DVD.

41. Manny Coto and Wendy West, "Do You See What I See?" *Dexter*, season 7, episode 11, directed by John Dahl, aired on December 9, 2012 (New York: Showtime Networks, 2013), DVD.

42. Arika Lisanne Mittman, "Dress Code," *Dexter*, season 8, episode 7, directed by Alik Sakharov, aired on August 11, 2013 (New York: Showtime Networks, 2013), DVD.

43. Manos Jr., "Dexter."

44. Smith, "Our Serial Killers, Our Superheroes, and Ourselves," 391.

REFERENCES

Arellano, Lisa. "The Heroic Monster: *Dexter*, Masculinity, and Violence." *Television and New Media* 20, no. 10 (2012): 1–17. doi:10:1177/1527476412450192.

Braxton, Greg. "*Dexter* Finale Breaks Ratings Record for Showtime." *Los Angeles Times*, September 23, 2013. http://articles.latimes.com/2013/sep/23/entertainment/la-et-st-dexter-finale-breaks-ratings-record-for-showtime-20130923.

Buck, Scott. "Circle Us." *Dexter.* Season 5. DVD. Directed by John Dahl. Aired on November 7, 2010. New York: Showtime Networks, 2011.

———. "Hello, Bandit." *Dexter.* Season 5. DVD. Directed by John Dahl. Aired on October 3, 2010. New York: Showtime Networks, 2011.

Buck, Scott, and Tim Schlattmann. "Left Turn Ahead." *Dexter.* Season 2. DVD. Directed by Marcos Siega. Aired on December 9, 2007. New York: Showtime Networks, 2008.

Campbell, Karen, Scott Buck, and Tim Schlattmann. "Hop a Freighter." *Dexter.* Season 5. Directed by John Dahl. Aired on December 5, 2010. New York: Showtime Networks, 2011.

Coto, Manny. "Practically Perfect." *Dexter.* Season 5. DVD. Directed by Ernest Dickerson. Aired on October 10, 2010. New York: Showtime Networks, 2011.

Coto, Manny, and Wendy West. "Do You See What I See?" *Dexter.* Season 7. DVD. Directed by John Dahl. Aired on December 9, 2012. New York: Showtime Networks, 2013.

Donnelly, Ashley M. "The New American Hero: Dexter, Serial Killer for the Masses." *Journal of Popular Culture* 45, no. 1 (2012): 15–26.

Goldman, Eric. "*Dexter*'s CBS Debut Date Announced." *IGN*, January 7, 2008. http://www.ign.com/articles/2008/01/07/dexters-cbs-debut-date-announced.

Gorman, Bill. "*Dexter* Returns to Its Highest Rated Premiere Ever, Up Double Digits." *TV by the Numbers*, September 27, 2010. http://tvbythenumbers.zap2it.com/2010/09/27/dexter-returns-to-its-highest-rated-premiere-ever-up-double-digits/65350.

Green, Stephanie. "Desiring *Dexter*: The Pangs and Pleasures of Serial Killer Body Technique." *Continuum: Journal of Media and Cultural Studies* 24, no. 4 (2012): 579–588. doi:10.1080/10304312.2012.698037.

Gussis, Lauren. "Do the Wrong Thing." *Dexter.* Season 7. DVD. Directed by Alik Sakharov. Aired on November 4, 2012. New York: Showtime Networks, 2013.

———. "Shrink Wrap." *Dexter.* Season 1. DVD. Directed by Tony Goldwyn. Aired on November 19, 2006. New York: Showtime Networks, 2007.

Johannessen, Chip. "My Bad." *Dexter.* Season 5. Directed by Steve Shill. Aired on September 26, 2010. New York: Showtime Networks, 2011.

Johannessen, Chip, and Manny Coto. "The Big One." *Dexter.* Season 5. DVD. Directed by Steve Shill. Aired on December 12, 2010. New York: Showtime Networks, 2011.

Manos, James, Jr. "Dexter." *Dexter.* Season 1. DVD. Directed by Michael Cuesta. Aired on October 1, 2006. New York: Showtime Networks, 2007.

Maynard, Kevin R. "Seeing Red." *Dexter.* Season 1. Directed by Michael Cuesta. Aired on December 3, 2006. New York: Showtime Networks, 2007.

Mittman, Arika Lisanne. "Dress Code." *Dexter.* Season 8. DVD. Directed by Alik Sakharov. Aired on August 11, 2013. New York: Showtime Networks, 2013.

Reynolds, Scott. "In the Beginning." *Dexter.* Season 5. DVD. Directed by Keith Gordon. Aired on November 28, 2010. New York: Showtime Networks, 2011.

Richdale, Jace. "Buck the System." *Dexter.* Season 7. DVD. Directed by Stefan Schwartz. Aired on October 14, 2012. New York: Showtime Networks, 2013.

Rosenberg, Melissa. "Father Knows Best." *Dexter.* Season 1. DVD. Directed by Adam Davidson. Aired on November 26, 2006. New York: Showtime Networks, 2007.

Schlattmann, Tim. "First Blood." *Dexter.* Season 5. Directed by Romeo Tirone. Aired on October 24, 2010. New York: Showtime Networks, 2011.

Smith, Victoria L. "Our Serial Killers, Our Superheroes, and Ourselves: Showtime's *Dexter*." *Quarterly Review of Film and Video* 28, no. 5 (2011): 390–400. doi:10.1080/10509200902820688.

West, Wendy. "Everything Is Illumenated." *Dexter.* Season 5. DVD. Directed by Steve Shill. Aired on October 31, 2010. New York: Showtime Networks, 2011.

Chapter Six

"These Are Their Stories"

Olivia Benson as Victim on
Law and Order: Special Victims Unit

In the series premiere of *Law and Order: Special Victims Unit* (*SVU*), Detective Olivia Benson is still a new addition to the unit. Alongside her partner Elliot Stabler, Olivia investigates cases that involve minors, the elderly, and, most frequently, sexual violence. For the first twelve seasons of the show, the duo shared the spotlight. While there were other main characters that also played significant roles, Olivia and Stabler were the focal point. When the Season Thirteen premiere announces Stabler's retirement, the scope of the whole show shifts, and *SVU* becomes a chronicle of Detective Benson's career as an SVU detective.

Dick Wolf's *Law and Order* franchise began in 1990; the original *Law and Order* ran for twenty seasons and spawned four different spin-off series, the most successful of which is *SVU*.[1] First airing in 1999, *SVU* is the longest-running series considered in *Assault on the Small Screen*, with a total of 343 episodes comprising the first fifteen seasons. Of those episodes, 171 (49.85%) meet the criteria for consideration here: they contain rape narratives about victims age eighteen and over that aren't also victims of sex trafficking. Given the show's specialized theme, it comes as no surprise that *SVU* provides not only more rape narratives but also a higher percentage of them. Viewers might also expect that, given the frequency and centrality with which the show addresses sexual assault, the representations contained in these episodes would be approached more consciously and, perhaps, more carefully. In their article "Television's 'New' Feminism: Prime-Time Representations of Women and Victimization," authors Lisa M. Cuklanz and Sujata Moorti explore the way rape narratives are presented in the first five seasons of *SVU*: *SVU* "positions itself as a dramatic series with feminist sympathies, addressing a subject that was long a focus of feminist activism. It is uniquely issue-oriented, building its emotional and dramatic appeal from a political issue rather than focusing on an eponymous protagonist [. . .]. *SVU* highlights power in gender relations, including within the family, and provides evidence of 'rape culture' as a potential factor in the commission of the crime."[2] While their article, which was published in 2006, could only have taken the third of the show's episodes into consideration, many of the arguments made by Cuklanz and Moorti hold true throughout the course of the series.[3] The only exception, I would argue, would be not a shift to but the addition of a focus on the protagonist, Olivia Benson. Over the course of the first fifteen years of *SVU*, there are multiple times when the rape narratives put Olivia in a position where she stands in for or nearly becomes one of the rape victims she works with. Olivia is portrayed as an advocate for victims; she works closely with them, and they trust her. She stands up for them and fights to see justice done for them. The times when Olivia becomes the victim rather than the advocate serve to remind viewers that anyone, regardless of how well prepared they might be to address sexual assault, can be victimized. The nature of Olivia's role, which is so central to the show, also prevents viewers—who may become desensitized to what other, less familiar victims go through—from dismissing either the short-term or lasting effects of sexual assault.

On a show that takes a feminist approach to representing rape and has, as Cuklanz and Moorti point out, a female lead who "is often regarded as a feminist hero,"[4] it is significant that one of the first personal details viewers learn about Olivia Benson is that she is the product of a rape. Her career, and in fact her character, is situated through the frame of what happened to her mother, and this frame begins to take shape in the series premiere. Season One, Episode One, "Payback,"[5] introduces two rape narratives. The first is the case the SVU investigates: the murder and castration of a man discovered to be a Serbian war criminal who participated in the systematic rape of sixty-seven women before coming to New York. While the specifics are enough to horrify viewers, of interest here are two conversations. The first, which happens early in the episode, is between Stabler and Captain Donald Cragen. Olivia is not a participant in the conversation, but she is the subject of it. Cragen is concerned about how Olivia will react to the case and tells Elliot to remind his partner that they don't get to choose the victim. This interaction begins the process of training viewers to recognize Olivia as a strong advocate for rape victims, occasionally to the extent that it worries her captain. The fact that his concerns prove to be well-founded when Olivia allows Marta Stevens, the murder suspect, to get away with lying about her crime because she is also a rape victim, resonates with viewers as they are first getting to know these characters.

The cause of Olivia's tendencies to identify—possibly over-identify—with rape victims becomes clearer toward the end of the episode when the second rape narrative is introduced. This narrative will carry through quite a bit of the first season of *SVU* and will continue to have an impact on the show as a whole for much longer. After solving the rapist war criminal's murder, Olivia has dinner with her mother, Serena Benson. They discuss the case, which leads to what is clearly a familiar argument for the two women.

Serena: I really wish you would consider getting out of that unit.

Olivia: Come on, Mother. Let's not tonight.

Serena: Do you think this is healthy for you?

Olivia: You were raped, for god sakes. Are you telling me you don't understand why [Marta Stevens] did what she did?

Serena: Oh, I understand it. That does not mean I condone it.

Olivia: Wait. Are you saying you wouldn't have done exactly the same thing if you'd had the chance?

Serena: Is that what you would have wanted me to do?

Olivia: Yes. [. . .] I hate him for what he did to you.

Serena: So do I. And if he hadn't, you would not be here.

It isn't just that Serena Benson was raped when she was in college, a detail viewers learn later in the first season. The detail that will have the most lasting effect within the universe of the show is the result of that attack: Olivia herself. Not only does learning about Olivia's history with rape explain her reactions within the scope of the investigation from "Payback," but it also introduces the first of several significant rape narratives throughout the series that directly involve Detective Olivia Benson.

While there are some close calls, Olivia is never actually raped. In addition to two specific instances when she is sexually assaulted, there are a handful of rape narratives over the course of the show where Olivia fills in for the victim rather than playing the role of savior or advocate. A closer look at the times when she becomes the victim offers insights into how the character, and the show insofar as it can be construed as a showcase for Olivia's career, evolve.

SERENA BENSON

Serena Benson's status as a rape victim plays a more significant role on *SVU* than the character herself does. Olivia's mother only appears that single time in the premiere episode, just long enough to be the one to inform viewers that her daughter, the detective whose career they will follow for the next fifteen seasons, is herself the product of a rape. The fact of her birth led Olivia to the Special Victims Unit, and her sustained concern over whether violence can be passed down genetically influences the kind of cop she is. Olivia's background makes her a more effective advocate for rape victims, a role she is just settling into in the series premiere and that becomes more comfortable for her as the show continues. The sustained narrative of Serena Benson's rape and its effects asks viewers to expand their thinking about what is at stake not just for rape victims themselves but also for the people closest to them.

The second episode to draw on this particular rape narrative is Season One, Episode Eight, "Stalked."[6] When a man accused of stalking, raping, and murdering women becomes fixated on Olivia, an exchange between them in interrogation draws connections between the way he tried to victimize her and the trauma Serena faced: "About your mother, though. Serena, isn't it? Is she still carrying around all the scars from that rape? Is she still having nightmares?" When Olivia attempts to steer the conversation back to the case at hand, which includes the murder of Karen Fitzgerald, he persists: "I'm fixed on you. And until I'm dead, I'll always be in your head, just like your mother has somebody in her head."[7] In this episode, Olivia is stalked and the SVU uses her as bait to lure out the suspect. He never gets close enough to sexually assault her, but the fact that he is a rapist and the way he draws a connection between their interaction and what Serena experienced focuses viewers' attention on the ways Olivia fills a role in this crime that is, in at least some small ways, similar to what her mother experienced. Olivia's connection to Karen Fitzgerald, who worked for another district attorney's office, plays a larger role in "Stalked," but the conversation between Olivia and this suspect is just the beginning of how *SVU* draws connections between Serena's victimization and her daughter's experiences.

Olivia's status as a child conceived through rape and the details viewers learn about what specifically happened to Serena (and to Olivia as a result of Serena's response to her trauma) asks viewers to consider ways rape can and does effect more than just the individual who directly experienced the sexual assault. This connection is explored further in Season One, Episode Eleven, "Bad Blood."[8] When Detective John Munch learns that Serena was raped and that her case was never closed, he asks some questions and is able to present Olivia with some new evidence. It is then that viewers learn Olivia has been investigating her mother's case as well, that she has read the reports and listened to her mother's statement, gone through pictures of potential suspects.

The next scene begins in Olivia's apartment where she sits alone, listening to an audiotape. As two voices go back and forth, viewers listen to Serena Benson tell a police officer the details of her attack and watch Olivia sift through pictures and files until the cut scene when she is following the path her mother describes on the tape—the shortcut Serena took on her way home after the campus library closed. Viewers see Olivia holding her tape player, standing in an alley just below street level, staring at the ground where her mother would have woken up after being knocked unconscious, to find a man on top of her, pulling up her dress. Olivia puts herself into the physical space where her mother experienced the worst moment of her life, the same moment when the idea of Olivia Benson first entered the world, and her mother's voice is the soundtrack of the moment for both Olivia and viewers. The way her focus is broken from the past by a car horn and the way the street noise immediately floods back into the scene grounds Olivia in the present and shows viewers just how closely she identified with the retelling of her mother's story. Between her close personal connection to the victim and the way her work in the SVU has given her a deeper understanding of rape as a crime, there is likely no one (with the exception of Serena herself) capable of making a stronger connection between the physical space of that alley and the violent crime that occurred there all those years earlier. Olivia's presence there and the way she loses awareness of the present moment serves as another example of how Olivia is affected by the crime committed against her mother.

The Season One finale, Episode Twenty-Two, "Slaves,"[9] uses a trope that will become familiar as the seasons of *SVU* progress: psychological evaluations that give viewers access to the inner thoughts of the detectives. In this evaluation, Olivia admits that the circumstances surrounding her conception do affect her: "I'm walking a tightrope. I, ah, got too close to a case once, um, a Serbian rapist was killed by his victims, and I got my ass in a sling over it." Referring to the events of the series premiere, "Payback," also draws viewers by the justification that episode gave for Olivia's reaction to those events: her mother's rape. When the psychologist asks whether her mother's rape has ever interfered with her judgment on the job, though, Olivia answers with an adamant no. It is unclear whether Olivia is aware that she seems to be contradicting herself.

In Season Two, Episode Eight, "Taken,"[10] Olivia's mother dies, and this is also the point when viewers begin to learn more about the ways her response to the trauma she suffered affected Olivia. The episode does not mention Serena's rape, but it does reveal that Serena Benson had a drinking problem. When Olivia shows up in the squad room immediately after her mother's funeral, Cragen tries to send her home. But Olivia is not interested:

"Look, Captain, it took me years to accept the fact that my mother was an alcoholic. When I did, I had to accept all the consequences. I can handle it."[11] The issue doesn't come up again for several seasons, but eventually Olivia will make it clear that she believes her mother's alcoholism was a result of the trauma she suffered during and after her rape. Due in part to her drinking, Serena was by turns a controlling or neglectful mother, a causality that may have turned Olivia into a victim of her mother's rape as well. If Serena's drinking was her attempt to cope with the trauma she suffered in a time when she would have received very little support from her community, then her treatment of Olivia also becomes a result of her assault.

Viewing Serena through this lens fits with the conclusion Cuklanz and Moorti draw in "Television's 'New' Feminism" about the ways *SVU* vilifies women, particularly within families and as mothers, even as it takes a feminist approach to the presentation of rape narratives. Season Six, Episode Nineteen, "Intoxicated,"[12] aired after the article was written but is, in some ways, a perfect fit for much of what Cuklanz and Moorti had to say about "the monstrous maternal storylines."[13] "Intoxicated" is also the episode in which viewers see a fairly clear picture of what life was like for Olivia as a teenager. In this episode, fifteen-year-old Carrie Eldridge's mother discovers her in bed with her twenty-one-year-old boyfriend, Justin. Carrie and Justin are naked, and the episode begins with a statutory rape investigation. The focus shifts, though, when Carrie's mother ends up dead. Carrie killed her after years of emotional and physical abuse that was if not caused by then certainly exacerbated by Denise Eldridge's drinking. In one scene, Olivia visits the Eldridges' empty apartment and searches it. The way the scene is shot, it seems to viewers that Olivia finds a bottle of booze in every place she looks, making it clear that she knew exactly where to search. The connections Olivia is making between Denise Eldridge and her own mother are pretty clear to viewers. Olivia took an immediate disliking to Denise Eldridge, and Olivia was the one to call a child rights attorney to represent Carrie. These are just glimpses, but the end of the episode spells out exactly how much Carrie's situation reflected what Olivia experienced as a teenager.

When she explains how she knew the child rights attorney in the first place, Olivia reveals her past to Assistant District Attorney Casey Novak. Serena Benson was an English professor, and when Olivia agreed to marry one of her mother's students, the two women fought. After her mother dropped a half-full bottle of vodka, "it shattered all over the floor and then she picked up the jagged edge of the bottle and she came at me screaming 'I'll never let anyone else have you!' And so I kicked her. Hard. And then I kicked her again, and she went flying across the room into the wall and she slid down to the floor. I'd never hurt her before."[14]

JOSEPH HOLLISTER

Serena Benson's rape narrative doesn't have an ending, at least not the way that most rape narratives addressed in police dramas do. Instead of wrapping up neatly by the end of a single episode, Serena's 1967 rape isn't solved until 2007, forty years later and seven years after Serena's death. In Season Eight, Episode Fifteen, "Haystack,"[15] Olivia, after illegally running a sample of her own DNA, discovers that she has a half brother, and, in some ways, the focus of the Benson family rape narrative shifts from Serena to Olivia's father, Joseph Hollister.

In Episode Sixteen, "Philadelphia,"[16] Olivia tracks down her brother, Simon Marsden, to discover that he is the prime suspect in a series of stalking incidents in the New Jersey town where he lives. Even though the evidence convinces Olivia that her brother is guilty, when he shows up at her apartment with a picture of her that he found among his father's things, she confesses why she has been interested in him. When Simon shows Olivia a picture of their father, she tells him the truth: "This man raped my mother."[17]

After an evening of drinking and bonding between the newfound siblings, Olivia is awoken in the middle of the night by her ringing telephone. The New Jersey stalker has escalated, and he has now raped a woman, Donna Leonte. To this point, Olivia has been worried primarily that her father's violence may have been passed down through genetics to her, but now she believes it is Simon who may have inherited the trait—that, or the possibility that being raised by a rapist influenced his behavior. Olivia demands that he admit it: "You're a rapist like your father."[18] Simon, however, maintains that he is innocent, that he would never hurt a woman. While viewers wouldn't expect him to confess to committing a rape, this second rape narrative to affect Olivia's family turns out to be a lie—Simon is being framed.

"Philadelphia" ends with DNA evidence that links Simon to Donna Leonte, and Olivia's half brother jumps bail. Three episodes later, in Episode Nineteen, "Florida,"[19] an FBI agent Olivia once worked with, Dean Porter, shows up in the squad room. He is looking for Simon and believes Olivia knows where he is. While she claims not to, it becomes clear that even though Olivia believes Simon to be guilty of stalking and of rape, she has been sending him money. Olivia Benson, who is also portrayed as a crusader for justice for victims, is actively helping a person she believes to be a rapist avoid capture. The fact that the plot of the episode eventually absolves Olivia because Simon was being framed does not actually change the fact that she didn't know that when she sent the money, though it might make it easy for viewers to forgive her atypical behavior.

Another example of how Olivia acts uncharacteristically in the face of this rape narrative involving her brother is the way that it leads her to question what she has always believed to be true about her mother. After she asks

George Huang, an FBI psychiatrist who plays a recurring role on *SVU*, to dig
into Simon's background, she reveals that she found other cases similar to
her mother's and also that she is doubting whether or not Serena was actually
raped.[20] This conversation takes place before the episode reveals that Simon
was framed.

Huang: You think your mother lied about being raped?

Olivia: He kept track of me. What rapist does that?

Huang: The evidence against Joe Hollister is just as strong as the evidence against your brother.

Olivia: I don't know for sure that Joe Hollister attacked these women and
my mother.

Huang: You've got to face the truth, Liv.

Olivia: My mother lied to me about so many things. What if this was one
of them? She's dead. I can't ask her. I need to know if the man that
fathered me was really a rapist.[21]

While the evidence against Simon is strong, it is also fabricated, but Huang
has no way of knowing that when he draws the connection. Simon is eventually cleared of all suspicion, but the results of Olivia's investigation into her
mother's rape support Serena's version of events. One of the victims in a
similar case that Olivia uncovered was able to identify Joseph Hollister as
her rapist. Once she has a definitive answer, or at least as definitive as she
can hope to achieve after all this time, Olivia's doubt of her mother's story
proves unfounded and also significant. *SVU* includes examples of rape narratives with false complainants, but for the most part, SVU detectives, Olivia in
particular, take up for victims until they are forced to change their beliefs
about what happened. The fact that Olivia does not afford her mother the
same courtesy as she does most of the victims she comes in contact with in
what is arguably the most significant rape narrative of the series to this point
contradicts many of the assumptions viewers have about her character.

Simon's rape narrative may be the most immediate in "Philadelphia," but
the emphasis of the episode is on Olivia and investigating the forty-year-old
case of what happened to Serena Benson. One of the most interesting things
about that case in terms of how the narrative is presented to viewers is that
both the victim and the rapist are dead. Instead of carrying any expectation of
justice for Serena or punishment for Joseph, viewers focus on their children
and the ways Olivia and Simon serve as stand-ins for their parents. The ways
in which Olivia's life is affected by her mother's rape have been made clear

in earlier seasons of the show, and the accusations Simon faces align him closely with his father—a point that Olivia makes several times. Really, this episode isn't about either Serena or Joe; it is about the legacy of Serena's rape and the impact that attack has on both the Benson and Marsden families (Marsden instead of Hollister because Simon's mother took back her maiden name after she and Joseph divorced). To this point, Olivia has not been sexually assaulted, but the way the rape narrative about her mother develops, it might make sense to consider her an indirect victim of sexual assault. In her brother, viewers glimpse the opposite side of the coin: where Olivia's close ties to a rape victim led her to seek justice and advocate for victims (most of the time), Simon was raised by a rapist. Whatever the ramifications of that, Simon turning out to be a rapist himself was not one.

LOWELL HARRIS

Up until Season Nine, Olivia's personal involvement in sexual assaults has been pretty constant but mostly indirect—she comes in contact with rape narratives either through her work or through the members of her family. While she is never raped, at least not in the first fifteen seasons of the show, it is a very close call on two separate occasions. The first is in Season Nine, Episode Fifteen, "Undercover,"[22] when Ashley Tyler, a sixteen-year-old rape victim, attacks Olivia in the back of an ambulance and sets in motion a chain of events that lead to an undercover investigation in Sealview Correctional Facility.

The first detective to go into Sealview undercover is Elliot Stabler. Posing as a lawyer, he attempts to speak with Risa Tyler, Ashley's mother, who refuses to talk to him out of fear. It was a guard who raped Ashley, after all, and the SVU detectives have no way of keeping Risa safe from the prison guards. When Elliot can't get Risa to talk, he appeals to the prison's warden, who claims there are no rapes occurring within her facility. Munch discovers the truth, however; due to the Prison Rape Elimination Act (which was signed into real-world law by then-president George W. Bush in 2003), all prisons are required to submit a list of rape complaints to the Department of Justice. There were forty-two complaints out of Sealview, none of which led to prosecution of the accused. Olivia fights Cragen for the opportunity to go in undercover.

Cragen: It's not our job to police the prisons.

Olivia: What should I tell Ashley? That your mother is an inmate so she doesn't really count? She's not a real victim?

Cragen: The warden stonewalled Elliot. She's not going to go along with this.

Olivia: So don't tell her. [23]

In addition to setting up an instructive moment for viewers—yes, prison inmates are real victims of rape—Olivia wins. As Katrina Rae Lewis, [24] she is sentenced to five years at Sealview on drug-related charges. Viewers watch as she is processed: In full view of a roomful of other inmates and fully clothed guards, she must strip down and shower. When she is made to endure a body and cavity search, the male guard grabs her butt, and when Olivia fights back, she is thrown to the ground and hit several times with a baton. When the guard wielding the baton is pulled off her, viewers recognize Fin Tutuola, another SVU detective, who is also undercover on his first day as a corrections officer.

Though Olivia has additional run-ins with the guard who grabbed her during processing, he isn't the one who takes her down to an isolated wing in the prison's basement, who tells her to "shut up and do what you are told" [25] just before she (and viewers) see the dirty mattress on the floor behind her, just before he grabs her face and pulls her body up against his then shoves her down onto the mattress. Captain Lowell Harris is the man who laughs as Olivia screams for help.

At her first opportunity, Olivia fights Harris off and runs away, but she has nowhere to go. The way she is trapped in that basement with him serves as a physical reminder of the fact that, when it comes to rape, victims are not to blame for what happens to them. Instead, they find themselves in situations where all of their control is stripped away. This truth is highlighted by the fact that Olivia understood, as well as she was able, what she was volunteering for when she fought to go into Sealview undercover. Even with the forewarning of exactly what might happen to her and all the training she had as an NYPD detective, she was still unable to maintain control of this situation. Nor should she have had to; nothing Olivia did should have to change. Instead, the blame for what nearly happens to her should be placed solely on Lowell Harris.

As he searches the basement for her, Harris keeps a running dialogue that displays for viewers just how vulnerable an inmate in Olivia's position would be: "You want to play a game? Good, because I know them all. You have two choices. You can come out now and make it up to me, or I can tell them that you tried to escape and I had to use necessary force. And you end up dead." [26] Even as Harris discovers Olivia's hiding place, viewers know that Fin is searching for her, but they have no way of knowing whether he will find them in time to rescue Olivia from being raped.

When she manages to free herself a second time, Olivia scrambles to a locked door where Harris catches up to her again. After he punches her, Harris forces Olivia to her knees and handcuffs her to the door as she yells no. Harris unzips his pants inches from Olivia's face. "Bite me, and you're dead,"[27] he tells her, and then Fin arrives, just as Harris reaches for Olivia's face again. This depiction of Olivia's sexual assault is unsettling partly because of who the victim is—her familiarity to the viewers and the futility of her training and struggle make it hard to watch—but the other aspect that makes it difficult is the fact that as much as *SVU* focuses on rape and sexual assault, there are very few actual representations of it. Instead, the detectives typically come on the scene after the attacks have occurred and are rarely even the first officers on the scene due to their specialization. Viewers don't know that Fin is going to arrive in time, and neither does Olivia, which is made extremely clear through close-up shots of her expression while the frame is shot to include Harris' left hip and Olivia's face.

Fin: Police! Move away from her!

Harris: She's trying to escape!

Fin: And you had to drop your pants to stop her?

Olivia: Lowell Harris, you're under arrest for the rape of Ashley Tyler . . .

Fin: And the attempted murder of a police officer.

Harris: You're a cop?

Olivia: Who's the bitch now?[28]

Whatever else is true of Olivia's response here, the fact that she is the one who places Harris under arrest returns all the power in this situation to the sexual assault victim, even though it is all too easy for viewers to imagine how many times, in similar situations, there would have been no recourse for an inmate who wasn't secretly an undercover NYPD detective.

Though viewers watch Olivia Benson's sexual assault in this episode, when Elliot asks her what happened in that basement, she tells him nothing. It isn't until she comes up with a way for Ashley to identify her rapist that Olivia has to admit out loud to medical examiner Melinda Warner that something did happen. Apparently, Harris has a mole on his penis that Ashley remembered when Olivia asked her whether her rapist had any distinguishing marks on his penis. When Warner asks Olivia how she could have known

Ashley was right about the mark, Olivia admits that she saw Harris' penis herself.

Warner: Olivia. Did he rape you?

Olivia: It's the closest I've ever come.[29]

At no point in this episode does Olivia label what happened to her, and she doesn't have to because when she arrests Harris a second time, it is specifically for the rape of Ashley Tyler. So while Olivia frequently convinces rape and sexual assault victims of the importance of facing their attackers in court, when it would be her turn to do the same, she doesn't. In fact, not only does she not do it herself, she sets up a sixteen-year-old girl whose mother was recently murdered (because Risa Tyler is killed at Sealview) to take the stand instead. For all the good work Olivia does with most rape victims, she is unable to follow her own advice in this episode. While it might be uncomfortable to be critical of her behavior in the same episode that she experiences a traumatic event, because all sexual assault survivors deserve the space in which to make their own decisions about how to move forward after their assaults, the show itself might have considered taking more responsibility for the situation Olivia ends up in and used the opportunity as an example of a narrative that falls more into line with the counsel Olivia has been giving other victims for years.

One thing *SVU* does that balances the scales a bit is follow through with the effects of Olivia's sexual assault into the tenth season. While the four episodes that wrapped up Season Nine immediately following "Undercover" didn't say much about it, Season Ten, Episode One, "Trials,"[30] shows how Benson's sexual assault is affecting her. Not only does she explain to Elliot that she hasn't been sleeping well and that she has repeatedly canceled plans to go out, but she zones out and has flashbacks to what happened in the basement of that prison. She also has a conversation with a rape victim about rape trauma syndrome, which she describes as a form of PTSD. Olivia bonds with Caitlin Ryan with a thinly veiled confession: "I sleep on my couch quite often. Do you need to have the TV on?"[31] While Caitlin may not be aware that what Benson is really saying is that she understands, being in a similar position herself, viewers are. Caitlin's story is much different from Olivia's, but when she describes the months following her rape, viewers have been given enough clues from what has taken place earlier in the episode that they recognize what could have happened to Olivia. Caitlin explains, "At first, I could function, and then I just started reliving it all the time, you know? I couldn't concentrate at work, so I lost my job."[32] Benson encourages Caitlin to seek help—a support group or counseling—and explains that a lot of rape victims feel the way Caitlin does.

While *SVU* has included psychological professionals many times by this point in the show, "Trials" ends with the first time Olivia seeks out that kind of help. The story she tells the therapist mirrors Caitlin's fairly closely—fine at first, began reliving the assault, can't sleep, feels out of control. So the episode ends with Olivia explicitly asking for help dealing with what she is feeling after being assaulted. While she could have taken a more proactive role in pursuing a case against Harris, she admits she needs help and then asks for it. This representation of a sexual assault victim, particularly when it is someone *SVU* viewers are so familiar with and care so much about, is important not just because Olivia seeks that help but also because she articulates the same kinds of concerns she has heard from hundreds of rape and assault survivors, giving voice to the emotional trauma that can arise months after a sexual assault, the kinds of issues that most shows cannot take the time to address if they include victims who only appear in a single episode that takes place immediately after an attack. In Olivia's case, some of her emotional response, and something the show seems committed to reiterating, stems from the fact that she wasn't actually raped.

Therapist: Olivia, you were sexually assaulted.

Olivia: He came so close, and there was nothing I could do to stop him. He had a weapon, and he completely overpowered me. And I never should have let him take me down there. Because I know better than that.

Therapist: Rape victims often blame themselves. You know how misplaced that blame is.

Olivia: I know, I know that here [points to her temple]. I've told that same thing to a lot of women. But now I feel like I don't deserve to be here.[33]

So even in this moment, when Olivia doubts all of the things she has told countless rape victims in the past, the therapist is there to remind her, and viewers, of the things Olivia knows but does not feel.

This is not the only time in Season Ten that Olivia is shown in therapy,[34] and the consistent reminder that she is seeking professional help to sort through her response to being assaulted is both a narrative tool, because of the way it serves as a device to convey particular kinds of information, and an important model of behavior for individuals who find themselves in positions similar to Olivia's. Though she shows some derision when it comes to dealing with psychologists earlier in the series, the fact that she asks for psychiatric help even though she was "only" assaulted and not raped might act as a kind of permission to encourage more survivors to seek out the same kind of help.

BRADY HARRISON

The emphasis in "Undercover" might be on the trauma Olivia suffers in the second half of the episode, but the commentary on prison rape throughout the episode is also important. It serves as a reminder to viewers that the detectives working in the SVU recognize all different victims of rape, regardless of a wide variety of factors that are sometimes used to dismiss rape complaints—people under the influence of drugs and/or alcohol and sex workers are asking for it, a man can't rape his wife, and prisoners deserve what they get as a form of punishment for the crimes they have committed. While what happens to Olivia asks viewers to reevaluate the last idea in particular, one of the more troubling recurring tropes throughout *SVU* is the threat of prison rape as an interrogation tactic. While *SVU* is fairly adept at handling rape narratives in a way that is sympathetic to victims, these threats seem to condone the practice instead of fighting against it, and just about every major character working in the SVU resorts to them at one point or another.[35]

Prison rape threats during interrogation are not unique to *SVU*. In fact, most of the shows included in *Assault on the Small Screen* make use of such threats at least once, regardless of how well or poorly other rape narratives represent victims or feminist understandings of rape. *SVU*, though, is singular in the fact that it actually considers not just the reality and existence of prison rape but also law enforcement officers attempting to address the issue. That work is undercut by the continued use of prison rape in interrogation, but the show also has an episode that addresses the threats themselves: In Season Eleven, Episode Nine, "Perverted,"[36] Brady Harrison attempts to frame Olivia for murder after the threats of prison rape she levels against him during his interrogation prove prophetic.

During their final confrontation, when Harrison breaks into Olivia's apartment and confronts her with a taser, she discovers that the man she is being framed for murdering was the same man who raped and brutalized Harrison in prison. She also learns that Harrison believes that she was the one to arrange the whole thing.

Harrison: You couldn't stand that I had no remorse for what I did to those women, so you, you set me up!

Olivia: Who told you that?

Harrison: You did! Don't you remember? "A pretty boy like you is gonna be real popular in prison. Maybe when you're raped, you'll understand what you put those women through."[37]

Of course Olivia apologizes and swears that she did not arrange for him to be raped, but he does not believe her. Viewers, though, know that she wouldn't do such a thing and also understand how this episode fits into the larger narrative about Olivia's own sexual assault while she was undercover and the resulting emotional trauma she experienced.

The truth of the matter, however, is that even though the threats Olivia made to Harrison happened well before her own assault, as a detective who typically identifies with the victims on a show dedicated almost exclusively to telling stories about sex crimes, Olivia should have known better than to make rape threats. While her motivation, even according to the threatened man himself, is that she over-identified with his victims, no one deserves to be raped or even threatened with rape, regardless of prior bad acts. That this is true in no way excuses the crimes Brady Harrison admitted he felt no remorse for or the crimes he has committed since being released, but it does highlight for viewers an understanding that there is no need for the SVU detectives to use interrogation tactics that contribute in any way to the cycle of prison rape.

WILLIAM LEWIS

The second rape narrative that leads to Olivia Benson nearly being raped begins in Season Fourteen, Episode Twenty-Four, "Her Negotiation,"[38] on an ordinary Sunday. All of the SVU detectives are enjoying their leisure time when Amanda Rollins, one of the two detectives who joined the SVU after Stabler's retirement between Seasons Twelve and Thirteen, gives chase to a man in the park. She has no idea who he is or what is about to unfold, but she does know something is very off about him. He has no identification and no fingerprints—viewers watched him burn them off on a hot stovetop in the episode's opening scene. Rollins calls in the whole squad.

What follows is the unraveling of Lewis' identity and the list of heinous crimes he committed and got away with in the past. Through a combination of luck and manic genius, Lewis has on at least three separate occasions successfully maneuvered his way through the legal system after kidnapping, torturing, and repeatedly raping his female victims. In "Her Negotiation," Lewis adds Alice Parker, the sixty-year-old woman who witnessed the initial flashing incident that brought him to Rollins' attention, to the list. The description of what Lewis did to her—burning her with cigarettes, keys, and coat hangers that had been boiled in water, sexually degrading her—and the list of what he had done to all his previous victims—an ex-girlfriend's mother, a pair of roommates, and a current girlfriend who was also his former defense attorney—make it clear to viewers exactly what is in store for Olivia when she enters her apartment at the very end of the Season Fourteen finale and Lewis is waiting for her there.

Olivia knows as well, since she was the one to draw out all the details of what he did to Alice Parker in interrogation. Lewis is careful to couch everything he says in hypotheticals so none of it will hold up as a confession in court, but both Olivia and viewers are aware of the way Lewis manipulates the truth. The other part of the interrogation that takes on a new meaning with Lewis' presence in Olivia's apartment is what can now be recognized as a threat: "What I did? You should be so lucky someone does that to you."[39]

For viewers, four months pass between the moment Lewis shoves Olivia offscreen in the Season Fourteen finale and when she wakes up lying on the floor with duct tape over her mouth in the Season Fifteen premiere, "Surrender Benson." While it may feel longer given all Olivia has been through in that time, it has only been a matter of hours. Lewis holds her captive for four days. In addition to the physical abuse she endures before they leave her apartment, during their time "together," Lewis forces Olivia to watch him rape Liz Mayer, the mother of his defense attorney. Mrs. Mayer gives her statement to Rollins: "She had duct tape on her mouth. Anytime she tried to close [her eyes], he put a lit cigarette on me."[40] Given Olivia's dedication to assisting rape victims, making her watch a woman be raped with no ability to fight back or protect her may just be the perfect way for Lewis to torture Olivia without even having to touch her. Lewis keeps Olivia incapacitated by force-feeding her vodka and Vicodin, and when Olivia tries to refuse at one point, Lewis is very clear: "Hey, hey, you don't get to say no anymore. [. . .] I'm a man of my word. Like when I told you about that lady and about what I was going to do to her, right? I told her everything, and then I did everything that I said, didn't I?"[41] This kind of psychological attack is one of the things Lewis does best; while what he has done to Olivia physically to this point shouldn't be dismissed, the awareness of all that Lewis is capable of makes what is still to come much more frightening.

Olivia has clearly become one of Lewis' victims. But she is not a rape victim. Even though Lewis repeatedly threatens to rape her, forcing her to watch what he does to Mrs. Mayer like a promise of what he plans to do to her, four days pass before he actually attempts the act. When Lewis begins unbuckling his belt, however, a housekeeper and her young daughter show up to clean the beach house where he is holding Olivia. As she explains later, fear about what he might do to the little girl or her mother gave Olivia the time and motivation to break an iron bar off the bed she was handcuffed to; she is able to use the bar to knock Lewis out. From that point, Olivia has regained most of the control over her situation. But Lewis is not helpless. He is restrained, but he is still able to goad Olivia into using that iron bar to beat him rather severely.

Lewis: All your life you've been listening to stories, women telling you about the worst night of their life. What about you? What are you working through?

Benson: Shut up! Shut up!

Lewis: Something your daddy did to you? Is that it? I'm on to something, aren't I? Call me what you want, but I can always smell a victim.[42]

And while, technically, he may be wrong—it's nothing Joseph Hollister did to Olivia directly that haunts her—there is just enough truth to what Lewis says to create exactly the reaction he was looking for. Olivia may have subdued Lewis, but he has had her under his control for four days as he tortured her. She hasn't eaten or slept. He retains enough control over her to force Olivia into taking physical, violent action against him even though he doesn't pose any immediate danger to her. Even at this point in the narrative, when Lewis is the one being beaten and Olivia is the one holding the weapon, he has still managed to turn her into the victim because he manipulates her into acting in a way that, under normal circumstances, she never would. That kind of manipulation might just be what Lewis is best at.

Season Fifteen, Episode Two, "Imprisoned Lives,"[43] serves as the second part of the series premiere; the two episodes aired on the same night. The episode takes place two months later, and viewers see flashes of all that has happened in that time. There is a scene where Olivia cuts off her own hair while staring in a mirror, another where she returns to her apartment for the first time since the attack, and several of her visiting her therapist's office. Then she returns to work. More than the specific case that plays out when Olivia first returns to the SVU, her recovery and adjustment after her ordeal with Lewis are important to the development of her near-rape narrative because viewers most likely assume that a trial is coming. The emotional reactions and setbacks that Olivia goes through in this episode really do work to highlight all of the times in previous seasons of the show when viewers have heard about the struggles faced during recovery. Through Olivia's story, they actually see glimpses at least of what that recovery might look like.

There are enough mentions throughout the next part of Season Fifteen to remind viewers that the William Lewis narrative isn't over yet. In Episode Three, "American Tragedy," there is a minor subplot involving street harassment. When a man tells Olivia to smile[44] and moves into her personal space as she walks down the sidewalk, she reacts violently. She visits her therapist, Dr. Peter Lindstrom,[45] and explains that, because she is a police officer, she can't go around overacting like that and physically assaulting people in the street. Lindstrom ties her reaction to this man back to when she was assaulted by Lewis: He says she blames herself "for underreacting to Lewis and now for overreacting to this guy"[46] and doesn't give her valid emotional responses enough credit. Olivia struggles in the role of victim, and viewers think of all the times they have heard her say similar things to other victims.

Olivia continues her therapy, and the show continues to remind viewers that Lewis' story isn't over yet; he goes to trial in Episode Ten, "Psycho/Therapist." Viewers watch Olivia and Assistant District Attorney Rafael Barba practice her testimony in the courtroom and discuss legal strategy. The two also talk about Mrs. Mayer's plans to testify. When Barba takes a moment to clarify for Olivia that he is charging Lewis with attempted murder and rape, her response is immediate: "He didn't rape me." Her statement is redundant; Barba is charging Lewis with the attempt, which makes clear that no actual rape occurred. While it might seem facetious, Olivia did not feel the need to clarify that Lewis didn't murder her, just that he didn't rape her. Barba's response calls even more attention to the redundancy: "I understand that that is important to you, but he's going to claim those four days were consensual."[47]

Olivia has taken the stand before. She has testified somewhat regularly within the scope of her job as an SVU detective. She has sat with numerous victims for the announcements of verdicts. There were times when a defense attorney cast suspicion for a murder onto her to create reasonable doubt as to his client's guilt. Olivia was in court as a defendant when she was nearly framed for murder in "Perverted." But even though she has been sexually assaulted before, Olivia has never been in court for a case in which she is the victim.

The change of setting forces viewers to see Olivia's victimization in a new light as well. In this episode, Olivia's status as a victim becomes a matter of public record. Her case is now at trial, and to this point, most of the people who know about what happened to her she didn't have to tell. Everyone she works with knew as much as she did about what Lewis was capable of before he abducted her, and everything she tells her therapist is protected by privilege and should never come out. Bringing the case to court means shining a spotlight on what happened to her, and viewers will see the way others respond to her account of events—the jury in particular.

Before the trial officially begins, though, Lewis attempts one more manipulation. Barba explains the plea deal Lewis is offering: He will plead guilty and give a full allocution if Olivia agrees to let him plead guilty to multiple counts of rape and sodomy.

Olivia: He wants to stand up in open court and give graphic details of what he did not do to me?

Barba: He will get twenty-five years to life. He will die in prison. Olivia, you will avoid a trial and having to testify.

Olivia: No, no, no, he does not get to do that to me. He did not rape me. He did not sodomize me. You looked at that rape kit. After four days, he did not have the balls to rape me. And now he wants to stand up in open court? Now? No. No.[48]

It is difficult to believe that a master manipulator like William Lewis believed that Olivia would allow him to lie on the record about what he hadn't done to her body. Olivia's choice of whether to accept his plea offer might seem like a way for her to retain some measure of control over the situation, but when Lewis is likely sure of the outcome and benefits from it regardless of what she decides—because either she will have to listen to his allocution or he will have the opportunity to face her on the witness stand—it amounts to little more than another avenue to inflict further trauma.

When Lewis uses the fact that the prosecution rejected his plea as reason to fire his attorney and represent himself, he creates another situation in which he gains control over his victims. The fact that he will be doing the questioning convinces Mrs. Mayer to change her mind about testifying, and it is difficult to blame her. When Olivia takes the stand, Lewis doesn't even have to begin questioning her in order to show her that he has regained control; after Barba has finished questioning her, Olivia braces herself as Lewis rises from his seat. All he does, though, is ask the judge for permission to recall her at a later time, drawing out the same emotional trauma he sustained over the four days he held her captive—the fear of what comes next.

Eventually Olivia does take the stand, and Lewis leads her through the events that took place almost eight months earlier.[49]

Lewis: Only two people know what happened over those four days.

Olivia: I know exactly what happened, and that's what I told the jury.

Lewis: I can see how that's the story you'd want the jury to believe. The truth's embarrassing.[50]

To that point, he has only spoken the truth. He hasn't denied her account of what happened, and she would be embarrassed, given all of her training, to have been abducted and physically assaulted. In this particular instance, however, there are more than two people who know most of what happened during those days: Olivia, Lewis, and all *SVU* viewers. Typically viewers don't have as much access to the truths of what happened between the victims and the perpetrators in the cases they see in trial, so there is always at least a little room for doubt. In this particular instance, though, viewers know exactly what Lewis did and exactly what Benson lies about. They see how words and legal tactics can be used against her and how the truth can be manipulated, in this case, in favor of the perpetrator. Viewers know that Olivia was a victim; they witnessed enough of her abduction to be sure of that. So every legal maneuver Lewis uses becomes a trick, and critical viewers may wonder how these same tricks are used against other victims who are just as damaged and just as traumatized as Olivia. When the accused rapist is the one asking the questions in particular, a trial can retraumatize victims by forcing them to repeat and relive the events in open court, and all the while, the person responsible for their suffering is not only witnessing the event but managing how the moment unfolds.[51]

When the jury finds Lewis guilty on two of the charges—assaulting a police officer and kidnapping—Barba tells Olivia he will ask for the maximum sentence: twenty-five years to life. After the verdict, Olivia excuses herself from the courtroom, finds an empty stairwell, and breaks down. Whether her tears are caused by trauma or relief, the episode doesn't say. But the very end of "Psycho/Therapist" tells viewers that even this trial and the two guilty verdicts aren't the end of William Lewis' narrative: He is shown four months in the future, laid out on a gurney in an orange jumpsuit, sweating and clearly ill but with a smile on his face.

Those four months pass in the *SVU* universe over the course of ten episodes. Lewis returns in Olivia's dreams and during her therapy appointments in the interim, but Lewis himself doesn't come back until Season Fifteen, Episode Twenty, "Beast's Obsession."[52] Viewers have been aware that something more is coming, but the show's main characters aren't until Olivia receives a video chat message from Lewis the morning he escapes custody.

After chasing him through the city, Olivia eventually slips the protective detail she was assigned and goes to meet Lewis on her own. He has abducted Amelia, the twelve-year-old daughter of the female prison doctor he seduced while in custody. While there are still lasting effects from the trauma Olivia suffered, she voluntarily gives up control of her physical self for a chance to protect Amelia—Lewis holds a gun on her and has searched her to ensure that she is unarmed. But she maintains some control. When Lewis attempts to rile her—"What's the matter, Olivia? Don't feel like talking? What? Oh Lord, you're not having flashbacks now, are you? PTSD, I mean, it's real. You're in your bed at night, wake up in a cold sweat thinking I'm in the room with a gun to your head"[53]—she refuses to be baited. When they arrive at the abandoned granary where he has Amelia tied up, Olivia chooses whom Lewis will rape first, her or Amelia. Olivia chooses to go first: "Do what you're gonna do," she says.[54] Then she stops fighting. She doesn't resist; she doesn't even move. He has tied her to a table, steps up right behind her, grabs her breasts, and kisses her face. She doesn't respond in any way. He starts to unbutton her pants, but stops. "That's it? That's all you're gonna give me, huh? You're just gonna stand there, play possum? All right. You know what? New game. My rules. Not yours."[55] Lewis and the viewers all know that

Olivia isn't going to turn control back over to him, and her volunteering to go first was calculated. No one would know better than Olivia Benson that rape is an act about control and power. For William Lewis, neither counts if they are given freely instead of taken by force.

Lisa M. Cuklanz and Sujata Moorti assert that "as the key female protagonist, Benson is a singular figure through which [*SVU*] espouses identifiably feminist attitudes toward rape and police work."[56] This is perhaps even truer after fifteen seasons than it was after five, for Olivia Benson has become the singular protagonist on the show. She is the only one of the characters who has been around for all fifteen seasons,[57] and in the majority of episodes, she plays the hero. It is a role in which Olivia is fairly adept and that viewers expect to see her play.

Part of the reason she does her job so well is because she is able to empathize with victims of sexual assault. When the series begins, viewers learn this empathy comes in part from her family history with rape—Olivia herself is the product of her mother's rape. The effects of that truth have a lasting impact on Olivia, her relationship with her mother, and her relationship with her job—at times putting Olivia into the position of standing in place of a victim. It isn't until later seasons that Olivia herself becomes the victim.

It is important to consider what it means that Olivia Benson is never raped. She is sexually assaulted and nearly raped on three separate occasions—once by Lowell Harris when she is undercover as a prison inmate and twice by William Lewis. Yet on a show that focuses on how the legal system works for and (at times) against rape victims, Olivia herself never becomes one. She repeatedly puts herself into situations where she knows there is a threat of rape. That kind of language when talking about a sexual assault victim usually amounts to victim-blaming, but when the victim being discussed works for the Special Victims Unit of the NYPD, all it means is that she is literally walking into situations she knows to be dangerous in that way. She volunteers to do it. She even wins arguments in order to be able to do it.

After she is assaulted, Olivia seeks professional psychiatric help. The role of these professionals is important because when Olivia has to take on the role of victim, someone needs to fill her shoes, say to her the things that she would say if she were on a case. For instance, in Season Fifteen, Episode Twenty-One, "Post-Mortem Blues,"[58] Olivia says that Lewis has won since he continues to manipulate her even after his death.[59] It is her psychiatrist, Dr. Lindstrom, who breaks down the reality of her situation: "He's dead, and you are alive. And so is Amelia. Now this trap you're in, he didn't trick you into it. You chose to walk into it."[60]

All of the times that Olivia has been forced into the role of victim by the narratives of the episode, she has actually been in the position to put herself at risk. She takes on some of the role of victim when she refuses to let her mother's rape case remain unsolved. She chooses to keep searching for her biological father, to follow her half brother in a way that leaves her vulnerable within the context of another rape narrative. She insists that Cragen send her to Sealview, and she does her job with William Lewis. She willingly gives herself up to him a second time in order to save Amelia. That she is never actually raped is significant when considering the sheer number of rapists she has interacted with in fifteen seasons.

The overarching narrative of *Law and Order: Special Victims Unit* shows that even Detective Olivia Benson, with all her training and resources, with the forewarnings and the awareness of the threat, is still vulnerable to sexual assault. The specific sets of circumstances within these episodes mean that she doesn't (or maybe hasn't yet) become a rape victim, but none of the things viewers know to be true about Olivia protect her fully from the possibility of rape. In order to fight for justice, she has put herself in vulnerable positions. It's enough to make viewers wonder what chance any other potential sexual assault or rape victim would have when even Olivia Benson is vulnerable.

NOTES

1. One simple way to define "most successful" would be to look at longevity: As of 2015, *SVU* is the only *Law and Order* spin-off still on the air and has had sixteen seasons. *Law and Order: Criminal Intent* had ten seasons before going off the air in 2011, and the *Trial by Jury* and *LA* (for "Los Angeles") spin-offs each only had a single season.

2. Lisa M. Cuklanz and Sujata Moorti, "Television's 'New' Feminism: Prime-Time Representations of Women and Victimization," *Critical Studies in Media Communication* 23, no. 4 (October 2006): 317.

3. Other arguments made by Cuklanz and Moorti that hold true throughout the seasons of *SVU* include feminist depictions of rape that don't treat sexual assault victims as sex objects, highlight the deficiencies in the justice system, and prioritize consent when defining an act as rape. *SVU* also "[inscribes] the presence of sexual assault in all spaces, perpetrated by strangers and acquaintances." Cuklanz and Moorti, "Television's 'New' Feminism," 309.

4. Cuklanz and Moorti, "Television's 'New' Feminism," 305.

5. Dick Wolf, "Payback," *Law and Order: Special Victims Unit*, season 1, episode 1, directed by Jean de Segonzac, aired on September 20, 1999, http://www.hulu.com/watch/159156#i0,p0,s1,d0.

6. Roger Garrett, "Stalked," *Law and Order: Special Victims Unit*, season 1, episode 8, directed by Peter Medak, aired on November 22, 1999, http://www.hulu.com/watch/159171#i0,p4,s1,d0.

7. Ibid.

8. Lisa Marie Petersen and Dawn DeNoon, "Bad Blood," *Law and Order: Special Victims Unit*, season 1, episode 11, directed by Michael Fields, aired on January 14, 2000, http://www.hulu.com/watch/159168#i0,p8,s1,d0.

9. Dawn DeNoon and Lisa Marie Petersen, "Slaves," *Law and Order: Special Victims Unit*, season 1, episode 22, directed by Ted Kotcheff, aired on May 19, 2000, http://www.hulu.com/watch/159157#i0,p20,s1,d0.

10. Dawn DeNoon and Lisa Marie Petersen, "Taken," *Law and Order: Special Victims Unit*, season 2, episode 8, directed by Michael Fields, aired on December 15, 2000, http://www.hulu.com/watch/159180#i0,p4,s2,d0.

11. Ibid.

12. Jonathan Greene, "Intoxicated," *Law and Order: Special Victims Unit*, season 6, episode 19, directed by Marita Grabiak, aired on March 15, 2005, http://www.hulu.com/watch/159250#i0,p16,s6,d0.

13. Cuklanz and Moorti, "Television's 'New' Feminism," 318.

14. Greene, "Intoxicated."

15. Amanda Green, "Haystack," *Law and Order: Special Victims Unit*, season 8, episode 15, directed by Peter Leto, aired on February 20, 2007, http://www.hulu.com/watch/275495#i0,p12,s8,d0.

16. Patrick Harbinson, "Philadelphia," *Law and Order: Special Victims Unit*, season 8, episode 16, directed by Peter Leto, aired on February 27, 2007, http://www.hulu.com/watch/159305#i0,p12,s8,d0.

17. Ibid.

18. Ibid.

19. Jonathan Greene, "Florida," *Law and Order: Special Victims Unit*, season 8, episode 19, directed by David Platt, aired on May 1, 2007, http://www.hulu.com/watch/275470#i0,p16,s8,d0.

20. In a visit with Simon's mother, Sharon, who has early-onset Alzheimer's, Olivia learns that Joseph Hollister claimed her as his daughter and even tried to call her once but hung up the phone when her mother answered. Olivia and FBI agent Dean Porter agree that is odd behavior for typical rapists.

21. Greene, "Florida."

22. Mark Goffman, "Undercover," *Law and Order: Special Victims Unit*, season 9, episode 15, directed by David Platt, aired on April 15, 2008, http://www.hulu.com/watch/196730#i0,p12,s9,d0.

23. Ibid.

24. Coincidentally, Lewis, Olivia's surname when she is undercover in Sealview, is the same last name as that of the second man who will nearly rape her in Season Fifteen.

25. Goffman, "Undercover."

26. Ibid.

27. Ibid.

28. Ibid.

29. Ibid.

30. Dawn DeNoon, "Trials," *Law and Order: Special Victims Unit*, season 10, episode 1, directed by David Platt, aired on September 23, 2008, http://www.hulu.com/watch/159194#i0,p0,s10,d0.

31. Ibid.

32. Ibid.

33. Ibid.

34. Season Ten, Episode Nine, "PTSD," for instance, begins with Olivia attending a meeting of a support group for survivors of military sexual trauma, which leads to a case involving Jessica Crewes, a woman who was raped in Iraq, became pregnant from the attack, and was murdered after returning to New York. While seeking her rapist and murderer, Olivia attempts to break up a fight between two marines, and after she is shoved back and slams her head against the wall, she pulls a gun on one of the marines and presses her weapon against the back of his head. Fin has to talk her down, and as a result of the incident, Cragen tells Olivia to take some personal time to sort herself out.

35. In Season Two, Episode Eight, "Taken," Cragen makes a comment about how a man accused of rape—falsely, it turns out—"won't be doing much sitting down in prison." That man is raped and eventually killed in prison. In Season Six, Episode Eleven, "Contagious," Elliot Stabler tells a suspect that other inmates "are gonna rip your cherry ass apart." In Season Ten, Episode Eighteen, "Baggage," Fin and Elliot use the threat of prison rape in an interrogation. These are just a few examples; there are others.

36. Dawn DeNoon, "Perverted," *Law and Order: Special Victims Unit*, season 11, episode 9, directed by David Platt, aired on November 18, 2009, http://www.hulu.com/watch/159201#i0,p8,s11,d0.

37. Ibid.

38. Julie Martin and Warren Leight, "Her Negotiation," *Law and Order: Special Victims Unit*, season 14, episode 24, directed by Norberto Barba, aired on May 22, 2013, http://www.hulu.com/watch/493220#i0,p20,s14,d0.

39. Ibid.

40. Julie Martin and Warren Leight, "Surrender Benson/Imprisoned Lives," *Law and Order: Special Victims Unit*, season 15, episodes 1 and 2, directed by Michael Smith, aired on September 25, 2013, http://www.hulu.com/watch/537726#i0,p0,s15,d0.

41. Ibid.

42. Ibid.

43. Ibid.

44. Men attempting to police the emotions of women they do not know is a prime example of street harassment that society too frequently suggests should be taken as a compliment or brushed aside. While Olivia's reaction may be over-the-top in its violence, her emotional response is and should be considered valid.

45. Peter Lindstrom is played by Bill Irwin, the same actor who plays Nate Haskell, the Dick and Jane Killer, on *CSI*.

46. Julie Martin, Warren Leight, and Jill Abbinanti, "American Tragedy," *Law and Order: Special Victims Unit*, season 15, episode 3, directed by Fred Berner, aired on October 2, 2013, http://www.hulu.com/watch/450451#i0,p0,s15,d0.

47. Julie Martin and Warren Leight, "Psycho/Therapist," *Law and Order: Special Victims Unit*, season 15, episode 10, directed by Michael Slovis, aired on January 8, 2014, http://www.hulu.com/watch/580385#i0,p8,s15,d0.

48. Ibid.

49. Olivia is first discovered to be missing on May 23; the trial began on January 3.

50. Martin and Leight, "Psycho/Therapist."

51. This idea about trials, particularly in which defendants represent themselves, will be elaborated on in the next chapter.

52. Julie Martin and Warren Leight, "Beast's Obsession," *Law and Order: Special Victims Unit*, season 15, episode 20, directed by Steve Shill, aired on April 9, 2014, http://www.hulu.com/watch/620378#i0,p16,s15,d0.

53. Ibid.

54. Ibid.

55. Ibid.

56. Cuklanz and Moorti, "Television's 'New' Feminism," 309.

57. Fin Tutuola comes in a close second; he joined the SVU in Season Two.

58. Julie Martin and Warren Leight, "Post-Mortem Blues," *Law and Order Special Victims Unit*, season 15, episode 21, directed by Michael Slovis, aired on April 30, 2014, http://www.hulu.com/watch/629156#i0,p16,s15,d0.

59. After forcing Olivia to play Russian roulette with him, Lewis killed himself, holding the gun in the exact right position to make it appear as if Olivia had shot him. Her refusal to lie about what caused Lewis' death creates problems for her with the Internal Affairs Bureau.

60. Martin and Leight, "Post-Mortem Blues."

REFERENCES

Cuklanz, Lisa M., and Sujata Moorti. "Television's 'New' Feminism: Prime-Time Representations of Women and Victimization." *Critical Studies in Media Communication* 23, no. 4 (October 2006): 302–321.

DeNoon, Dawn. "Perverted." *Law and Order: Special Victims Unit*. Online. Directed by David Platt. Aired on November 18, 2009. http://www.hulu.com/watch/159201#i0,p8,s11,d0.

————. "Trials." *Law and Order: Special Victims Unit*. Online. Directed by David Platt. Aired on September 23, 2008. http://www.hulu.com/watch/159194#i0,p0,s10,d0.

DeNoon, Dawn, and Lisa Marie Petersen. "Slaves." *Law and Order: Special Victims Unit*. Online. Directed by Ted Kotcheff. Aired on May 19, 2000. http://www.hulu.com/watch/159157#i0,p20,s1,d0.

————. "Taken." *Law and Order: Special Victims Unit*. Online. Directed by Michael Fields. Aired on December 15, 2000. http://www.hulu.com/watch/159180#i0,p4,s2,d0.

Garrett, Roger. "Stalked." *Law and Order: Special Victims Unit*. Online. Directed by Peter Medak. Aired on November 22, 1999. http://www.hulu.com/watch/159171#i0,p4,s1,d0.

Goffman, Mark. "Undercover." *Law and Order: Special Victims Unit*. Online. Directed by David Platt. Aired on April 15, 2008. http://www.hulu.com/watch/196730#i0,p12,s9,d0.

Green, Amanda. "Haystack." *Law and Order: Special Victims Unit*. Online. Directed by Peter Leto. Aired on February 20, 2007. http://www.hulu.com/watch/275495#i0,p12,s8,d0.

Greene, Jonathan. "Florida." *Law and Order: Special Victims Unit*. Online. Directed by David Platt. Aired on May 1, 2007. http://www.hulu.com/watch/275470#i0,p16,s8,d0.

————. "Intoxicated." *Law and Order: Special Victims Unit*. Online. Directed by Marita Grabiak. Aired on March 15, 2005. http://www.hulu.com/watch/159250#i0,p16,s6,d0.

Harbinson, Patrick. "Philadelphia." *Law and Order: Special Victims Unit*. Online. Directed by Peter Leto. Aired on February 27, 2007. http://www.hulu.com/watch/159305#i0,p12,s8,d0.

Martin, Julie, and Warren Leight. "Beast's Obsession." *Law and Order: Special Victims Unit*. Online. Directed by Steve Shill. Aired on April 9, 2014. http://www.hulu.com/watch/620378#i0,p16,s15,d0.

————. "Her Negotiation." *Law and Order: Special Victims Unit*. Online. Directed by Norberto Barba. Aired on May 22, 2013. http://www.hulu.com/watch/493220#i0,p20,s14,d0.

————. "Post-Mortem Blues." *Law and Order Special Victims Unit*. Online. Directed by Michael Slovis. Aired on April 30, 2014. http://www.hulu.com/watch/629156#i0,p16,s15,d0.

————. "Psycho/Therapist." *Law and Order: Special Victims Unit*. Online. Directed by Michael Slovis. Aired on January 8, 2014. http://www.hulu.com/watch/580385#i0,p8,s15,d0.

————. "Surrender Benson/Imprisoned Lives." *Law and Order: Special Victims Unit*. Online. Directed by Michael Smith. Aired on September 25, 2013. http://www.hulu.com/watch/537726#i0,p0,s15,d0.

Martin, Julie, Warren Leight, and Jill Abbinanti. "American Tragedy." *Law and Order: Special Victims Unit*. Online. Directed by Fred Berner. Aired on October 2, 2013. http://www.hulu.com/watch/450451#i0,p0,s15,d0.

Petersen, Lisa Marie, and Dawn DeNoon. "Bad Blood." *Law and Order: Special Victims Unit*. Online. Directed by Michael Fields. Aired on January 14, 2000. http://www.hulu.com/watch/159168#i0,p8,s1,d0.

Wolf, Dick. "Payback." *Law and Order: Special Victims Unit*. Online. Directed by Jean de Segonzac. Aired on September 20, 1999. http://www.hulu.com/watch/159156#i0,p0,s1,d0.

Chapter Seven

"Separate Yet Equally Important"

Prosecuting Rape Narratives on Prime Time

Maybe it isn't surprising that so many individuals who have been raped choose not to report the crimes committed against them. Deciding to report a rape carries with it additional layers of potential trauma: the necessity of retelling specific events of an attack repeatedly for months at a time to multiple and potentially hostile audiences. Individuals who have been raped must first tell their stories to the police, who may or may not believe them. Then the district attorney's office gets involved, and that person decides whether to press charges. Then judges and juries need to hear what happened and will or will not find accused rapists guilty. As all this happens, months pass, and each new person a victim tells is another person who may not be sympathetic or supportive.

Media representations of rape narratives, including several from the shows considered in *Assault on the Small Screen*, suggest that most of society is aware of the difficulties that accompany a rape trial, at least within the universes created on the shows. Paul Bergman's "A Third Rapist? Television Portrayals of Rape Evidence Rules" explores the possibility of three layers of assault that occur in television rape narratives—the first being the rape itself, the second the report of the rape and any resulting trial, and the third the presentations of the rape narratives themselves and rape evidence rules in particular.[1] While the third point is worth further consideration, the first is undeniable, and the second seems like common knowledge. At least within the universes of the police dramas considered so far, it is generally assumed that reporting a rape and all that an investigation and a trial can entail will serve as a retraumatizing experience. One clear example of how the system designed to obtain justice for the victims can act as a source of revictimization is from *CSI*. In Season One, Episode Four, "Pledging Mr. Johnson,"[2] criminalist Warrick Brown is blackmailed by a judge, who wants him to tamper with the evidence in a case identified only as "the Henderson rape case." Viewers don't get much more information than that, but here is an obvious example of a narrative in which the system a victim put her trust in actively works to deny her justice. While the case could be made that this is a very specific and corrupt individual working within the criminal justice system (as opposed to the system itself), it seems as though the majority of rape victims across these shows anticipate an uphill battle when they decide to pursue charges against their rapists. None of the shows demonstrates the potential results of said battle as well as *Dexter*; the rape narratives that don't directly affect women Dexter is involved with chronicle Dexter's quest for violent and bloody vigilantism against rapists when the system cannot offer victims the justice they deserve.

But there are additional, less flagrant examples of rape narratives that recognize the potential for retraumatization. *Criminal Minds* has multiple episodes of rape narratives with victims who are distrustful of the authorities, from Season One, Episode Nineteen, "Machismo,"[3] to Season Seven, Episode Twelve, "Unknown Subject,"[4] in which one of two rapists uses his victims' insecurities about being believed by authorities to keep them from reporting a second attack. When both the victims and the second rapist use the exact same phrase—"No one believes a slut who cries wolf"[5]—to describe the reason the women aren't to be believed, SSA Emily Prentiss is able to solidify the connection between them. In that same episode, when the BAU discovers that Regina Lampert has taken the man she believes to be her rapist hostage, viewers see another victim express a similar understanding of how the system works. After Prentiss tells Regina she has the wrong man to keep her from killing her rapist, she will not give her statement to anyone else. Prentiss admits that she lied to keep Regina out of prison.

> **Regina:** As opposed to where I am right now? I mean, while he gets a lawyer and a fair trial.

> **Prentiss:** He will never see the light of day. Ever.

> **Regina:** Can you guarantee that? You know, when they talk about victims getting revictimized by the system, they mean you.[6]

And while this example is clearly complicated by the fact that Regina is most likely under arrest for kidnapping at least, the whole episode highlights the ways society in the *Criminal Minds* universe expects that victims will get caught up in a cycle of revictimization.

Viewers don't see what happens when the case(s) in "Unknown Subject" or any other case on *Criminal Minds* actually ends up in court. There are no examples of rape narratives that end up in courtrooms in *NCIS*, either. When it comes to narratives that include the prosecution of rape, *Law and Order: Special Victims Unit* has an enormous advantage just in terms of sheer numbers. This makes sense to viewers; the original *Law and Order* was based on the premise that "there are two separate yet equally important groups: the police who investigate crime and the district attorneys who prosecute the offenders." In that series, episodes were typically split more or less evenly between investigations in the first half and prosecution in the second. While *SVU* takes some liberty with the equity of the divide, this spin-off series creates a viewer expectation that there will frequently be more to the story than the police catching the perpetrator. Viewers don't just want to see the investigation reach a reasonable conclusion about who is responsible; they want a jury's verdict and a sentence handed down from a judge. When a case goes to trial, the details of the offenses committed against the state and the victim it represents become a matter of public record in the universe of the show. When cases move into the courtroom, viewers can watch justice being served and punishment being levied.

While other shows may offer that kind of closure occasionally on specific cases, *SVU* does it habitually. *SVU* presents rape narratives of a wide array of victims in terms of gender, sexual orientation, class, race, and profession in its fifteen seasons, and throughout them all, at least one of the regular characters serves as a representative of the district attorney's office. As individual assistant district attorneys assigned to SVU, these characters play an important role in furthering the interests of the state whenever they appear, which happens frequently even before the point when a given case goes to court. The ADAs—particularly Alex Cabot, Casey Novak, and Rafael Barba—present legal angles and strategies to the detectives and viewers whenever they contribute to an episode, and they frequently take a hard stance when it comes to victims' accounts of what happened: The ADA is not interested in what Benson or the other SVU detectives believe. They are interested in what they can prove in court and what they can convince a jury of, beyond a reasonable doubt, and they serve as a constant reminder that the legal system comprises more than just the mostly sympathetic detectives in the SVU.

Because of their stance and the ADA's focus on whether a case can be made at trial, the prosecution fulfills a significant role in *Law and Order: SVU*, even in episodes where they do not appear. Over time, viewers are trained to expect that each case will likely end up at trial whether it is shown, and as such, viewers can anticipate the ADA's questions for and expectations of the detectives and the victims. Viewers frequently see the ADA asking victims difficult questions based on the understanding that the defense will ask those same questions and worse in court if they can get away with it. In those scenes, even the ADAs seem to recognize the ways in which a trial can serve as a revictimization, and in the broader scope of representing rape narratives, the prosecution in this role often ensures that by the time episodes reach the courtroom, viewers are firmly in support of the victim. Viewers have heard the victim's account multiple times, seen it tested from various angles by the SVU and the ADA, and are usually satisfied that the victim is credible.

By the time a case reaches trial in an episode of *SVU*, rape victims have already made it through two rounds of investigation. They have worked with Olivia and the other SVU detectives to determine who committed the crime, and both the victim and the evidence have convinced the ADA to move forward to trial. Because these two rounds of investigation are conducted by familiar characters that viewers see as allies in the quest for justice, viewers align themselves with the victims even more readily than they might if they determined their alliances based solely on the victim or the case itself. Whatever might or might not be true of the specifics of the case, the majority of viewers want a win in the courtroom for Olivia and for Cabot or Novak or Barba, depending on the season.

This alignment with the prosecution is visually reinforced by the orientation of the camera during the trial. In the physical space of the courtroom, viewers are almost always closest to the ADA and the jury. The defense table is typically shown from across a large room, and that distance serves as a reminder of the separation that exists between the defense's version of events and what viewers know to be true based on the investigations they witnessed earlier in the episode. This distance is also significant because it serves as a buffer between viewers and the individuals responsible for the crimes that have been committed. Frequently, viewers believe they know what really happened, and the drama in the courtroom comes from trying to determine what the jury will believe—and whether the episode will include the verdict at all. That tactic is used just often enough that the question exists in the back of viewers' minds as episodes draw to a close.

SVU viewers are familiar with the risks a rape victim takes when deciding to testify against a rapist in open court. Season Four, Episode Twenty-Two, "Futility,"[7] serves as a good example of several ways pursuing criminal proceedings can retraumatize people who have been raped. "Futility" begins when the accused, Michael Gardner, punches Olivia Benson in the face after she announces he is being arrested for rape.[8] That act of physical violence alone may have been enough to convince some viewers of his guilt, but there are three ways the justice system itself revictimizes the four women Michael Gardner is accused of stalking and raping. In order to provide his victims, who include Carrie Huitt and Karen Leighton, with orders of protection while Gardner is out on bail awaiting trial, the court must first provide Gardner with their home addresses. Some of the attacks happened in or near the women's homes, but not all of them. In those cases, the system itself hands Gardner information and access to these women that he may not have already had. The rationale makes sense—Gardner needs to know where he cannot go in order to avoid the women—but Carrie, Karen, and the others feel and potentially become more vulnerable once Gardner knows where they live.

"Futility" prominently features Bethany Taylor, a rape crisis counselor Carrie confides in after she is raped. When a question arises about the veracity of the lineup identification, the defense subpoenas Bethany, who refuses to discuss what Carrie told her in confidence. The judge orders Olivia to arrest her, and in a legal maneuver to get Bethany out of jail, Olivia goes to Carrie to convince her to waive her right to confidentiality. The following is Carrie's response to Olivia's request.

> **Carrie:** You're all sitting around waiting for me to shake this off and get back to normal. You have no idea. I can't sleep more than twenty minutes a night. I hate to be alone, but god, I hate to be around people more. And I am so afraid to walk outside or be in a crowded place, because you know, I might run into him. And all I can think to myself is it would have been so much better if he had just killed me. So, ah, that's what I talked to Bethany about. Because she told me that I could say anything to her and no one would ever know.[9]

As Carrie speaks, it is clear to viewers through her body language that she is extremely uncomfortable. While many rape victims turn to Olivia with these kinds of confidences, Carrie has not been one of them up to this point. Neither Olivia nor viewers were ever supposed to have access to these thoughts or feelings, and now that they do, it is likely that everyone involved feels the new sense of violation. Carrie believed she was safe when she told her counselor her fears and put words to the trauma she experienced. Instead, she has been forced to share them with Olivia, whom she does not view as a confidante, to say nothing of the fact that there are millions of people watching the narrative unfolding on television. If Carrie's own words quoted above weren't enough to make it clear to viewers that the system failed to protect her, Bethany makes it explicit that Olivia in particular contributed to not just Carrie's additional trauma but that of other victims as well. Six of Bethany's clients quit counseling, and she fears they won't seek the help they need from other avenues. Olivia attempts to rationalize the events that took place:

> **Olivia:** I did what I had to do to stop Michael Gardner from raping another woman.

Bethany: [. . .] You got your win. Who cares if it's at everyone else's expense?[10]

The third way in this episode the system enables the revictimization of women who have been raped is when Michael Gardner decides to exercise his right to represent himself in court. Whenever a defendant chooses to appear pro se, the victims of the crime being tried must not only face their attacker in court but also respond to their attacker directly. The defendants question their victims and gain no small amount of control over how the victims relive and also present to the jury their accounts of the crimes committed against them. In the case of Michael Gardner, the thought of facing him and having to answer his questions was enough to change Carrie's mind about testifying until Olivia convinced her to do so, another time when Olivia acts as a representative of the system and contributes to Carrie's retraumatization.

Eleven seasons later, Olivia finds herself in a position similar to Carrie's when she has to face William Lewis in a courtroom in Season Fifteen, Episode Ten, "Psycho/Therapist,"[11] as discussed in the previous chapter. Lewis eventually chooses to represent himself, and Olivia is forced to answer his questions about the four days he held her captive and the things he made her do and did to her. Lewis decides when Olivia will speak—asking the judge to compel her to speak at times, talking over her at others. He also has control over when she takes the stand; after Barba questions her for the prosecution, Olivia might have mentally prepared herself to face Lewis' questions, but he instead requests permission to recall her at a later time.

In addition to the amount of control Lewis' defense gives him over Olivia, this trial is significant because viewers have a much higher awareness of what transpired between the two of them during the four days in question. They know exactly what did and did not happen to Olivia, and they see how Lewis frames the specific details of those events in a way that twists them far enough from the truth to call Olivia's version into question but still fit the testimony of other witnesses. Unaccustomed to seeing Olivia in such a vulnerable position on the stand as the victim, viewers could draw connections between how Lewis works the system to twist Olivia's words and the way the same can be done to twist other victims' statements in other cases. Viewers know in "Psycho/Therapist" that Lewis is manipulating the truth, and in this particular example, they know he has done it before, to more victims than just Olivia. Nevertheless, there are still brief moments in which it is almost understandable that the jury believes Lewis' story, calling attention to the ways in which society—represented by a jury of Lewis' peers—believes stories even less masterfully manipulated than William Lewis'.

In addition to the role it sometimes plays as a physical space for revictimization, the courtroom, and the preparation that leads up to it, also serves as a place to explore real-world issues surrounding the prosecution of rapes. In her chapter "Popular Re-presentations" from *Rape on Trial*, Lisa M. Cuklanz explains that "in the fictionalized texts, the characters, their stories, and the accompanying problems and tensions are presented in personal or interpersonal terms rather than in generalized, social terms. In other words, the exigencies of a tightly controlled plot are at odds with the full expression of a political message, and each story stops short of suggesting radical changes in power structures or cultural practices."[12] While her contention that there is no call for radical change may be accurate, one way rape narratives that play out in the courtroom can be effective is by shining a spotlight on and giving a face to what might otherwise be easily dismissed statistics about the realities of rape. For instance, *SVU* is the only one of the shows considered in this project—including *The Good Wife*, which will be discussed in the next chapter—to give a man who has been raped the opportunity to put his account of what happened to him on the record. In Season Three, Episode Ten, "Ridicule,"[13] *SVU* addresses how men who report being raped, especially when the perpetrators are women,[14] as is the case in this episode, are treated. When he first meets Olivia and Elliot, Peter explains that when he reported his rape, "the cops treated [him] like dirt, made fun of [him], brought [him] to the hospital and told the nurse it was a scam."[15] In addition to that account, the SVU detectives are not actually investigating Peter's rape; they are investigating him as a potential suspect in the murder of one of his rapists. The case does eventually end up in court and the other two women who raped Peter eventually confess, but this representation of how male victims can be treated by the system that is supposed to help them is significant. Another reason this episode is important is because of Elliot's lack of compassion for Peter. Not only does Elliot attempt to argue that Peter's arousal equals consent, but the episode also suggests that his job as a stripper does the same. There are plenty of episodes in which the detectives assure female victims that neither of those factors serves as consent, and that Elliot argues differently because of the gender of the victim points out one of the ways that even the SVU detectives get the investigation and prosecution of rape wrong.

Even earlier, in Season Two, Episode Seven, "Asunder,"[16] a rape narrative addresses not only a defendant who is a police officer, but also the fact that at the time of this trial, ADA Alex Cabot is the only lawyer in the *SVU* universe's New York to have successfully convinced a grand jury to indict in a case of spousal rape. "Asunder" aired on December 1, 2000, so to that point, at least in the *SVU* universe, raping one's spouse had never been brought to trial. While "Ridicule" was the first mention of the real-world 1984 case *People v. Liberta* in an episode, the results of it are relevant here as it was the case that criminalized spousal rape in the United States.[17] So while it is true that marital rape had been criminal for sixteen years by the time this episode aired, *SVU* blatantly calls attention to the lack of criminal proceedings that address it.

Another rape-related issue brought up through a rape prosecution narrative is in Season Fourteen, Episode Eighteen, "Legitimate Rape," [18] regarding the parental rights of a rapist whose victim conceives a child during the assault. The title is an acknowledgment of Todd Akin's infamous comments from 2012, and the episode, which aired in March 2013, not only includes a defendant who represents himself in court and a woman who becomes pregnant as a result of her rape but a second trial, a custody battle in family court, between Avery Jordan, the mother, and her rapist.

In this episode, a former congressman, also a medical doctor, takes the stand on behalf of the defendant to explain how "the body has a mechanism for shutting down ovulation in response to stress."

> **Defendant:** And if a pregnant woman came to your office claiming she had been raped, your response would be?
>
> **Congressman:** I would tell her, Honey, if you need to lie to yourself or your family, okay. But don't lie to Doc Showalter or the Lord. [19]

When this argument strikes a chord with a deeply religious juror, the jury splits the charges—they declare the defendant not guilty of rape but guilty of stalking. If the criminal trial weren't retraumatizing enough, Avery must then face her stalker (because the man was acquitted of the rape charge) in family court when he sues for custody of her son. "When does it end? Do I have to live with the man who raped me in my life forever?" Avery asks. While her stalker is granted minimal supervised visitation, Avery has the financial resources to flee the country, which she does at the end of the episode. But in addition to all that her trials have called attention to throughout the episode, the show calls attention to the laws addressing custody of children conceived through rape. According to ADA Barba, a rapist can sue for custody in thirty-one states: He has even "seen [a custody suit] used in acquaintance rape cases just to get the victim to drop charges. And they call that law?" [20]

Throughout the fifteen seasons of *SVU*, there are also several instances of rape trials in military court, at least two episodes that focus on trials over freedom of speech and rape jokes, and a variety of other rape-related issues that have made headlines in the real world as well as in the SVU universe. Because of the variety of issues considered and also due to the way those issues are presented—by characters with whom viewers have established relationships—the rape narratives that account for the prosecution of those crimes can be instructive for viewers who are sympathetic to the struggles faced by the victims themselves but also for more skeptical viewers who are likely to side with Olivia and Barba (or whichever character serves to represent the prosecution) for reasons that may have little to do with the specifics of a case and more to do with their investment in those recurring characters.

Perhaps not too surprisingly, this is also true for all of the shows considered before this point that include prosecution. With the possible exception of *CSI*, all these police dramas follow the development of characters whose professional lives are dedicated to serving the state, and as such, viewers find themselves siding with the prosecution more often than not in the legal battles. And realistically, even though characters on *CSI* repeatedly state that the criminalists are not investigators, that they are impartial and merely interpret evidence, they are accused frequently enough by the defense of working in conjunction with the state (and seen by viewers actually doing so) that the line is blurred even as dialogue attempts to convince viewers otherwise.

The presentation of courtroom drama in these shows is significant because the frequency with which viewers see the state fighting for rape victims does somewhat obscure the fact that, when it comes to reporting a rape, representatives of the state are often the first battle in a long series victims will have to face. For every example of the various ways in which some aspect of the system serves to revictimize, there is a mention of how successful the Manhattan SVU and ADAs are in prosecuting rape. For instance, in Season Eight, Episode Fifteen, "Haystack,"[21] Elliot Stabler and Casey Novak end up in court as defendants in a police harassment suit, and their attorney states that Elliot has a 97% closure rate for his cases while Novak's is 71%, both well above the national average. The detectives and attorneys on *SVU* are presented as highly successful professionally, and viewers see enough examples to believe those numbers.

The criminal rape trials portrayed on *Law and Order: Special Victims Unit* and other shows shine light on two different perspectives of individual crimes. While it is clear from the beginning of any given trial which side most viewers will take, these trials are also used in an instructive capacity that calls attention to the rape myths and narratives that the defense—either attorneys or the accused themselves—use to attempt to discredit victims' statements. Paul Bergman's discussion of a possible third rapist—the representations themselves—addresses a concern about the effects these narratives might have in the real world. He explains that "to the extent that rape complainants' reluctance to report their attackers to the police is due to their beliefs that the formal legal system will treat all rape complainants like them harshly and unfairly, the television portrayals do constitute a third rapist."[22] While there is room yet to definitively tie television portrayals to the reluctance of real-world rape complainants, the representations themselves and the messages they spread give viewers clear and specific ways to align themselves with the victims and play instructive roles about rape-related issues while portraying clear examples of the ways the criminal justice system does not always best serve the interests of the rape victims it is meant to represent.

NOTES

1. Paul Bergman, "A Third Rapist? Television Portrayals of Rape Evidence Rules," in *Law and Justice on the Small Screen*, ed. Peter Robson and Jessica Silby (Portland, OR: Hart Publishing, 2012), 154, 155.

2. Josh Berman and Anthony E. Zuiker, "Pledging Mr. Johnson," *CSI*, season 1, episode 4, directed by Richard J. Lewis, aired on October 27, 2000 (Hollywood: Paramount Home Entertainment, 2003), DVD.

3. Aaron Zelman, "Machismo," *Criminal Minds*, season 1, episode 19, directed by Guy Norman Bee, aired on April 12, 2006 (Hollywood: Paramount Home Entertainment, 2006), DVD.

4. Breen Frazier, "Unknown Subject," *Criminal Minds*, season 7, episode 12, directed by Michael Lange, aired on January 25, 2012 (Hollywood: Paramount Home Entertainment, 2012), DVD.

5. Ibid.

6. Ibid.

7. Michele Fazekas and Tara Butters, "Futility," *Law and Order: Special Victims Unit*, season 4, episode 22, directed by Alex Zakrzewski, aired on April 25, 2003, http://www.hulu.com/watch/159299#i0,p20,s4,d0.

8. Michael Gardner is played by Fred Savage, the actor still best known for his role as Kevin Arnold in *The Wonder Years*. It is interesting that one of the very first things viewers see his character in *SVU* do is perpetrate an act of violence against a beloved character; it forces viewers who recognize the actor to immediately adjust their thinking about him.

9. Fazekas and Butters, "Futility."

10. Ibid.

11. Julie Martin and Warren Leight, "Psycho/Therapist," *Law and Order: Special Victims Unit*, season 15, episode 10, directed by Michael Slovis, aired on January 8, 2014, http://www.hulu.com/watch/580385#i0,p8,s15,d0.

12. Lisa M. Cuklanz, "Popular Re-presentations," in *Rape on Trial: How the Mass Media Construct Legal Reform and Social Change* (Philadelphia: University of Pennsylvania Press, 1995), 87.

13. Judith McCreary, "Ridicule," *Law and Order: Special Victims Unit*, season 3, episode 10, directed by Constantine Makris, aired on December 14, 2001, http://www.hulu.com/watch/159299#i0,p8,s3,d0.

14. Coincidentally, Diane Neal, the actress who plays ADA Casey Novak beginning in Season Five, also has a small role as one of three female rapists in "Ridicule."

15. McCreary, "Ridicule."

16. Judith McCreary, "Asunder," *Law and Order: Special Victims Unit*, season 2, episode 7, directed by David Platt, aired on December 1, 2000, http://www.hulu.com/watch/159188#i0,p4,s2,d0.

17. *People v. Liberta*, 64 N.Y.2d 152, 474 N.E.2d 567, 485 N.Y.S.2d 207 (1984).

18. Kevin Fox and Peter Blauner, "Legitimate Rape," *Law and Order: Special Victims Unit*, season 14, episode 18, directed by Jonathan Herron, aired on March 27, 2013, http://www.hulu.com/watch/472480#i0,p16,s14,d0.

19. Ibid.

20. Ibid.

21. Amanda Green, "Haystack," *Law and Order: Special Victims Unit*, season 8, episode 15, directed by Peter Leto, aired on February 20, 2007, http://www.hulu.com/watch/275495#i0,p12,s8,d0.

22. Bergman, "A Third Rapist?" 172.

REFERENCES

Bergman, Paul. "A Third Rapist? Television Portrayals of Rape Evidence Rules." In *Law and Justice on the Small Screen*, edited by Peter Robson and Jessica Silby, 153–172. Portland, OR: Hart Publishing, 2012.

Berman, Josh, and Anthony E. Zuiker. "Pledging Mr. Johnson." *CSI*. Season 1. DVD. Directed by Richard J. Lewis. Aired on October 27, 2000. Hollywood: Paramount Home Entertainment, 2003.

Cuklanz, Lisa M. "Popular Re-presentations." In *Rape on Trial: How the Mass Media Construct Legal Reform and Social Change*, 85–113. Philadelphia: University of Pennsylvania Press, 1995.

Fazekas, Michele, and Tara Butters. "Futility." *Law and Order: Special Victims Unit*. Online. Directed by Alex Zakrzewski. Aired on April 25, 2003. http://www.hulu.com/watch/159299#i0,p20,s4,d0.

Fox, Kevin, and Peter Blauner. "Legitimate Rape." *Law and Order: Special Victims Unit*. Online. Directed by Jonathan Herron. Aired on March 27, 2013. http://www.hulu.com/watch/472480#i0,p16,s14,d0.

Frazier, Breen. "Unknown Subject." *Criminal Minds*. Season 7. DVD. Directed by Michael Lange. Aired on January 25, 2012. Hollywood: Paramount Home Entertainment, 2012.

Green, Amanda. "Haystack." *Law and Order: Special Victims Unit*. Online. Directed by Peter Leto. Aired on February 20, 2007. http://www.hulu.com/watch/275495#i0,p12,s8,d0.

Martin, Julie, and Warren Leight. "Psycho/Therapist." *Law and Order: Special Victims Unit*. Online. Directed by Michael Slovis. Aired on January 8, 2014. http://www.hulu.com/watch/580385#i0,p8,s15,d0.

McCreary, Judith. "Asunder." *Law and Order: Special Victims Unit*. Online. Directed by David Platt. Aired on December 1, 2000. http://www.hulu.com/watch/159188#i0,p4,s2,d0.

———. "Ridicule." *Law and Order: Special Victims Unit*. Online. Directed by Constantine Makris. Aired on December 14, 2001. http://www.hulu.com/watch/159299#i0,p8,s3,d0.

People v. Liberta, 64 N.Y.2d 152, 474 N.E.2d 567, 485 N.Y.S.2d 207 (1984).

Zelman, Aaron. "Machismo." *Criminal Minds*. Season 1. DVD. Directed by Guy Norman Bee. Aired on April 12, 2006. Hollywood: Paramount Home Entertainment, 2006.

Chapter Eight

"If It Forces You to Prosecute" [1]

The Good Wife *and Helping Victims*
Take Back Their Voice

It makes sense to talk about *The Good Wife* last when this conversation started with *NCIS*. The shows work well as bookends, separated by all the shows between that offered either fumbling or empowering representations of rape narratives—sometimes a combination of both in the same show, the same episode. Whatever else *NCIS* is, it is certainly the show that works the hardest to silence or discredit the stories of women who are raped. *The Good Wife* is the opposite: nearly every instance of a rape narrative throughout the first four seasons of the series depicts main characters working to amplify the voices of rape victims, help them tell their stories, and give them their day in court.

Maybe that makes sense in a show that, in a lot of ways, is centered around controlling various narratives. The opening scene [2] of *The Good Wife* features a press conference in which Peter Florrick, the Illinois state's attorney, resigns from office and publicly apologizes to his wife Alicia and his constituents in an attempt to get ahead of the sex scandal and ethics violation that will eventually send him to prison. Alicia stands at his side, silent, impeccably dressed, and unreadable; she is, in that scene at least, the "good wife" of the show's title. And while her position as Peter's wife continues throughout the first four seasons of the show, it frequently takes a backseat to her other roles: mother, woman, and lawyer once she obtains a job practicing law at Lockhart/Gardner. [3] It is through her job that Alicia comes into contact with the various rape narratives presented on the show, and though her response to every victim is not perfect, she frequently works in a professional capacity to create and maintain a space in which rape victims are given the opportunity to have their voices heard.

While *The Good Wife* borrows elements from the legal-procedural format, it also relies heavily on serial plots—like the ongoing struggles and triumphs in Alicia's relationship with her husband and her associate Will Gardner. The show is well received by critics and was ranked the fourteenth top broadcast drama for its 2013–2014 season.[4] Julianna Margulies has won two Primetime Emmy Awards for her portrayal of Alicia Florrick, in 2011 and 2014, and the show itself has been nominated twice, in 2010 and 2011. In 2013, *The Good Wife* was described as "the deftest portrayal of technology on TV" by *Wired* magazine[5] and "miles ahead of anything else that's on at the moment" by the *New York Times*.[6] That last comment is particularly true in the one area of greatest concern here: representing and portraying rape narratives.

Whereas the first ten seasons of *NCIS*, a show that deals with investigating military crimes, contain zero episodes that directly address military sexual trauma, the first four seasons of *The Good Wife* contain several—while it is only one case, the victim becomes a recurring character on the show, appearing in seven episodes during Season Four. Army Captain Laura Hellinger is introduced in Season Four, Episode Six, "The Art of War,"[7] and what happened to her presents a clear example of military sexual trauma. While serving in Afghanistan, Captain Hellinger was raped. She received no justice through military court and, with encouragement from Colonel Leora Kuhn, who has worked with Alicia before, she seeks Alicia's help in a civil suit against her attacker and the military contractor who employs him. The narrative arc of the episode gives Captain Hellinger, a member of the Judge Advocate General's (JAG) corps, a very real voice as a part of her own defense. Not only can she accuse her rapist and testify about what happened to her in a court of law, but she is also able to stand in the courtroom and participate in questioning and cross-examining witnesses as a part of the suit. In just this one episode, *The Good Wife* does more to address military sexual assault than ten seasons of *NCIS*, all while simultaneously showing an example of a rape victim who participates actively in the quest for her own justice.

Of course, there is more to "The Art of War" than just a comparison with *NCIS*. Though she has argued before military court in earlier episodes, Alicia Florrick is a civilian. Captain Hellinger must bring her case to civilian, civil court because she has already exhausted her options within the military justice system, and she has no grounds for a criminal trial outside of it. Colonel Kuhn, a military judge before whom Alicia has previously argued, explains that while Captain Hellinger cannot sue the military, "the attacker was an employee of Martinell Security, one of the independent contractors in Afghanistan." She continues: "Given the evidence was deemed insufficient for criminal prosecution, [Hellinger] decided to sue in civil court."[8]

The investigation into what happened to Captain Hellinger in Afghanistan as Alicia searches for evidence she can use to win in court definitively supports the claim that the woman was raped, yet she found no justice within the system set up by the military, even with a sympathetic senior officer's involvement in the case. Additionally at issue is the fact that Captain Hellinger would have no recourse in civilian court had her rapist been a military serviceman. Bucky Stabler, counsel representing the army, Martinell, and ultimately Hellinger's rapist, uses *Feres v. the United States* to establish precedent, as Feres protects the military from being sued:

> **Bucky:** *Feres vs. the United States*, your honor. A serviceman, or woman such as the plaintiff, cannot sue the military, therefore by extension they cannot sue a contractor which is deemed an arm of the military.
>
> **Alicia:** Your honor, the military contractor must prove their aims and independence are subjected to the military, and unless Martinell can prove that the military ordered this rape—
>
> **Bucky:** Excuse me. That is offensive, your honor.
>
> **Alicia:** No. The offense here is you are trying to protect one of your employees from facing his accuser in court. Captain Hellinger has served her country for twelve years. At the very least, she deserves to face her rapist.[9]

Alicia's response, particularly at the end of this exchange, seems reasonable whether the accused is military personnel, but that is exactly the issue at stake: Does Captain Hellinger have cause to bring civil suit against the man who raped her in a civilian court? Alicia obtains her first win in this case when she convinces the judge that Ricky Waters, Captain Hellinger's accused rapist, is not immune to prosecution. The judge demands that he be made available for questioning, and Captain Hellinger's response to the ruling is telling.

> **Hellinger:** We won!
>
> **Alicia:** Not yet.
>
> **Hellinger:** You don't understand. Seeing him in court? We won.[10]

Because that is the justice available to victims of military sexual trauma in the version of the military that exists in the universe of *The Good Wife*— regardless of the outcome of a trial, just facing the man who raped her in a civilian court is more than Captain Hellinger expected to achieve.

The second win comes later as a part of Lockhart/Gardner's investigation into what actually happened to Captain Hellinger in Afghanistan. After Waters does what he can in court to turn Hellinger's account of events into a familiar "he said/she said" distortion of the facts (she was drunk, I walked her home, she must be angry that I turned down her advances), Kalinda, an investigator with Alicia's firm, discovers a witness to the attack who was afraid to come forward previously. Even though Sergeant Wade Compton is only a witness to the crime, he explains he feared retribution from his superiors if he reported what he heard. When Alicia questions him about why he didn't come forward, Sergeant Compton responds, "Mr. Waters is kind of like my boss. I mean, he's close with my [commanding officer]."[11] A discussion of Compton's fear for his job follows a comment Alicia made earlier about the fact that Captain Hellinger was being pressured to quit her own job and the military altogether as a result of her attack. The discovery of this witness to the attack not only solidifies Captain Hellinger's account of what happened, a clear boon for Alicia's case, but gives name to the fear felt by someone who only witnessed the crime, and a male witness at that. The specifics of this story arc as it unfolds make the situation faced by Captain Hellinger, and other potential victims of military sexual trauma, even clearer to viewers; if the male witness felt threatened in that manner, how must the female victim have felt?

Securing the testimony of the witness and forcing the accused to appear is as far as the court can go toward redressing the wrongs committed against Captain Hellinger. Judge Abernathy, a recurring character consistently portrayed as an outspoken liberal who refuses to allow his political opinions to color his judgments, delivers the ruling:

> I have given this a great deal of thought. And I want you to know, Captain Hellinger, that I am truly sympathetic to your plight. To be denied justice in military court was tragic. To be denied justice again in civilian court is just cruel. But I'm afraid the Supreme Court has spoken very clearly in Feres as much as I may personally disagree. Mr. Waters was an Army reservist at the time of the attack, and therefore he is immune from liability. As such, I'm afraid I must dismiss this case.[12]

Speaking through Judge Abernathy and the specifics of Captain Laura Hellinger's story, *The Good Wife* takes on the idea that it is the very structure of the military justice system that makes it impossible for there to be any justice in this scenario. The military courts couldn't do anything for Captain Hellinger, and then the very fact that the accused was military keeps the civilian justice system from being able to do anything either.

After Abernathy announces his ruling—that even though it is clear something happened, legal precedent has tied his hands—Alicia and Laura sit in the courtroom. Everyone else has gone. When Alicia announces that they can appeal, Laura says no. Alicia apologizes, but Laura responds, "Hey, you got me into court. That's more than I thought we'd do."[13] And that might be the worst of it all. Because even though Captain Laura Hellinger found herself in a position that gave her a loud, clear voice in seeking justice against her rapist, she had little to no expectation of being able to actually achieve it. Her defeatist attitude—in this case, well earned—is just one of the instances in which characters on *The Good Wife* show an awareness of the realities of contemporary rape culture.

In terms of a broader discussion about rape narratives on *The Good Wife*, there are several additional reasons why this particular case is significant. As mentioned previously, Laura Hellinger becomes a recurring character on the show after this first introduction—she leaves the military, goes to work for Peter Florrick (who is back in the state's attorney's office), and briefly dates Will Gardner, a partner at Alicia's firm, with whom Alicia herself has history. Viewers are given ample opportunity to see Laura Hellinger respond to what happened to her and then move on with her life. She is portrayed as more than just a victim; she is a survivor who plays a role in the overall narrative of the show that transcends her status as "victim." Laura Hellinger's case also fits the trend of most rape narratives addressed on the show: although most of Lockhart/Gardner's work revolves around defending the rights of the accused, more often than not, Alicia and the other lawyers at her firm find themselves arguing for the victims in the eighteen episodes that portray rape narratives in the first four seasons. Given the firm's business model, and the fact that among Alicia's clients are suspected murderers and drug dealers, an attorney at Lockhart/Gardner should most likely argue for someone being accused of rape, not someone doing the accusing.

This pattern is established in the first episode of *The Good Wife* to deal with a rape narrative: Season One, Episode Two, "Stripped."[14] When Alicia is called into a meeting with a potential client, she learns that four months prior, Christy Barbosa was raped while working as a stripper at a bachelor party. Christy is asking Lockhart/Gardner to file a civil suit against her rapist as the state's attorney has declined to prosecute, but Will expresses concern over taking Christy's case.

> **Will:** Well, the problem here, Christy, is that any civil suit could be seen as opportunistic.
>
> **Christy:** Because of their money?
>
> **Will:** Yes.
>
> **Christy:** I'm sorry, but I didn't choose my rapist.[15]

The accused is a member of the McKeon family, a wealthy and influential family in *The Good Wife*'s Chicago. In addition to raising the question of Christy's perceived motives, Will refers to similarities between Christy's case and the rape scandal involving Duke University's lacrosse team.[16] Calling attention to this real-world controversy in the context of this episode ties what happens in the universe of *The Good Wife* to events that viewers could easily be familiar with through other avenues, developing connections between the show's representations of rape narratives and those of real-world media.

Will's final concern is that Christy's case really belongs in criminal, not civil, court. The decision not to prosecute made by Peter Florrick's replacement offers a glimpse into the world of rape prosecution; low reporting rates are only one part of the problem. Even after a victim reports, there is always the possibility that her story won't be believed or that the powers that be will decline to prosecute for lack of evidence, which is what happened to Christy. Will highlights this problem when asked whether he believes Christy's story: "I believe a lot of things I can't prove."[17]

Because "Stripped" is the first episode of *The Good Wife* to address a rape narrative, it sets the tone for how the rest of the show will address similar story lines. Lockhart/Gardner agrees to take on the victim's case in civil court, and while they might be in it for the money, the show does maneuver the narrative enough that the main characters end up fighting on the side of the victim, a trend that continues throughout most of the first four seasons. Viewers will repeatedly, and almost exclusively, see Alicia, Will, Diane Lockhart, and other familiar faces advocating for rape victims in the courts. Additionally, this episode showcases the ways in which the criminal justice system can fail people who have been raped. It addresses the prosecutor's prerogative to decide whether a case is winnable, and in instances where the case is dropped, victims are left with little recourse other than costly civil litigation. Another issue addressed specifically in "Stripped" is the processing of rape kits. While the civil suit in this episode is decided in favor of the defendant, the ruling is due to the cross-contamination of a DNA sample collected as evidence. While on the stand testifying in open court, the doctor who tested the contaminated sample explains that his lab handles "an immense backlog of untested rape kits from crime labs all across the country."[18] This narrative shines light on the real-world problem of somewhere around four hundred thousand untested rape kits across the United States,[19] a number that comes from the Department of Justice.

This first episode goes even further in addressing frequent issues in rape narratives. Will's early questions about Christy's motives—whether she is just going for money—are underlined by her profession. Employed by the accused as a stripper for his bachelor party when she was raped, Christy also worked for a time in the recent past as an escort. Kalinda reveals this fact to Alicia, and they have the following exchange:

Alicia: So what's your point, a call girl can't get raped?

Kalinda: Yeah, that's my point, thanks. Look, she lied to us. Why believe her now?

Alicia: Because she walked away from half a million dollars? And when did she ever lie to us?[20]

Though Kalinda's tone is difficult to read—she was likely being sarcastic in her response to Alicia—the real point is that with zero prompting, the main character of *The Good Wife* not only affirms that strippers and escorts can be victims of rape but also solidifies the fact that throughout this whole episode, Alicia has believed Christy's account of events, and nothing has happened to change her mind—or, if they identify with Alicia's perspective, the minds of the viewers.

Christy's refusal to settle out of court for five hundred thousand dollars is important not only because it apparently convinced Alicia but also because it sends a message that there is more to Christy's quest for justice against her rapist than a payday: she turns down the money because if she doesn't, "he'll know how much it costs to rape somebody and get away with it, that's all. This is about him admitting that he did this to me."[21] And while the outcome of the civil suit isn't what Christy and Alicia had hoped for, they were able to achieve justice in the end. McKeon is met outside the courtroom by the press and begins to give a statement: "This is all I want to say. I have been falsely accused by a woman who wanted nothing more than a quick payday. But every year, there are thousands of women who are abused, and I don't think we should let this false accusation . . ."[22] His supremely hypocritical speech is interrupted by the police who arrive to arrest him for the rape of Christy Barbosa. Glenn Childs, the new state's attorney, is there to gloat over his predecessor's wife.

Childs: Must be hard to lose, Mrs. Florrick.

Alicia: Not if it forces you to prosecute.

Childs: I'm coming out of this with a criminal case I'll win. You're coming out with a loss. Nice job.[23]

Though Alicia may have lost, Christy didn't. Alicia stood next to her, helping Christy fight for her voice as a victim, first in civil court and then again in the promise of a criminal case that the prosecution will likely win, since the state's attorney's office has discovered an uncontaminated DNA sample, new evidence that should convict the rapist. So even while reaching a conclusion that means justice for Christy Barbosa, this first episode of *The Good Wife* to incorporate a rape narrative takes the time to address the fact that the system does not always work for rape victims. That may be enough to get viewers thinking about all the other rape victims in the *The Good Wife* universe for whom the state's attorney's office declines to prosecute and who might not have the resources to pursue other avenues of legal recourse; it may also get viewers thinking about rape victims who find themselves in similar circumstances in the real world.

As far as viewers are aware, Alicia Florrick has no prior history with sexual violence. She is a private person, almost always reserved and guarded, and it is never suggested that she was raped or sexually assaulted. Her motivation for becoming a lawyer is never considered either; it is just what Alicia does. Even so, it becomes clear early on in *The Good Wife* that Alicia aligns herself with rape victims. She seems to understand what they face during the process of a trial, and she works to ensure they have as much of a voice as they want within the justice system. Season Two, Episode Five, "VIP Treatment,"[24] is an important episode to consider in terms of this idea because not all victims will choose to pursue legal recourse.

In "VIP Treatment," Alicia is pulled out of a formal event to meet with a massage therapist considering a civil suit after having been sexually assaulted by a client. Laura White explains: "I went to the police, and they, um, I guess I sounded nuts so I came here. Because of you."[25] While the majority of Alicia's reputation arose from her husband's scandal, there is a trend throughout the series of rape victims turning to her specifically for help. Viewers see that story line play out in all three of the episodes that have been introduced so far, and there are more to come.

In this particular episode, Laura White was not raped, but she was sexually assaulted. And her attacker is even more famous in the universe of *The Good Wife* than Christy Barbosa's: Laura was attacked while providing massage services for Joe Kent, a name immediately recognized by Alicia and the partners at her firm as that of a man world-renowned for his work with women's rights issues, particularly in third-world countries. In fact, he is in Chicago after recently receiving a Nobel Peace Prize for that work. While Alicia is surprised and nearly dismisses Laura's claims, she ultimately calls in the partners.

Surprisingly, it is Diane Lockhart, who leans hard left politically, who most strongly opposes taking the case. She is the one who sends an investigator out to determine whether Laura is lying. Will and Derrick Bond, who buys in as the third named partner for part of Season Two, see the case as an opportunity to make quite a lot of money. Whether they believe Laura's story, they are willing to move forward and work for her; they also send out an investigator, but Kalinda is to investigate Kent. The partners then question Laura, asking her about the specific details of her attack, about her profession, and about whether she is the kind of massage therapist to provide other, sexual services. Laura makes it very clear that behavior would get her fired and that she was unable to extract herself from the situation earlier for the same reason: her job is dependent on her ability to keep the hotel's VIP guests happy. After she has fully recounted the details of her assault, Diane questions her demeanor.

> **Diane:** Miss White, don't take this the wrong way, but given that this happened five hours ago, you seem remarkably calm.
>
> **Laura:** I'm not sure how I'm supposed to take that the right way.
>
> **Diane:** Take it as the first of a long line of hard questions.
>
> **Laura:** Would it make a difference if I was crying?
>
> **Diane:** You were sexually assaulted. Wouldn't that make sense?
>
> **Laura:** When I was kicked out of college, I cried for an hour. Then I stopped, and I never cried again. That's who I am. But if it helps, I wish this had happened to somebody who cried a lot. [26]

Whether viewers could go so far as to suggest that some of the questions lean in the direction of victim-blaming, it is interesting that under the guise of posing the difficult questions, some characters can attempt to mask their distrust of victims in the name of preparing the victim for the kinds of questions she would face in a courtroom.

That is not Alicia, though. In this episode, Alicia isn't the character posing those questions. Instead, she is the one viewers see sitting alone in a room with the victim while the partners discuss whether they believe Laura's story and whether they will take on her case. The conversation the two women have in private calls more attention to the uphill battle faced by sexual assault victims—particularly in high-profile cases:

> **Laura:** Is this a mistake?
>
> **Alicia:** It's a process, Laura. We have to go through it.
>
> **Laura:** Yeah. My friends will be like "what are you doing? He's helping women. Suck it up. I thought you were on our side." [27]

It is at this point that Laura provides Alicia with a piece of physical evidence to support her version of events: a towel into which Joe Kent ejaculated. Later in the episode, Lockhart/Gardner is able to further corroborate Laura's claims when the investigation uncovers another massage therapist with a similar complaint against Joe Kent.

But in the end, whatever evidence they have doesn't matter. Laura White makes a decision to get up and walk away. At no time does she recant her story or try to explain away what happened to her. She makes no excuses for herself or for Joe Kent. The specifics of her assault, who was where and when, are complicated, and when faced with Kent's reputation and the possibility that she won't be believed, Laura decides against filing suit. By this point in the episode, viewers know she came to Alicia and Lockhart/Gardner after talking with Cary Agos, a former associate at the firm who now works for Peter Florrick at the state's attorney's office. The state's attorney declined to press criminal charges, and when Laura sees what she is up against in the response she receives at Alicia's firm, she makes a decision about how she will move forward.

> **Alicia:** We tried to do too much in one night. You get some sleep, give me a call in the morning.
>
> **Laura:** No. I'm done.
>
> **Alicia:** We found another masseur he molested.
>
> **Laura:** She didn't bring charges.
>
> **Alicia:** No. Same thing happened to her. She was giving him a massage, and he attacked her.
>
> **Laura:** Why didn't she bring charges?
>
> **Alicia:** She was afraid.[28]

The conversation continues briefly, but Laura's decision in the end is to walk away. And Alicia lets her. There are plenty of reasons, several considered in this episode, that sexual assaults don't get reported. None of them exactly apply here since Laura did report the crime committed against her, but her decision not to pursue legal action against Joe Kent in the end is important because it was exactly that: her decision. Laura White's agency was stripped from her when she was assaulted and again by the criminal justice system when the state's attorney declined to prosecute her case—they made that decision; she did not. By watching her walk away, Alicia acknowledges Laura's right to make up her own mind. Laura has told her story, and she knows there are people who believe her. Whether the feeling will last, she has convinced herself that is enough. And Alicia supports her by spending most of their time together listening, allowing Laura to determine which silences to fill and which stories to tell, and watching her leave.

The last instance of a similar rape narrative—Lockhart/Gardner representing a victim in a civil case—is Season Four, Episode Twenty, "Rape: A Modern Perspective."[29] In this episode, high school student Rainey Selwin was raped and her attack was captured on video and then disseminated through social media. There are many similarities between this case and the real-world events that took place in Steubenville, Ohio, when an underage Jane Doe was repeatedly raped by several football players who recorded the events.[30] About a month before "Rape: A Modern Perspective" aired in April 2013, the media coverage of the Steubenville sentencing included anchors on CNN lamenting the rapists' lost potential and their promising futures, another specific facet of the real-world case of which the episode does seem aware.[31] That isn't the only real-world news headline the universe of *The Good Wife* draws on in this episode, either.

The episode opens with a visual representation of a tweet: "I don't care if they put me in jail. Todd Brasher RAPED ME."[32] Viewers are then introduced to Rainey when she is on the stand being questioned by her attorney, Will Gardner, who addresses the fact that the proceedings are taking place in civil, rather than criminal, court.

Will: So, Rainey, why are you suing your rapist . . . your accused rapist?

Rainey: He's not in jail. He raped me and got a plea bargain with the prosecution so he's going to Princeton, not prison. I don't think he should get off scot-free.

Will: So the money, the amount you are suing him for?

Rainey: It's going to rape victim advocates. I just want it to cost him something. I don't want anything.[33]

At this point, Judge Robert Parks interrupts Rainey's testimony and has the jury removed from the courtroom. Judge Parks has just received a copy of the previously mentioned tweet, which violates the gag order he put on the case to keep it from being tried in the press. He wants to know whether Rainey wrote the tweet.

Against Will's advice that Rainey insist on her Fifth Amendment right against self-incrimination, she tells the truth: "Todd Brasher raped me so I wrote that."[34] When Parks holds her in contempt of court, a sheriff takes her into custody. In order to secure her release, Judge Parks demands Rainey apologize and promise not to tweet again. She refuses.

Rainey: Let's say this goes against me.

Alicia: We have a good case.

Rainey: But the prosecutors had a good case, and Todd Brasher is free, so let's say this goes against me. Then what's out there is not "Todd Brasher is a rapist." What's out there is "I'm sorry for calling Todd Brasher a rapist."[35]

By refusing to apologize, Rainey gives up her freedom for the length of the trial, but she retains control of her own speech, of what she will do with the voice she has been given within the scope of this second trial of Todd Brasher.

Another way Rainey's case mimics the Steubenville case is the involvement of Anonymous, a hacker collective, which leaked evidence and announced the names of the rapists on the Internet in both cases. For Rainey, Anonymous hacked into Brasher's cell phone and sent Alicia's teenaged son Zach incriminating video and photographs. Those online activities are combined with courtroom activism—showing up for court wearing Guy Fawkes masks and chanting "Justice for Rainey" until Judge Parks has them removed. While their actions are disruptive, and some are even illegal, these Anonymous supporters of Rainey help her achieve a kind of justice that the actual justice system seems to be standing in the way of, since Rainey is the one in custody and her rapist received a plea bargain.

Some of the evidence uncovered by Anonymous is introduced into court and proves to be both detrimental (as their actions cause Judge Parks to declare a mistrial) and essential (as new information forces Parks to reconsider his position) to Will and Alicia's case. A second video, this time of Todd's police interview, includes what is essentially a confession that Will uses to secure Rainey's release: "Rainey is being imprisoned for speaking the truth. And that is wrong. This video proves it."[36] The episode ends with Rainey being released from jail, but with no official word on the outcome of the trial. While viewers have enough information to make certain assumptions about the results, the real focus of this episode, from the opening tweet to the final scene of Rainey's release, is Rainey retaining her voice in the face of a second rape trial, and this time it is Will, not Alicia, who takes point with the victim.

One more aspect of "Rape: A Modern Perspective" worth consideration is the way that it draws on other real-world rape headlines beyond Steubenville. When Todd's defense attorney calls to the stand a doctor who testifies that Rainey's external injuries were sustained during "rigorous gymnastics training," Alicia uses another piece of evidence provided through Anonymous: a paper written by the doctor that calls his credibility into question.

Alicia: Didn't you write a paper arguing that women could not get pregnant when raped?

Brasher's Lawyer: I'm sorry! Objection! Relevance.

Alicia: Your Honor, the defense expert's attitude toward rape is directly relevant to his testimony on rape.

Judge Parks: Seems inarguable.

Dr. Brinks: I don't know where you got that.

Alicia: Doctor, did you argue that the female anatomy of ducks has evolved to the point where the reproductive tract can resist rape?

Dr. Brinks: That's a draft. I never submitted it.

Alicia: And that the same has happened in adult women.

Dr. Brinks: I wrote that when I was very young. I was positing intellectual theories.

Alicia: Theories that women can't really be raped?

Dr. Brinks: No. That female reproduction uses trauma as a block to pregnancy.

Alicia: Good. As long as we know how you really think.[37]

The theories posited by this doctor and exposed by Alicia's line of questioning might sound familiar. In August 2012, Todd Akin, then a Republican member of Congress from Missouri, controversially said, "If it's a legitimate rape, the female body has ways to try to shut that whole thing down."[38] The media at the time made several connections between Akin's comments, which may have contributed to his loss in an election that cost him a seat in the Senate, and the reproductive system of female ducks. Not only does *The Good Wife* establish a connection between Rainey's case and this misguided commentary on rape from a real-life legislator, but it takes the opportunity to establish the ridiculousness of such comments by framing them in a courtroom and putting an argument against them on record in the universe of *The Good Wife*. This is another example of this series blurring the line between the narrative of the show and real-world politics and attitudes toward rape.

Out of eighteen episodes of *The Good Wife* that deal with rape narratives, only two include Alicia's firm representing rapists. Given that the nature of their law practice is defense, this detail is particularly significant. It isn't until

Season Three, Episode Six, "Affairs of State,"[39] that viewers first see Lock-hart/Gardner representing a rapist. It is worth noting that, for the majority of the episode, Alicia has reason to believe her client is innocent. Also, the case doesn't progress far enough to actually reach trial. In addition to shifting where Alicia's loyalties lie—from the victim to the rapist—this episode raises several significant issues regarding consent.

Lockhart/Gardner's client is the son of a Taiwanese diplomat accused of the murder of Mya Nickels, whose body was found aboard a ship during a party; she had been sexually assaulted prior to her death. In several episodes during the third season, *The Good Wife* added a new associate, Caitlin, at Lockhart/Gardner. Alicia serves as her mentor, but Caitlin is the first to arrive on scene when Mya's body is found. Chen Pin, their client, and a friend who is connected to the Dutch embassy have been accused of showing Mya unwanted attention, and while the Dutch friend had diplomatic immu-nity, Chen Pin does not. Cary Agos, in his role at the state's attorney's office, is pursuing charges.

Alicia meets up with Caitlin and Chen at the hospital. In a reversal of what rape episodes often show, instead of the invasive evidence collection victims typically endure for the camera, this episode shows the suspect's examination. While standing on a large piece of white paper, Chen is made to remove his clothing, scrapings are taken from under his nails, his hair is combed, and everything is gathered as evidence. During most of this exam-ination, Caitlin waits on the other side of a curtain, but when Alicia arrives, she immediately announces her presence to Chen and pushes the curtain aside. "Did they tell you you have the right to remain silent?" she asks her client. "I didn't do it," he replies.[40] He is naked and clearly distraught, and this representation of what a rape suspect goes through is unique in all the episodes considered as part of this project.

Considerations of consent are less unique, but the specifics of the argu-ments in this episode are relevant to *The Good Wife*'s representation of rape narratives. The first way "Affairs of State" addresses consent is through the theme of the party where Mya was killed. It was a stoplight party, Caitlin informs Alicia after discovering pictures from the party posted online. The color of a person's cup indicates their relationship status: a person drinking from a red cup is in a relationship and unavailable, a yellow cup means the person's relationship status is complicated or in flux, and a green cup means the holder is available. Various cell phone pictures from that night show that the color of Mya's cup changed from red early in the party to green later on. Caitlin's explanation is framed within the firm's attempt to prove that any sexual contact between Mya and Chen Pin was consensual. Chen Pin claimed that he had made out with the victim, but that it was a consensual act. Caitlin's exact words before she shows Alicia the pictures and explains the significance of the cups are "I think I have something on the consensual.

Chen? We have to prove he made out with her consensually?"[41] Alicia responds in the affirmative, and Caitlin then explains what the color of Mya's cup means. This is problematic for two reasons: First, a green cup, regardless of its significance in the party theme, does not actually signify consent to sexual activity. The color of Mya's cup in no way proves anything about the nature of her interactions with Chen. Second, while they aren't actually accusing the victim of lying, since the physical evidence has to speak for her, their job here is to do what they can to pick out the flaws in Cary's version of what happened.

As it turns out, though, Mya's voice hasn't been silenced completely. Kalinda and Cary both gain access to a voicemail message Mya left for the boyfriend she'd had at the beginning of the party (red cup) but had broken up with by the end (green cup). In it, Mya tells someone at the party: "Hey, I said don't touch me." A male voice they all identify as Chen's replies: "I'm not touching you."[42] Cary believes this voicemail will be all the evidence he needs for a conviction, and whatever else is true in this specific episode, *The Good Wife* has maintained its commitment to making the voices of rape victims heard and giving rape (or in this case attempted rape and murder) victims substantial roles to play in the cases built against their attackers.

In fact, Mya's input doesn't end with the voicemail. Kalinda also discovers that Mya and the friend she attended the party with worried about losing each other so they kept in contact using an app on their phones called the Rape App. Mya's friend explains the app to Caitlin: "We both had it installed on our phones so we could keep track of each other. See? A GPS shows you where your friend is." The app also includes a panic button. "That's what sucks," Mya's friend explains. "The phone vibrated when Mya pushed it, but the music was so loud and I was dancing so I didn't feel it."[43] There is a time stamp, though, and a digital record of when Mya hit the panic button.

With the information they have, Alicia and Caitlin seem confident that Chen Pin wasn't involved in Mya's attempted rape and her death—he signed a bar receipt a minute after Mya pushed the panic button. Cary, though, recognizes that Chen Pin didn't actually sign the receipt. Regardless of what Cary knows, Alicia and Caitlin both seem to reasonably believe that it was Chen Pin's Dutch friend with the diplomatic immunity who attacked Mya Nickels up until the point when they pass their client—who is supposed to be on house arrest—headed in the opposite direction in a car. They follow him for a short while until it becomes apparent to Alicia that he is most likely headed for the airport. At that point, she pulls the car over so that she and Caitlin both have plausible deniability.

Caitlin: I thought he was innocent.

Alicia: I know. Sometimes the guilty ones look like the innocent ones.

Caitlin: Well, that's depressing. [44]

While there is clearly some resistance when it comes to believing in their client's guilt, it does not come at the expense of the victim's voice. Instead, both Alicia and Caitlin believe there is a second plausible suspect who should be held accountable for what they believe he did. And in the end, Cary does track Chen Pin down in the airport and takes him into custody before he flees the country. It is unclear whether Alicia's firm will continue to represent him, but the episode never shows any of the lawyers from Lockhart/Gardner defending Chen Pin after it becomes clear that he truly is the guilty party, which creates a distance between their work and his guilt.

The second episode of *The Good Wife* that has Alicia working with a rapist is also in Season Three. Episode Eight, "Death Row Tip," deals with a tip from a documentary being shot in a prison that leads to the discovery of two buried bodies. The man who gave the interview is on death row for abducting and raping two fourteen-year-old girls over a period of three days. Though she is assigned to work the case with a Legal Aid attorney, Alicia makes it very clear that she does not want to defend this man.

Alicia: Did you see what he did to their bodies?

Legal Aid Attorney: But you don't execute him.

Alicia: Why not? [45]

The episode is a bit heavy-handed when it comes to highlighting Alicia's justification for her question. The victims were the same age as Alicia's own daughter, for one. Additionally, it seems that the rapist actively works to justify her disgust—first through the nature of his crimes and then by convincing Alicia to bring his mother and brother to see him as he is headed for his execution just so that he can tell them to burn in hell.

There are at least three aspects of the narrative at work in this episode that keep Alicia's involvement in this case from negating the good work she has done and will do to amplify the voices of rape victims. The first is that justice has been done for the two girls who were raped and killed by this man. He is not even just in prison; he is on death row for what he has done to them. Second, neither Alicia nor the Legal Aid attorney is interested in trying to free this man. They are instead working to stop his execution. There is no doubt of his guilt at any point throughout the episode. The third aspect is Alicia's reticence. She struggles as the audience might; maybe this man does deserve to die. While Alicia seems fairly comfortable with that idea, the show itself complicates the matter through the task set before her. Her entire career at Lockhart/Gardner has been ethically murky insofar as it is Alicia's job to defend people who may in fact be, and often are, guilty. Alicia's reticence to do her job in this episode brings into stark clarity the moral and emotional complexity of this particular case.

There are two more episodes of *The Good Wife* that fit into this discussion of rape narratives and creating space for the voices of victims. These two episodes are different than all that have come before as they focus on what specific voices—not rape victims' voices—should and should not be allowed to say about rape. In Season Two, Episode Eighteen, "Killer Song,"[46] the man who tortured, raped, and killed Mallory Cerone thirty years ago is about to be released from the treatment center where he has been held ever since he was found not guilty by reason of insanity all those years ago. The victim's daughter, Rhonda, wants to stop her mother's killer from making money off a song he wrote about what he had done. The episode contains much analysis of the content of the lyrics, since the civil suit Rhonda is bringing requires proof that the song was actually written about her mom. The song, titled "Drive On Out," includes lyrics like "not too far in the trunk of my car where no one else can hear her scream."[47] While there is the potential for a First Amendment argument, that an artist's work is protected under freedom of speech, it is unlawful to profit off the commission of a crime. That is what Alicia and Rhonda are working to avoid. Because as graphic and disturbing as even that limited selection from "Drive On Out" is, in the show's universe, it is number three on the Billboard Top 200.

By the end of the episode, Alicia and Will achieve a favorable result in the civil case and set events in motion for a criminal trial, since a close reading of the song lyrics led to the discovery of a second rape/homicide committed by the same man. In this episode, instead of amplifying the voice of the victim, the goal was to diminish, if not eliminate, the voice of the rapist. By shifting the emphasis in this way, the end result is similar to the cases where victims need a platform from which to speak. Here, silencing the rapist and keeping him from earning money off of Mallory Cerone's death work to ensure that she—or her daughter at least—retains control of her story.

While "Killer Song" addressed issues concerning rape narratives in song, Season Four, Episode Seven, "Anatomy of a Joke,"[48] considers another form of popular culture. When comedian Therese Dodd, a client of Lockhart/Gardner, takes her top off on a late-night television show to perform a breast exam, the Federal Communications Commission fines the network, and they turn around and sue Therese for two million dollars. Alicia and Cary, who is back at Lockhart/Gardner, get the case. The main focus of this episode is on the limits of what can be said or done on television; however, there are three different times when rape becomes a topic of discussion.

First, there are two moments when the characters discuss how rape is represented in popular culture. One is less direct. Alicia, Cary, and Therese spend a portion of the episode meeting with various FCC representatives. While discussing the threshold for what is shown on television, the following conversation occurs:

> **FCC Representative:** I've always thought you network folks were too terrified of us at the FCC anyway. We're not the ones infantilizing entertainment.
>
> **Therese:** That's what I told him.
>
> **FCC Representative:** So hypocritical. You allow yourselves to show naked bodies just as long as they're bruised and covered in blood.[49]

The focus of this commentary is on the physical violence portrayed in popular culture, but the fact that the bodies mentioned are "naked" adds a sexual undertone and suggests rape or sexual assault. While the comment is only loosely connected to a discussion of rape narratives, the fact that this perspective comes from a representative of the FCC, even if it is a fictional representative from *The Good Wife*'s version of the FCC, lends it a bit of weight. The fact that it rings true as a reality in most television programming in the real world helps as well.

The second moment is much more direct. After Therese's attempts at humor complicate their situation with some of the other FCC representatives, the FCC commissioner cancels their scheduled meeting. Alicia and Cary decide to attend anyway, as if they never received notice of the cancelation. While the issue at stake essentially comes down to obscenity and what is considered appropriate for television viewers, Commissioner Martinez has several questions regarding Therese's brand of humor.

> **Martinez:** What I have trouble reconciling is this new Therese with the Therese that told this joke: "Rape is never funny. Unless you're raped by a clown." How is this funny, Miss Dodd?
>
> **Alicia:** Sir, that wasn't part of the original act.
>
> **Martinez:** I understand that. But I find myself confused by Miss Dodd's sense of humor. Do you know that every forty-five seconds there is another sexual assault in America? So I'm not sure how rape is funny.
>
> **Cary:** The joke isn't about rape, sir, it is about a ridiculous juxtaposition.
>
> **Martinez:** But it makes light of rape, doesn't it? Shall I read it again?[50]

People who speak out against rape jokes are frequently told to lighten up, that it was just a joke, and asked whether they have a sense of humor. Although the way this conversation is set up, the condemnation of rape jokes is coming from the opposition (Alicia and Cary are, of course, on the side of Therese, their client), what *The Good Wife* has done here is raise the issue in a way that forces viewers to be critical of the very idea that such a thing could be viewed as funny. There's no room left to laugh over the supposed joke before the very heart of it is questioned and, as such, it is deemed unfunny. It is interesting how Alicia attempts to sidestep the issue, though perhaps it is for no other reason that she see or admit the relevance of that particular joke to this particular meeting since the matter at hand is Therese's nudity. Regardless of Alicia's purpose, though, the script doesn't put her in the position of arguing for rape jokes. Cary picks that up instead. And even then, it is in defense of his client, which might be excusable since viewers of legal dramas are trained to understand that good attorneys on television will say just about anything and make just about any legal argument in order to serve their clients.

Then the conversation continues:

Therese: You're right. It's not funny, Commissioner.

Cary: Therese . . .

Therese: What? He's right. Rape is never funny. And the association of clowns and rape is just offensive. And I feel terrible that I wrote it.[51]

While the concern might be the fact that this character has shown little respect or remorse for her actions, this particular moment is presented as genuine. Regardless of whether a viewer sees Therese's actions as vulgar or over-the-top, she does seem conflicted over the seriousness of the issues she confronts in these "jokes" and her desire to get a laugh.

Almost regardless of the end result of the episode—which has the network dropping its suit and Therese kissing Cary on the mouth to avoid answering the commissioner's question about whether she would behave in a similar manner on television in the future—this episode asks viewers to think critically about what they see on television and how they think about naked bodies, violence, and rape jokes.

The third way rape comes into consideration in "Anatomy of a Joke" is through the return of Laura Hellinger, the army captain Alicia attempted to help in court in "The Art of War." While Laura Hellinger's first appearance on the show was discussed at the beginning of this chapter, in the timeline of the *Good Wife* universe, it was the episode that immediately preceded "Anatomy of a Joke." Toward the beginning of "Anatomy of a Joke," Laura stops in to see Alicia at Lockhart/Gardner's offices. She is no longer wearing her army uniform. When Alicia asks about it, Laura explains that she is now out of uniform "permanently, unfortunately. My choice. I was losing my bearings, things soured."[52] The fact that this was the first of the three rape-related scenes from this episode may influence the way viewers approach the rest, or at least the earlier comment from the FCC representative. But even more importantly, this series is making a conscious effort here to deal with at least some of the aftermath of rape. Viewers aren't just seeing rape victims immediately after the fact, when they are still vulnerable and fragile, as is the case in most episodes of most of the shows discussed throughout this project. Instead, in Laura Hellinger at least, viewers see an example of what all rape victims really are: people trying to move forward in their lives.

It's not really as simple as that, though. While she won't come out and say so, the implication of "things soured" is that Laura Hellinger no longer felt suited to the military after she was attacked. Those things could align with the kinds of harassment and career ramifications military rape victims face as discussed in the documentary *The Invisible War*, which highlights the ways in which women who are raped are often treated more harshly in the system of military justice than men who rape.[53]

But whatever is or isn't true about the circumstances under which Laura Hellinger left the military, what *The Good Wife* viewers see is a woman who was attacked, who fought back in court, who fought to make her voice heard, moving on with her life. Not only does she appear in this episode, but after Peter Florrick gives her a job in the state's attorney's office, she eventually meets both Alicia and Will in the courtroom. She and Will even date for a short time. In her, viewers have an example of what can come next for a woman who was raped, even after she doesn't receive the kind of justice she deserves.

In fact, when it comes to *The Good Wife*, few representations of rape victims focus on the immediate aftermath of their attacks. This is partially due to the nature of the show—in most cases and on most shows, the only lawyers involved as early as the reporting process are the prosecutors. Even so, there are examples of rape narratives on the show that make the point that it could have been otherwise; the massage therapist in "VIP Treatment" finds herself in Lockhart/Gardner's offices within hours of her attack. The show has created a narrative space in which victims can and sometimes do find their way to Alicia and her firm right away, but the majority of the time, the victims represented on the show have already been through a criminal (or military) trial. So what viewers get from *The Good Wife* is a list of examples of the times in which reporting a rape and trusting the justice system to work isn't enough. Then Alicia and Lockhart/Gardner come in to work with rape victims to help them regain control and a voice, to help them take the next step, often into civil court.

Viewers of *The Good Wife* not only meet victims after they have already begun the work of recovering and moving on after experiencing trauma, but they also see how these women regain the control that has been stolen from them. In rape narrative after rape narrative, the attorneys at Lockhart/Gardner, and Alicia Florrick in particular, work to amplify the voices of rape victims and force the courts to pay attention to what these women have to say.[54] Lockhart/Gardner's role in these rape narratives asks viewers to question the way the court system works for or against rape victims, and the ways the narratives draw on and overlap with real-world rape scandals and headlines allow that same questioning to apply to more than the universe created for the show.

The fact that the show does this advocacy for victims without, at least through the first four seasons, falling back on the familiar idea that one of the show's recurring characters has a history with sexual assault is worth mentioning.[55] But whatever else is true about *The Good Wife*, in terms of advocating for rape victims, it is arguably the best of all the shows considered in this project. This show is still on the air, and it can only be hoped that any additional rape narratives will be treated with the same careful attention and awareness and that other shows might take some cues from *The Good Wife* in terms of how to address rape narratives.

NOTES

1. Robert King and Michelle King, "Stripped," *The Good Wife*, season 1, episode 2, directed by Charles McDougall, aired on September 29, 2009 (Hollywood: Paramount Home Entertainment, 2010), DVD.

2. Robert King and Michelle King, "Pilot," *The Good Wife*, season 1, episode 1, directed by Charles McDougall, aired on September 22, 2009 (Hollywood: Paramount Home Entertainment, 2010), DVD.

3. The firm Alicia Florrick works for goes through several name changes during the first four seasons of *The Good Wife*. In the beginning, it is Stern, Lockhart & Gardner. Briefly in Season Two, it is Lockhart/Gardner & Bond. The remainder of the time, Diane Lockhart and Will Gardner are the two named partners. For the sake of clarity, I have chosen to refer to the firm exclusively as Lockhart/Gardner.

4. For comparison's sake, other shows considered in this project also ranked included *NCIS* at #1, *Criminal Minds* at #7, and *CSI* at #11. Amanda Kondolojy, "CBS Wins the Season in Viewers for the Sixth Straight Year and 11 of the Last 12," *TV by the Numbers*, May 20, 2014, http://tvbythenumbers.zap2it.com/2014/05/20/cbs-wins-the-season-in-viewers-for-the-sixth-straight-year-and-11-of-the-last-12/266124.

5. Clive Thompson, "From Anonymous to Bitcoin, *The Good Wife* Is the Most Tech-Savvy Show on TV," *Wired*, September 27, 2013, http://www.wired.com/2013/09/screen-smarts.

6. Mike Hale, "Familiar Drama Shines among Guts and Gore," *New York Times*, November 8, 2013, http://www.nytimes.com/2013/11/10/arts/television/the-good-wife-stands-out-among-newer-fall-shows.html.

7. Robert King, Michelle King, and Ted Humphrey, "The Art of War," *The Good Wife*, season 4, episode 6, directed by Josh Charles, aired on November 4, 2012 (Hollywood: Paramount Home Entertainment, 2013), DVD.

8. Ibid.

9. Ibid.

10. Ibid.

11. Ibid.

12. Ibid.

13. Ibid.

14. King and King, "Stripped."

15. Ibid.

16. See Susannah Meadows, "What Really Happened That Night at Duke," *Newsweek*, April 22, 2007, http://www.newsweek.com/what-really-happened-night-duke-97835.

17. King and King, "Stripped."

18. Ibid.

19. Nora Caplan-Bricker, "The Backlog of 400,000 Unprocessed Rape Kits Is a Disgrace," *New Republic*, March 9, 2014, http://www.newrepublic.com/article/116945/rape-kits-backlog-joe-biden-announces-35-million-reopen-cases.

20. King and King, "Stripped."

21. Ibid.

22. Ibid.

23. Ibid.

24. Robert King and Michelle King, "VIP Treatment," *The Good Wife*, season 2, episode 5, directed by Michael Zinberg, aired on October 26, 2010 (Hollywood: Paramount Home Entertainment, 2011), DVD.

25. Ibid.

26. Ibid.

27. Ibid.

28. Ibid.

29. J. C. Nolan, "Rape: A Modern Perspective," *The Good Wife*, season 4, episode 20, directed by Brooke Kennedy, aired on April 14, 2013 (Hollywood: Paramount Home Entertainment, 2013), DVD.

30. See Richard A. Oppel Jr., "Ohio Teenagers Guilty in Rape the Social Media Brought to Light," *New York Times*, March 17, 2013, http://www.nytimes.com/2013/03/18/us/teenagers-found-guilty-in-rape-in-steubenville-ohio.html.

31. "Guilty Verdict in Steubenville Rape Trial; Matt Lauer Faults NBC; Iraq War Anniversary," *CNN Reliable Sources* transcript, aired on March 17, 2013, http://transcripts.cnn.com/TRANSCRIPTS/1303/17/rs.01.html.

32. Nolan, "Rape."

33. Ibid.

34. Ibid.

35. Ibid.

36. Ibid.

37. Ibid.

38. Charles Jaco, "Jaco Report: Full Interview with Todd Akin," *Fox 2 Now—St. Louis*, last modified August 20, 2012, accessed January 2, 2015, http://fox2now.com/2012/08/19/the-jaco-report-august-19-2012.

39. Corinne Brinkerhoff, "Affairs of State," *The Good Wife*, season 3, episode 6, directed by Dean Parisot, aired on October 30, 2011 (Hollywood: Paramount Home Entertainment, 2012), DVD.

40. Ibid.

41. Ibid.

42. Ibid.

43. Ibid.

44. Ibid.

45. Robert King, Michelle King, and Matthew Montoya, "Death Row Tip," *The Good Wife*, season 3, episode 8, directed by Joshua Marston, aired on November 13, 2011 (Hollywood: Paramount Home Entertainment, 2012), DVD.

46. Karen Hall, "Killer Song," *The Good Wife*, season 2, episode 18, directed by James Whitmore Jr., aired on March 29, 2011 (Hollywood: Paramount Home Entertainment, 2011), DVD.

47. Ibid.
48. Craig Turk, Robert King, and Michelle King, "Anatomy of a Joke," *The Good Wife*, season 4, episode 7, directed by James Whitmore Jr., aired on November 11, 2012 (Hollywood: Paramount Home Entertainment, 2013), DVD.
49. Ibid.
50. Ibid.
51. Ibid.
52. Ibid.
53. Kirby Dick, director, *The Invisible War* (Los Angeles: Docurama Films, 2012), DVD.
54. For all the good *The Good Wife* does to create opportunities for women who have been raped to speak out about the crimes committed against them, a point worth mentioning that the show does not address is that women are not the only victims of rape. Given the fact that many of the other shows discussed in this project that aired for more than four seasons made the same mistake, *The Good Wife* is certainly not alone in this oversight. Hopefully future seasons of the show will address this concern.
55. One relationship worth mentioning in this context is Lockhart/Gardner investigator Kalinda Sharma's with her husband. A shady figure, Nick first appears in Season Four, and their sexual relationship is sometimes violent and, one could argue, may involve some questionable consent. I have chosen not to do so here because neither Kalinda nor the show indicates that anything more than rough sex took place.

REFERENCES

Brinkerhoff, Corinne. "Affairs of State." *The Good Wife*. Season 3. DVD. Directed by Dean Parisot. Aired on October 30, 2011. Hollywood: Paramount Home Entertainment, 2012.
Caplan-Bricker, Nora. "The Backlog of 400,000 Unprocessed Rape Kits Is a Disgrace." *New Republic*, March 9, 2014. http://www.newrepublic.com/article/116945/rape-kits-backlog-joe-biden-announces-35-million-reopen-cases.
Dick, Kirby, director. *The Invisible War*. DVD. Los Angeles: Docurama Films, 2012.
Hale, Mike. "Familiar Drama Shines among Guts and Gore." *New York Times*, November 8, 2013. http://www.nytimes.com/2013/11/10/arts/television/the-good-wife-stands-out-among-newer-fall-shows.html.
Hall, Karen. "Killer Song." *The Good Wife*. Season 2. DVD. Directed by James Whitmore Jr. Aired on March 29, 2011. Hollywood: Paramount Home Entertainment, 2011.
Jaco, Charles. "Jaco Report: Full Interview withTodd Akin." *Fox 2 Now—St. Louis*, August 19, 2012. http://fox2now.com/2012/08/19/the-jaco-report-august-19-2012.
King, Robert, and Michelle King. "Pilot." *The Good Wife*. Season 1. Directed by Charles McDougall. Aired on September 22, 2009. Hollywood: Paramount Home Entertainment, 2010.
———. "Stripped." *The Good Wife*. Season 1. DVD. Directed by Charles McDougall. Aired on September 29, 2009. Hollywood: Paramount Home Entertainment, 2010.
———. "VIP Treatment." *The Good Wife*. Season 2. DVD. Directed by Michael Zinberg. Aired on October 26, 2010. Hollywood: Paramount Home Entertainment, 2011.
King, Robert, Michelle King, and Ted Humphrey. "The Art of War." *The Good Wife*. Season 4. DVD. Directed by Josh Charles. Aired on November 4, 2012. Hollywood: Paramount Home Entertainment, 2013.
King, Robert, Michelle King, and Matthew Montoya. "Death Row Tip." *The Good Wife*. Season 3. DVD. Directed by Joshua Marston. Aired on November 13, 2011. Hollywood: Paramount Home Entertainment, 2012.
Kondolojy, Amanda. "CBS Wins the Season in Viewers for the Sixth Straight Year and 11 of the Last 12." *TV by the Numbers*, May 24, 2014. http://tvbythenumbers.zap2it.com/2014/05/20/cbs-wins-the-season-in-viewers-for-the-sixth-straight-year-and-11-of-the-last-12/266124/.
Meadows, Susannah. "What Really Happened That Night at Duke." *Newsweek*, April 22, 2007. http://www.newsweek.com/what-really-happened-night-duke-97835.

Nolan, J. C. "Rape: A Modern Perspective." *The Good Wife.* Season 4. DVD. Directed by Brooke Kennedy. Aired on April 14, 2013. Hollywood: Paramount Home Entertainment, 2013.

Oppel, Richard A., Jr. "Ohio Teenagers Guilty in Rape the Social Media Brought to Light." *New York Times*, March 17, 2013. http://www.nytimes.com/2013/03/18/us/teenagers-found-guilty-in-rape-in-steubenville-ohio.html?_r=0.

Thompson, Clive. "From Anonymous to Bitcoin, *The Good Wife* Is the Most Tech-Savvy Show on TV." *Wired*, September 27, 2013. http://www.wired.com/2013/09/screen-smarts/.

Turk, Craig, Robert King, and Michelle King. "Anatomy of a Joke." *The Good Wife.* Season 4. DVD. Directed by James Whitmore Jr. Aired on November 11, 2012. Hollywood: Paramount Home Entertainment, 2013.

Conclusion

Mariska Hargitay's on-screen work with rape victims as Detective Olivia Benson on *Law and Order: Special Victims Unit* crossed over into the real world as well. As the founder of the Joyful Heart Foundation, Hargitay is directly responsible for the creation of a community whose "mission is to heal, educate and empower survivors of sexual assault, domestic violence and child abuse, and to shed light into the darkness that surrounds these issues."[1] Hargitay credits her decision to start the foundation to letters she received from fans of her show, real-world individuals who had been raped or sexually abused or assaulted, who wrote her to tell their stories. "I felt a great responsibility to these brave women and men and wanted them to know that they had been heard and that they could have hope. I studied the subject, trained to become a crisis counselor and used my visibility as an actress to become an advocate," Hargitay explains in the "Founder's Corner" of Joyful Heart's website.[2]

The glimpses of these stories (which can be found at www.joyfulheartfoundation.org) provide anecdotal evidence of the effects rape narratives presented on crime and legal television dramas can have on members of the audience. These individuals saw stories that resonated with their experiences and reached out to another person about them. Some of them were speaking about what was done to them for the first time. Hargitay is an actress on a television show, but the representations of rape narratives she is a part of have had a direct and real impact on lives outside of the *SVU* universe. It could be argued that when it comes to presenting rape narratives, *SVU* is in a category unto itself, and that the effects those rape narratives had on the presumably small percentage of viewers who took the time to write Hargitay should not be broadly applied. But that is not what I am suggesting. Rather, it is important that the possibility of that kind of impact be taken into consideration. There are so many examples of rape narratives within popular culture, it is hard to pick up a book, see a movie, or turn on the television without coming across one. In *Watching Rape: Film and Television in Post-feminist Culture*, Sarah Projansky opens her argument with the claim that "the pervasiveness of representations of rape naturalizes rape's place in our everyday world, not only as real physical events but also as part of our fantasies, fears, desires, and consumptive practices. Representations of rape form a complex of cultural discourses central to the very structure of stories people tell about themselves and others."[3]

The stories people know and tell influence what they see on television. Consider the number of narratives viewers might recognize as "ripped from the headlines" or at the very least recognizable nods to real-world happenings. For years, scholars like Susan L. Brinson, author of "TV Rape: Television's Communication of Cultural Attitudes toward Rape," have discussed the idea that "a symbiotic relationship exists between television and society. Whatever values or attitudes are current in society will eventually find their way to television. Television, through depictions that are perceived as realistic, will both reflect and in some manner shape those societal attitudes and values."[4] Recognizable stories—like the episode of *The Good Wife* from Season Four, "Rape: A Modern Perspective,"[5] that is clearly modeled after the Steubenville, Ohio, rape scandal—blur the distinctions between the presentations of rape in the universe of a show and the realities of it offscreen. *Assault on the Small Screen* draws on these ideas without the intention of contributing to their veracity. There are important arguments to be made about the ways society shaped television narratives and about how the abundance of rape narratives in popular culture could lead to desensitization or create an unrealistic distance between viewers and the crimes portrayed. The goal of this project, though, has been from the beginning to interrogate how rape narratives are being presented specifically in the eight shows considered here.

None of these shows is perfect, and how could any of them possibly be when dealing with subject matter as imperfect as rape? The scale by which these shows are measured here is a decidedly feminist one, and the judgments concern only how the shows deal with this one specific type of narrative. All of the shows considered offer glimmers of feminist ideologies in other aspects—most of the law enforcement agencies, district attorney's offices, and law firms include high-ranking female characters, for instance. Many of the female characters are well-developed, flawed individuals. Some of the most central female characters are bosses, and some of them even directly espouse feminist concerns. When it comes to the rape narratives, however, some of these shows take more care than others.

While the structure of *Assault on the Small Screen* was not intended to be nor did it really become a ranking, had it been, the two shows that serve as bookends would not have changed. *NCIS* does the least of any of these shows to present rape narratives that address feminist understandings of the issue in two ways. First, *NCIS* has fewer rape episodes than any other show despite being the third-longest-running series considered here. Second, the majority of the show's rape narratives attempt to distract viewers' attention away from rape—by refusing to name it, subverting viewers' expectations of it, ignoring its existence entirely, or ending rape narratives with complainants who have lied to investigators—to the point that even when a rape has actually been committed, viewers have to work to recognize it. Perhaps this overall approach to rape narratives is not surprising given the fact that the show's creator, Donald P. Bellisario, also wrote Season Two, Episode Twenty-Two, "SWAK,"[6] a rape narrative that ends when an emotionally distraught woman believed to be a rape victim admits she was too embarrassed to tell her mother about her sex life so she claimed to have been raped instead. In the episode, this rape narrative was secondary to another investigation after the woman's dying mother sent a biological weapon to NCIS through the mail as a form of revenge against the agents. The representations of these two women stand in fairly well for the majority of the show's treatment of rape victims.

On the other end of the spectrum from *NCIS* is another CBS show *The Good Wife*. Perhaps because its perspective is more clearly female—both the eponymous character of Alicia Florrick and showrunner Michelle King[7] potentially guide the show that way—this show works to do nearly the opposite of *NCIS*: The majority of rape narratives presented on *The Good Wife* focus on helping individuals who have been raped find a voice even after the criminal justice system has failed them. The majority of the rape narratives focus on civil suits against accused rapists, but when the show is actually a legal drama focused on defense attorneys, that the main characters even end up fighting for the victims at all reads like a conscious decision on the part of the show's creative team.

There isn't a clear progression through the rest of the book in terms of least to most feminist. Attempting to structure the book in such a way felt like an oversimplification of an issue that cannot be simplified. Neither rape nor its representations in popular culture are simple. Police and legal dramas like the ones considered in *Assault on the Small Screen* are meant to chronicle the quest for justice after a crime has been committed. These shows provide heroes—or antiheroes—who are hardworking law enforcement officers and lawyers and who right the wrongs that have been done in their fictional versions of society. They are, for the most part, the good guys. The criminals are the bad guys. And the viewers join the fight by aligning themselves with the good guys and trying to solve the mystery of who is responsible for the wrong that has been done.

For most crime narratives, the physical evidence makes certain things clear: what happened, for instance. When it comes to rape narratives, though, the question of "what" frequently supersedes the question of "who": The majority of rape narratives across all eight of these shows are about crimes committed by someone known to the victim. The problem becomes, then, whose version of events is most believable—the familiar trope of a "he said/she said" rape narrative. An element of feminist understandings of rape that most of the rape narratives considered in this project take into account is that consent is integral to the distinction between sex and rape. Shows like *Criminal Minds* and *SVU* include instructive narratives, teachable moments, in which the characters explain for other characters and for the audience that certain behaviors by the victims—such as the clothes they wear or the type of work they do—do not constitute consent. Quite a few of these shows, even the ones that should be considered the most feminist in their depictions of rape narratives, do make exceptions when it comes to rape taking place within the walls of a prison. *The Closer* and *SVU* both make use of prison rape threats as if they were an acceptable interrogation technique, and the shows that include prison rape narratives don't usually take strong stances against the issue itself.

In addition to prison rape, several other specific types of rape narratives make appearances on multiple shows: complainants who filed false reports, rape on college campuses, rape in the military, rape or sexual assault of one of a show's main characters. In the last instance, if the assault takes place during the timeline of the show, the victim is always female—*CSI*'s Catherine Willows, *The Closer*'s Brenda Leigh Johnson, *Rizzoli & Isles*' Jane Rizzoli, *Dexter*'s Rita Bennett and Lumen Pierce, *SVU*'s Olivia Benson. The male characters who have personal experience with sexual assault—*Criminal Minds*' Derek Morgan and *CSI*'s Nick Stokes—were both assaulted as minors. This fits the unfortunate truth that very few of the 342 episodes (across all eight shows) with rape narratives actually create a space for the representation of male victims. *Criminal Minds*, *CSI*, and *SVU* are the exceptions, with both *Criminal Minds* and *CSI* offering one or two episodes apiece. All three shows incorporated discussions of why men are so much less likely to report rape into those episodes.

One characteristic of police and legal dramas is that, by the end of a narrative, the bad guy has been either caught or at least identified with the promise of being caught in the future. This is part of what makes these shows rewarding for viewers: the opportunity to watch justice being served. Despite this, however, it is the shows that account for the prosecution of rape cases that tend to offer the most realistic representations of how rape is addressed offscreen. While *Dexter* rarely shows viewers the inside of a courtroom, the code that helps Dexter Morgan decide whom he can kill requires that he focus his attention on those who have fallen through the cracks of the legal system. The rapists he encounters have either successfully maneuvered through the legal system or haven't been caught. *SVU* creates the expectation of a trial through the continual presence of a representative from the district attorney's office, and trial preparation and the trials themselves provide many opportunities for the show's recurring characters to explain both the benefits and the pitfalls that await rape victims in court. *The Good Wife* also focuses primarily on what the legal system can and cannot do for rape victims—to the point that several of the cases Alicia tries end up back in criminal court once she has done what she can for the victims or their families in civil court. The ways in which the legal system fails rape victims—who in real life only see their attackers face prison in 2% of cases[8]—are perhaps the most accurate reflections of real-world rape culture that television has to offer.

Throughout this book, it has been my intention to present arguments in each chapter that represent as many different examples of rape narratives as possible. That being said, there are certainly episodes that could not be considered in these pages, a fact that is particularly true of the six shows that are still airing new episodes at the time I write this. With all those additional episodes, and even with the ones I included in my discussion, there are many more issues worth consideration. Had I the time and space, the overwhelming whiteness of the victims in rape narratives on these shows is worth further consideration, as is the significance of who exactly writes and creates these narratives. These ideas are, of course, in addition to the questions about the potential psychological effects these narratives have on viewers and their attitudes toward rape. Clearly, there is much left to say, but I will leave it at this: Rape isn't actually hard to define. It is difficult to prosecute, and sometimes it is tricky to recognize. It is a challenging thing to portray appropriately on television, but there are many people out there creating television content that tries. If depictions of rape narratives are going to play such a significant role on television[9] for audiences of so many millions of people, it is important that we pay attention to the messages those narratives are sending. Rape narratives both reflect and contribute to rape culture by further normalizing the ways rape exists within and permeates our daily lives up to and including our popular culture. Expanding the ways we examine and assess rape narratives shown on television seems like a small yet important step toward addressing how society constructs its ideas about rape.

NOTES

1. Joyful Heart Foundation, 2014, http://www.joyfulheartfoundation.org/.
2. Ibid.
3. Sarah Projansky, *Watching Rape: Film and Television in Postfeminist Culture* (New York: New York University Press, 2001), 3.

4. Susan L. Brinson, "TV Rape: Television's Communication of Cultural Attitudes toward Rape," *Women's Studies in Communication* 12, no. 2 (1989): 25.

5. J. C. Nolan, "Rape: A Modern Perspective," *The Good Wife*, season 4, episode 20, directed by Brooke Kennedy, aired on April 14, 2013 (Hollywood: Paramount Home Entertainment, 2013), DVD.

6. Donald P. Bellisario, "SWAK," *NCIS*, season 2, episode 22, directed by Dennis Smith, aired on May 10, 2005 (Hollywood: Paramount Home Entertainment, 2006), DVD.

7. Michelle King and her husband, Robert King, are co-creators, executive producers, and frequent writers of *The Good Wife*. Michelle King co-wrote five of the episodes considered in Chapter Eight of *Assault on the Small Screen*—all with her husband and two with an additional co-writer.

8. RAINN (Rape, Abuse and Incest National Network), "Reporting Rates," accessed May 14, 2013, http://www.rainn.org/get-information/statistics/reporting-rates.

9. Of the 1,409 episodes considered for this project, 342 of them contained rape narratives that fit the criteria I outlined in the introduction. That accounts for nearly a quarter, approximately 24%, of the total episodes in these eight shows.

REFERENCES

Bellisario, Donald P. "SWAK." *NCIS.* Season 2. Directed by Dennis Smith. Aired on May 10, 2005. Hollywood: Paramount Home Entertainment, 2006.

Brinson, Susan L. "TV Rape: Television's Communication of Cultural Attitudes toward Rape." *Women's Studies in Communication* 12, no. 2 (1989): 23–35.

Joyful Heart Foundation. 2014. http://www.joyfulheartfoundation.org/.

Nolan, J. C. "Rape: A Modern Perspective." *The Good Wife.* Season 4. DVD. Directed by Brooke Kennedy. Aired on April 14, 2013. Hollywood: Paramount Home Entertainment, 2013.

Projansky, Sarah. *Watching Rape: Film and Television in Postfeminist Culture.* New York: New York University Press, 2001.

RAINN (Rape, Abuse and Incest National Network). "Reporting Rates." Accessed May 14, 2013. http://www.rainn.org/get-information/statistics/reporting-rates.

Episode Index

Index

About the Author

Molly Ann Magestro has a master's degree from Iowa State University and a PhD from the University of Wisconsin–Milwaukee. She is a senior lecturer at the University of Wisconsin–Washington County, where she teaches composition and creative writing.

CPSIA information can be obtained at www.ICGtesting.com
Printed in the USA
BVOW08*0116140715

408201BV00003B/3/P